The Children's Author Blueprint Series

How To Market And Promote A Children's Book

YOUR COMPLETE TOOLKIT FOR GETTING THE WORD OUT BEFORE, DURING, AND AFTER LAUNCH

EEVI JONES

For my sweet Sunday Readers,
who keep showing up with open hearts, curious minds, and
big dreams for their stories. Thank you for walking this journey with me,
for trusting me, and for believing that your books deserve to be seen.

Published by LHC Publishing 2026

How To Market And Promote A Children's Book
Copyright © 2026 by Eevi Jones

All inquiries regarding permission should be directed to
www.LHCpublishing.com

ISBN: 978-1-952517-48-8 Paperback

LHC
P U B L I S H I N G

TABLE OF CONTENTS

INTRODUCTION

A NEW WAY TO THINK ABOUT MARKETING YOUR CHILDREN'S BOOK

Let's start by taking a deep breath together.

If the word *marketing* already feels heavy, intimidating, or a little uncomfortable, you are exactly where you're supposed to be, my friend. This book was written for you.

For so many children's book authors, marketing feels loud, overwhelming, and completely disconnected from why we wrote our precious book in the first place. We imagine ads, complicated funnels, social media pressure, and tactics that feel forced or misaligned. We imagine doing it wrong. Or worse, being told that if our book does not "take off," it must mean we failed.

This book exists to change that narrative.

———————————— • ◆ • ————————————

WHAT MARKETING REALLY IS

Marketing, at its core, is not about tricks or formulas. It is about generating interest and excitement for our book.

Because no matter how beautiful, meaningful, or magical our children's book is, readers can only fall in love with it if they know it exists.

We have worked incredibly hard to write, illustrate, and publish our story. It deserves to be seen. And I would love to support you in giving it the attention it deserves.

Traditionally, marketing is often presented as something we do *after* the book is finished. A separate, intimidating phase that kicks in once the creative work is "done."

But I don't believe in that definition.

In this book, marketing means anything that brings *awareness* to our book.

- *Talking about our story with enthusiasm.*
- *Sharing a copy of our book with someone who might love it.*
- *Mentioning our work in conversation.*
- *Connecting our story to a season, a moment, or a real-life need.*

All of that is marketing.

When we begin to see marketing this way, it suddenly becomes a lot less scary. And a lot less heavy. Because chances are, you are already doing far more marketing than you realize.

NINJA TIP:

A simple reframing is sometimes all it takes. If something helps our book become more visible, more understood, or more loved, it counts as marketing.

WHY THIS BOOK EXISTS

Over the past several years, I have worked closely with many one-on-one clients, helping them achieve their dream of bringing their children's books into the hands of little ones.

And while I absolutely love that work, I also realized something important.

Not every author can - or should have to - invest in one-on-one mentorship, especially when they are just starting out. And that realization is what led me to write this book.

Everything I have learned, everything I have taught, everything that has worked for me, for my clients, and for my *Children's Book University*® students - it's all in here.

This book only covers strategies I truly believe in and have seen work in real life. Not theory. Not hype. Not "one-size-fits-all" promises.

Because the truth is this:

There is no single right way to market a book. There is no magic strategy that works for everyone. Our best marketing approach will always be the one that fits us and our book!

THE GOAL OF THIS BOOK

The goal of this book is to change how you think about marketing altogether, so it can naturally become part of your everyday life. Talking about your book stops feeling awkward or forced and starts feeling like the most natural thing in the world.

By the time you reach the final page, you will have built your very own marketing toolkit - filled with strategies you understand, trust, and feel comfortable using.

Some will feel immediately aligned. Others may gently challenge you to stretch. You get to choose what to try, when to try it, and how deeply to lean in.

There is no pressure here. Only possibility.

NINJA TIP:

You are never meant to use all strategies at once. This is a toolbox, and the tools are here when you need them.

A HOLISTIC WAY TO THINK ABOUT MARKETING

Most marketing advice focuses only on what happens after the launch. This book, however, is not a post-launch-only book.

This is a holistic marketing guide.

We will look at what we can do throughout the *entire* book creation process. From the earliest stages of writing, to preparing for launch, to long-term, ongoing promotion.

Why?

Because when we bake marketing into the process from the very beginning, it no longer feels like an afterthought. It becomes part of the rhythm of creating and sharing our work.

There are countless things we do every day that we don't think of as marketing. This book will help you recognize them, embrace them, and use them intentionally.

! A NECESSARY PREREQUISITE:

Before we go any further, we need to be honest about one important thing.

Our marketing is only as effective as our book is good.

This book assumes that you care deeply about your craft - that you have written, revised, and polished your story to truly serve its readers.

Marketing cannot compensate for a weak story. But when paired with a strong book, it becomes incredibly powerful.

TWO ANGLES, ONE POWERFUL APPROACH

Throughout this book, we will look at marketing from two complementary angles.

- *One angle builds on our **branding**.*
- *The other strengthens our **strategy toolkit**.*

Some strategies help shape how you and your book are perceived. Others help expand its reach. Together, they create momentum.

This is also why this book looks different from anything I have created before.

You may recognize some ideas from my YouTube channel. Over the years, I've shared many strategies there. But this is the first time everything is brought together in one place, organized strategically, and aligned with *exactly when* to use each approach during your book's creation journey.

The value of this book is not just in the ideas themselves, but in their timing and context.

PICK WHAT WORKS FOR YOU

As you'll soon discover, this book holds a wide range of strategies. Please don't feel overwhelmed. And please don't feel like you need to do everything!

Every children's book is different. Every author is different. Some strategies will feel fun and energizing to you. Others may not - and that's okay.

If you love speaking, school visits or podcast interviews may be a wonderful fit. If you thrive on social media, you'll find ideas tailored to that strength.

Marketing can be time-consuming at times, yes. But it can also be deeply enjoyable when you choose strategies that align not just with sales goals, but with who you are.

NINJA TIP:

There is no single magic strategy that works for every book. Anyone claiming they've found "the one way" is not being entirely honest. This book exists because your best strategy will be *your* strategy.

—— ◆ ——

HOW THIS BOOK IS ORGANIZED

Because marketing looks different at different stages, I have organized this book into six distinct phases, based on the developmental stage of your book. I call this my *Lighthouse Marketing Framework*.

The strategies are organized by when they are best used; but they are not limited to those moments alone. I encourage you to read this book in its entirety, as each chapter contains strategies that can benefit you, regardless of where you are in your journey.

- **Phase 1: Pre-Manuscript**
  Everything you can do even *before* your book is written.

- **Phase 2: Creation Process**
  How to weave marketing elements directly into and around your book as you create it.

- **Phase 3: Preparing Your Launch Pad**
  Setting your book up for an initial boost through thoughtful pre-launch preparation.

- **Phase 4: Launch Window**
  Making the most of your launch moment.

- **Phase 5: Post-Launch**
  Reaching readers, influencers, and communities after publication.

- **Phase 6: Long-Term & Continuous Marketing**
  Strategies that support your book's success for months and years to come.

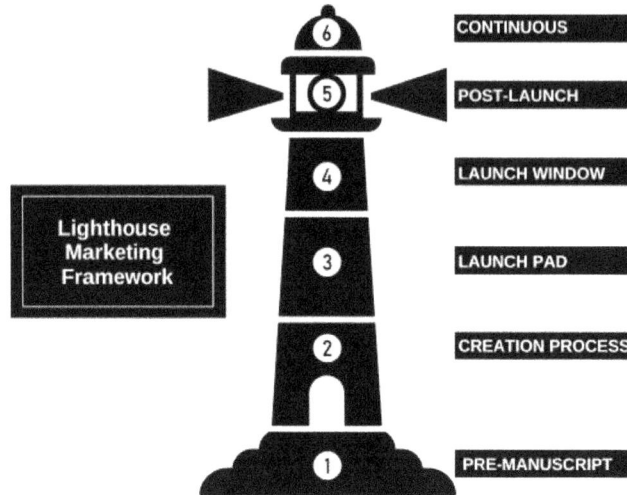

CONTINUOUS

POST-LAUNCH

LAUNCH WINDOW

Lighthouse Marketing Framework

LAUNCH PAD

CREATION PROCESS

PRE-MANUSCRIPT

Each phase is covered extensively in its own chapters.

No matter where you are in your journey - whether you haven't written a word yet, are deep in revisions, preparing to launch, or hoping to breathe new life into an already published book - this book has you covered.

———•✦•———

SHOWING UP FOR YOUR BOOK

One of the biggest differences between books that quietly disappear and books that find their readers is how actively the author is willing to share their work with the world.

Out of a hundred new authors, only a handful are willing to consistently show up. To experiment. To refine. To go the extra mile when others stop.

Be part of that handful! Put on your lab coat. Try things. Adjust. Stay curious.

Go where others are not willing to go, and I promise you, it will pay off.

I am so excited to walk this path with you.

But first…

WHO AM I?

Who am I, you might ask. What qualifies me to write this book? How can I help you? And perhaps more importantly, why should you listen to me?

Hi, I'm Yvonne. But as you may already know, my friends call me Eevi. Using a number of different pen names, I have written and ghostwritten more than seventy children's books, ranging from baby books all the way to middle-grade chapter books, many of which have made it onto Amazon's bestseller lists and the *USA Today* bestseller list.

I'm the author of the multi-award-winning book *How To Self-Publish A Children's Book*, and the founder of *Children's Book University*®, where I help aspiring children's book authors write, illustrate, and publish their books.

How To Market And Promote A Children's Book, then, is a natural extension of my first book on this topic.

You may be wondering if you could figure out all this information on your own. And the answer is, probably. But there's surprisingly little help out there that specifically pertains to the marketing and promoting of self-published children's books. And as you will soon see, the marketing of children's books differs greatly from that of all other genres.

I'm fortunate enough to be able to make a living doing what I love most. I truly adore what I do, and with this book, I'm trying to give back to the wonderful author community, so children everywhere can benefit from its incredible creativity.

Over the years, I've been able to secure highly sought-after interviews with outlets such as *Forbes, Huffington Post*, and *EOFire*, an award-winning podcast that has hosted guests like Tony

Robbins and Hal Elrod. I have also created courses and written articles for industry-leading sites such as *Reedsy* and *Kindlepreneur*, which have provided my work, services, and books with meaningful exposure.

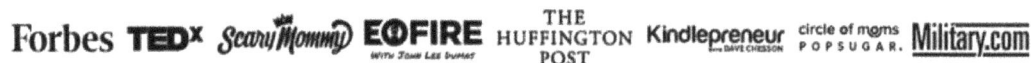

Forbes **TEDx** *Scary Mommy* **EOFIRE** THE HUFFINGTON POST Kindlepreneur circle of moms POPSUGAR. Military.com

And you can too.

No matter how far along you are in the creation process of your beautiful children's book, it is never too early, nor too late, to think about marketing it.

> *"It's never too early, nor too late, to think about marketing your children's book."*

So many set out to fulfill their dream of becoming a published children's book author, only to feel disheartened when initial sales slow down after friends and family have rushed to purchase their copies.

This book will help you create a continuous sales stream, month after month, and get your beautiful book into the hands of little boys and girls who will fall in love with your characters, your story, and your message.

To make this guide as comprehensive and actionable as possible, I have interviewed children's book authors at different stages of their journey, as well as school librarians and teachers. Together, their insights help showcase the methods that truly work for our genre.

This book also includes a number of swipe files, templates, and other resources designed to support you with the marketing aspects of your children's book.

To help you find these resources easily, I have indicated them with an arrow (↑) throughout the book. You can view and download each file at

https://www.eevijones.com/marketing-downloads

I recommend bookmarking this page so you can return to it quickly and easily whenever you need it.

HOW TO USE THE COMPANION RESOURCES

To help you stay organized and feel supported every step of the way, I have created two downloadable and printable companion resources for this book that are meant to bring clarity, focus, and ease to your marketing efforts.

1. Your Marketing Strategy Overview

This overview showcases my **Lighthouse Marketing Framework** at a glance. It visually lays out each phase of the journey and the marketing strategies that live within them, giving you a clear picture of what this book covers and how all the pieces fit together.

Think of this as your map.

As you move through the book, you can use this overview to see exactly where you are on your marketing journey. Over the coming weeks and months, feel free to check off the strategies you've explored or implemented. There is no rush and no expectation to do everything at once. This overview simply helps you stay oriented and intentional.

2. Your Personalized Marketing Strategy Plan

Throughout this process, my goal is for you to feel empowered, not overwhelmed. To support that, you'll also find a printable *Personalized Marketing Strategy Plan* that works hand in hand with your *Marketing Strategy Overview*.

Rather than trying multiple strategies all at once, I encourage you to approach your marketing in rounds.

Choose a small number of strategies to focus on at a time. I recommend starting with no more than **three strategies per round,** and giving each one enough space to truly show results. In most cases, that means allowing at least **three months** before deciding whether a strategy is working for you and your book.

At the end of each round, pause and evaluate.

- *Which strategies felt aligned?*
- *Which ones moved the needle?*
- *Which ones felt draining or ineffective?*

Strategies that work well can be carried forward into the next round. Those that don't can be gently released and replaced with new strategies you're ready to try.

NINJA TIP:

The goal is not to do everything at once. The goal is to discover what works for *you*. Over time, this process naturally filters out what doesn't serve you and leaves you with a clear, personalized, step-by-step marketing plan you can return to again and again.

By approaching your marketing in this intentional, methodical way, you prevent overwhelm and gain clarity. Step by step, you'll build a strategy that feels sustainable, effective, and uniquely yours.

I truly hope this book provides you with everything you need to propel your beautiful children's book to the next level and get you the sales you so deserve. I can't wait to see you succeed.

Once you've made it through these pages, I would love to hear from you and celebrate your wins and successes with you - no matter how big or small they may be. You can find, tag, and contact me on Instagram under **@eevi_jones**. I may not always be able to respond, but I read every message I receive.

ALWAYS REMEMBER: the number one thing that will set you apart is taking action.

So let's get started.

With my deepest gratitude,

~ Eevi

———————•✦•———————

YOUR TO DOs FOR THIS CHAPTER:

- ❏ Download & print the **Marketing Strategy Overview**
- ❏ Download & print the **Personalized Marketing Strategy Plan**

Find all your templates and swipe files using this link below. You may want to bookmark this page, so you can refer to it as quickly and easily as possible.

↑ *https://www.eevijones.com/marketing-downloads*

LINKS SHARED:

- Eevi's YouTube Channel - *https://www.eevijones.com/youtube*
- How To Self-Publish A Children's Book - *https://www.eevijones.com/book-release*

CHAPTER 1
The Mindset That Changes Everything

Before getting started, I want to take a moment to talk about our mindset in this first chapter. I felt it was important to begin here because so many aspiring authors are held back by limiting beliefs, a fear of not being good enough, and a reluctance to share their accomplishments. We worry about self-promotion, and about what others might think.

We may hesitate to promote our book because we don't want to feel like we're imposing on the people we love.

And I truly understand this fear, because I've been there.

But here's the thing: You're doing something amazing! Not only did you have the beautiful dream of wanting to write your very own children's book, but you also took the courage to follow through and turn that dream into reality.

You've worked incredibly hard for this. So please don't hide your accomplishments because you're worried about taking up space and drawing attention to yourself.

Here are a few things that have helped me change the way I view marketing my books and my work:

(1) If we don't talk about our book, nobody will. And if nobody talks about it, no one will know about it. And if no one knows about it, no one will buy it.
(2) You might be surprised how many of your friends have considered writing a children's book themselves, but thought they couldn't do it. Sharing our journey shows them that it *can* be done; and that it can be done successfully.
(3) It's very likely that you are the only person within our family or circle of friends who has written and published a book. Supporting us on this journey can actually feel exciting to others, not like a burden or nuisance. Many people will be delighted to learn about our beautiful undertaking.
(4) And if we don't ask, our loved ones won't have the opportunity to support us.

Yes, some people may roll their eyes privately. But here's what I want you to remember instead:

- It's not our business what others think of us.
- In the end, those opinions do not matter. So don't let them hold you back.

Because here's the truth:

1. There'll always be someone who doesn't like what we are doing, and that's completely okay. It doesn't mean our beautiful book is any less valuable.
2. As a society, we are often taught that talking about ourselves is boastful or selfish. When someone feels annoyed by self-promotion, it is usually not personal. It is cultural.
3. What if just one person told you, "Your book made my daughter so happy. Thank you so much for writing this meaningful story! I never would have found it if you hadn't shared it," while a dozen others rolled their eyes? That is a ratio worth embracing. Focus on the children who will love your book but never would have discovered it if you hadn't spoken up.

Shift your focus from thinking about yourself to what your book can do for little boys and girls.

———— • ◆ • ————

! **An Invitation as You Begin:**

While you may have heard me talk about some of these strategies before, I encourage you not to think, "I already know this." Instead, challenge yourself to look for something new in each one, whether it's a fresh angle, a new perspective, or a way to make it your own.

As you read, keep asking yourself: *How can I apply this to my book? How can I make this strategy feel like me?* **An open mind is indispensable to growth.**

So get ready to share your heart out, my friend. Because you are about to change a little someone's world with your beautiful work...

PART I
MARKETING BEFORE THE BOOK EVEN EXISTS

1

PRE-MANUSCRIPT

CHAPTER 2
Before the First Word:
Getting Started Earlier Than You Think

In the business world, it is often said that we have to build our network before we need it. This same principle applies to the marketing of a children's book as well. The most effective marketing does not begin after publication; it starts long before our book is released.

Many people call this creating buzz. What you will learn throughout this book will help you create real, and more importantly, lasting buzz that extends far beyond your launch date. And interestingly, some of the most powerful ways to create that long-term buzz actually begin long *before* launch - in fact, *before* our manuscript is even completed.

That is why I have added this chapter.

Before we talk about promotional strategies, outreach, or visibility, we need to look at what we can do in the pre-manuscript phase to increase our book's marketability before it is written or finalized.

To do that, we first need to understand how children's books are different from other genres, why this distinction matters so much when it comes to marketing, and how we can use it to our advantage.

———————— • ✦ • ————————

HOW ARE CHILDREN'S BOOKS DIFFERENT (AND WHY IT MATTERS)?

There are a lot of talented authors out there, but the most successful ones don't rely on their book to magically find readers. Instead, they actively seek out the readers and write with them *already* in mind.

As children's book authors, our marketing challenge is unique because our books must appeal to two very different audiences:

- the **children** the book is written for, and
- the **adults**, such as parents and grandparents, who purchase the book for them

The average buyer's age of children's books is between the ages of 30 and 44. More than 70 percent of these buyers are female. They are also more likely than readers of any other genre to discuss and recommend a book they and their children enjoyed. In fact, buyers of children's books are more strongly influenced by recommendations from family and friends than buyers in any other book category.

What does this mean for us as children's book authors?

It means that marketing does not start with ads or social media posts. It starts with intentional choices *during* the book creation process itself. Ideally, we keep both audiences in mind from the very beginning, including the storyline, wording, themes, and the underlying message of the book.

That is why, in this pre-manuscript phase of this book, I want to share my proprietary *Lead-With-The-Heart Method* with you. This is the method I personally use to ensure that a story resonates emotionally with children while also clearly communicating value to the adults who purchase it.

By the end of this chapter, your story will not only feel uniquely yours, but it will also be positioned in a way that makes it far easier to market later on.

! **Is your story already written or even published? Keep reading. I will show you how to apply everything you are about to learn, no matter where you are in the process.**

—————————• ✦ •—————————

LEAD-WITH-THE-HEART METHOD

When I write my books, my number one goal is to create something that makes children feel accepted, loved, and understood.

We all have different reasons for writing our children's books, but here is something incredibly important to understand from a marketing perspective: when we address both (1) the emotional needs of the child and (2) the desires of the adult buyer, we create a story that is much easier to promote, recommend, and sell.

When we address both (1) the emotional needs of the child and (2) the desires of the adult buyer, we create a story that is much easier to promote, recommend, and sell.

Loving parents, grandparents, and caregivers are constantly looking for books that help their little ones feel special, feel loved, or overcome challenges they are facing. These challenges might include bullying, potty training, patience, kindness, or navigating big emotions.

At the heart of it, we are all driven by the desire to help children grow into confident, compassionate little humans. Books play a powerful role in that journey.

My *Lead-With-The-Heart Method* consists of two main components which, when combined, help us write a book that is naturally aligned with its marketing: (1) a trend and (2) a value.

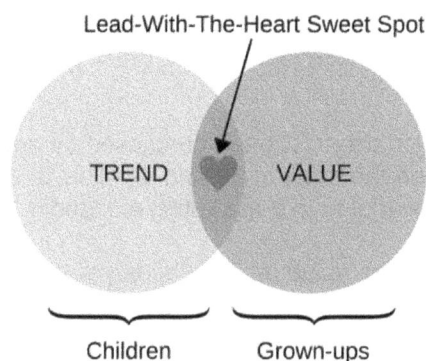

Lead-With-The-Heart Sweet Spot

TREND   VALUE

Children   Grown-ups

1. TREND

I love teaching this concept, because writing for children is usually never framed this way. We are often told to simply write what interests us (the author) and trust that the audience will follow.

But when we are intentional about trends, we increase the likelihood that children will be immediately drawn to our book, which in turn makes marketing significantly easier.

A trend refers to themes, characters, or topics that naturally capture children's attention. Sometimes these are widely visible in the toy, entertainment, and children's media space. Other times, they are the quiet, everyday fascinations that show up again and again in children's lives.

These are the things we see when we walk into a bookstore and spot the first display table in the children's section. They appear in toy stores, on kids' clothing, and across children's television and media. But they also show up at home, on the playground, and in everyday routines - in the things children ask for, talk about, and light up over.

For a time, unicorns were everywhere. They showed up on TV, on dresses and shirts, and across toy aisles. Similarly, when a new Jurassic Park movie was released, dinosaurs became wildly popular again. Suddenly, children were asking for dinosaur toys, dinosaur pajamas, and dinosaur bedding.

In the same way, if a child is obsessed with garbage trucks, construction vehicles, or fire engines, chances are they are not alone. Those interests often signal a shared fascination among many children of the same age.

When we identify a trend - whether it's a widespread cultural moment or a deeply loved everyday interest - and thoughtfully weave it into our story, we create a familiar, exciting entry point for young readers. That trend becomes the vehicle through which our message, theme, or value is carried.

And when children feel instantly drawn to the character or world, they are far more open to the story we want to tell.

2. VALUE

Now remember, children's books are most often purchased by adults, with more than 70 percent of buyers being women between the ages of 30 and 44. This is where the *Lead-With-The-Heart Method* becomes especially powerful from a marketing standpoint.

While the trend attracts the child, the value attracts the buyer.

Whenever I consider a book idea, I ask myself why a grown-up would choose this book for a child. Sometimes it is because the child is asking for it after spotting a unicorn or dinosaur on the cover. Other times, it is because the adult connects deeply with the message, the emotional tone, or the lesson the book teaches.

We buy children's books because we want to pass along values and social understanding. We look for stories about sharing, patience, kindness, inclusion, resilience, and empathy.

This second component of the *Lead-With-The-Heart Method* exists to fulfill the needs of the buyer, which directly supports our long-term marketing efforts.

COMBINING THE TWO

When our book speaks to both audiences, we are already ahead of so many other children's book authors. Many authors simply sit down and write without considering how their book will later be positioned, described, or shared.

But not us.

By thinking about marketing at this stage, we are setting ourselves up for success before the first promotional post is ever written. This approach strengthens our book's foundation and makes every future marketing decision more effective.

To brainstorm trending topics for your book, ask yourself:

"What do children already love and feel excited about?"

Sometimes that shows up as something that feels big and visible everywhere. Other times, it shows up in quieter, everyday ways. Here are a few places to look:

- Amazon bestseller lists, especially the top 10 in your category
- Current children's television channels and programming
- Popular themes on kids' clothing, pajamas, and accessories
- Displays and feature tables in bookstore children's sections
- Most importantly, what the children in your life cannot stop talking about

Paying attention to these patterns helps us identify trends that naturally resonate with young readers.

The values, on the other hand, come from you.

If you have children, think about the lessons you believe are most important for them to learn. If you do not have children, reflect on what you valued or needed most when you were young.

Let's look at an example. One of my books is called *The Garbage Trucks Are Here.*

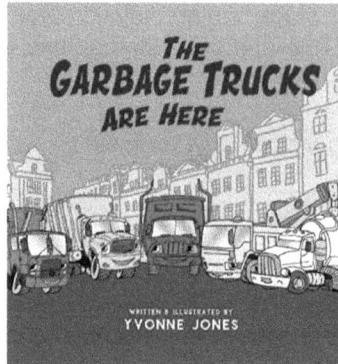

The trend I chose was garbage trucks, inspired by my then two-year-old who eagerly awaited trash day each week. Trends often start close to home. The key is confirming demand, which I did by researching Amazon.

The value I infused into the story was teamwork. Learning how to work together is an essential skill for young children.

By combining a strong trend with a meaningful value, the book became much easier to market to both children and adults. These elements later informed the book's cover, title, and description, which we will explore in upcoming chapters.

NINJA TIP:

WHAT TO DO IF THE STORY IS ALREADY WRITTEN?

If your story is already written, there is no need to start over.

Instead, revisit your manuscript with fresh eyes. Think about your two target audiences and see where you might strengthen either the trend or the value. Even small adjustments can significantly improve your book's marketability.

By simply thinking about these elements, you are already ahead of the vast majority of aspiring children's book authors.

Take what you have written and infuse it with this new awareness. When children want to read your book and adults want to buy it, marketing becomes a natural extension of the story itself.

YOUR TO DOs FOR THIS CHAPTER:

- ❏ Identify 3-5 trends for the age-group you're writing for
- ❏ Identify 3-5 of your most important values you would like to share with your little readers

Find all your templates and swipe files using this link below. You may want to bookmark this page, so you can refer to it as quickly and easily as possible.

↑ *https://www.eevijones.com/marketing-downloads*

PART II
MARKETING WHILE THE BOOK IS BEING CREATED

CREATION PROCESS

2

PRE-MANUSCRIPT

1

CHAPTER 3
Author Branding From The Inside Out

In the previous phase, we looked at a few small but important things we can do even *before* we begin writing a children's book. We talked about a research phase we should go through so we can tailor our beautiful book to an audience that already exists, rather than writing blindly and hoping our book will eventually find its readers.

I introduced you to an idea I share with all of my clients and students inside *Children's Book University*®: having marketing and audience awareness already in mind as you prepare to write your book.

I also shared my *Lead-With-The-Heart Method*, which provides you with a blueprint for writing a book that appeals to both children and the adults who purchase books for them.

In this chapter, I will show you some of the things you can do *during* the actual creation process of your children's book.

With my proprietary *Lighthouse Marketing Framework*, I want to show you that marketing does not have to be something we tack on at the very end. Instead, we can thoughtfully weave marketing into the *entire* writing and creation process. While others wait until publication to think about how to get their book into the hands of young readers, we will already be creating awareness, anticipation, and momentum along the way.

In this part of the book, I will introduce you to several powerful concepts. Some of them may feel familiar, while others may be completely new.

If this is where you currently are in your creation process, I encourage you to truly take these ideas to heart and implement as many of them as possible.

And if you have already published your children's book, don't worry. Most of these concepts can still be applied, adjusted, and implemented retroactively.

————— • ✦ • —————

AUTHOR IDENTITY & BRANDING YOURSELF

You are a brand. And great marketing always starts with you and how you present yourself.

As a children's book author, your name is your brand. Because of this, a well-crafted author profile is essential. It allows potential readers to feel like they know you. And getting to know someone is the first step in building trust.

If we want to build a lasting relationship with our readers, this is one of the first steps we need to take.

OUR AUTHOR BIO: *The Written Part*

Imagine your author bio written in a way that allows your personality to truly shine through. Very often, the author bio is the only thing readers know about us as authors. That makes it a powerful opportunity to connect.

Writing an author bio can feel intimidating, especially if it's your first one. Over the years, I have worked to make this process easier and more enjoyable for my clients and students by breaking it down into four clear objectives.

When drafting an author bio, we want to:

1. *Make it interesting and relevant*
2. *Make it informative*
3. *Use it to connect with the reader*
4. *Keep it extremely concise*

Anything beyond these objectives is optional and may be better suited for an "About" page on your website.

"About" pages differ from author bios in that they can be longer, more detailed, and more expansive. In this section, we are focusing specifically on an author bio that can be used:

- *inside the book itself, usually in the back*
- *on our Amazon sales page*
- *for media appearances that require a short bio*

Let's walk through these four objectives one by one.

1. INTERESTING & RELEVANT

An author bio becomes interesting and relevant when it connects *directly* to the reader. In other words, it should tie back to our book's topic whenever possible.

Readers did not find our book because of us. They found us because of what our book is about.

For example, if our children's book addresses bullying, we might begin a paragraph like this:

> *"Having been bullied for most of her childhood, ..."*
> *"As a teacher, [NAME] saw firsthand the impact bullying can have ..."*

These examples are written in third person, which is standard practice for author bios, even though we usually write them ourselves.

2. INFORMATIVE

To determine whether the information you are sharing is truly informative, ask yourself:

- *Does this help the reader decide whether or not to purchase my book?*
- *Does this encourage the reader to learn more about me? If so, how and why?*

Adding credibility markers can be very helpful to readers, because it shows that you are an expert in whatever topic you're writing about. Being an "expert" doesn't mean that you have to have a degree in something in order to be able to talk or write about it.

Credibility markers are incredibly helpful here. They signal experience, knowledge, and trustworthiness. And being an "expert" does not require a degree.

Credibility markers can include:

- *Working with children in the past or present*
- *Being a parent of a child with special needs, if that is relevant to your book*
- *Rescuing or fostering animals, if your book addresses that topic*
- *Personal experience related to the story's theme*
- *Media features*
- *Awards*

For example, if I were a parent looking for a book about adopting a dog, I would find it incredibly reassuring to know the author had gone through that experience personally. Even a single sentence can make a meaningful difference.

3. CONNECT WITH THE READER

Depending on our book's topic, connection may already be established in the "Interesting & Relevant" section. But there are additional ways to build rapport.

We can show readers that we are just like them, navigating similar joys and challenges. For example:

> *"As a mother of 3 little dragons, …"*
> *"As a stay-at-home dad, …"*
> *"Having always wanted to find her own unicorn, …"*

These small details allow our personality to shine through.

In the example above, saying "three little dragons" communicates that we are a parent of three, while also showing a playful sense of humor. Have fun with this. Creativity here builds warmth and memorability.

4. CONCISE

I hesitate to give a strict word count for author bios because length depends on context and topic. What matters most is clarity and relevance.

Short paragraphs are also visually more appealing and easier to read than large blocks of text.

To show how these guidelines work in practice, let's look at three examples.

EXAMPLE 1

More about the author

› Visit Amazon's Diane Alber Page

Biography 2. DIANA'S CREDIBILITY MARKER 3. CONNECT WITH READER

Diane Alber has had a passion for art since she held her first crayon at age two, which inspired her to subsequently earn a Bachelor's Degree in Fine Arts from Arizona State University. She is a wife and a mother of two young energetic children who love books. She became inspired to start writing and illustrating books because she saw a need for a book that inspired art and creativity in children. She also hopes that this book encourages parents to be proud of their children's art work no matter what it looks like!

1. RELEVANCY

4. CONCISE

BONUS: PHOTO

This author does a wonderful job weaving in credibility markers while remaining relatable and relevant. Everything that needs to be said is communicated concisely.

EXAMPLE 2

Breaking up longer text into shorter paragraphs can greatly improve readability. This version of my bio comes from one of my children's books co-authored with a well-known *Wall Street Journal* bestselling author and coach.

More about the author

› Visit Amazon's Eevi Jones Page

3. CONNECT WITH READER   2. CREDIBILITY MARKER

Biography

Writing under a number of pen names, Eevi Jones is a multi-award-winning & 9-time bestselling children's book author, and the founder of Children's Book University™, where she teaches loving moms, dads, grandparents, and teachers how to write & publish their own magical story.

1. RELEVANCY

Eevi has been featured in media outlets such as Forbes, Scary Mommy, Entrepreneur On Fire, Huffington Post, Exceptional Parent Magazine, SCBWI, and many more.

2. INFORMATIVE

She can be found online at EeviJones.com.

And for more books in the BRAVING THE WORLD series, visit BravingTheWorldBooks.com.

BONUS: PHOTO

Knowing many readers of the co-author's audience are entrepreneurs, I included credibility markers relevant to *them*, such as features in *Forbes* and *Huffington Post*, as well as my role as the founder of *Children's Book University*®.

I also shared my website, which is often overlooked but incredibly important. If you have a website, always include it when appropriate.

EXAMPLE 3

This example is by one of my readers, Andi Cann. Like the author in the first example, Andi has written and published multiple children's books.

More about the author

› Visit Amazon's Andi Cann Page

1. RELEVANCY

Biography

Andi loves writing children's books! She writes stories about friendship, love, and kindness children want to read again and again. With beautiful illustrations and heartfelt characters, Andi aims to enchant and inspire readers to feel confident, strong, and special about who they are.

Andi's memorable characters include Fancy Francie, Princess Pumpkin Patch, Mr. Hoopeyloops, Jojo, Puddles, Rex, Rory the Elf, Popsy, and MerryLyn, with many more on the horizon. Her non-fiction books for kids teach about animals and nature.

Andi lives in Arizona with her husband and two dogs named Beau and Francie. She treasures time with her two grown children and loves art, animals, and reading good books! Visit her website at https://www.andicann.com

BONUS: PHOTO   3. CONNECT WITH READER   2. INFORMATIVE

Her bio is short yet expressive. Through carefully chosen words, we quickly understand who she is and what she values. Most importantly, it feels genuine and reader-focused.

When I shared my own author bio with you earlier, you may have noticed I referred to it as "one of my bios." That was intentional.

Our bio is a living document that evolves as we grow. Awards, media features, series expansions, and milestones can all be woven in over time.

For example:

- If our book wins an award, we can add *"As an award-winning author, ..."*
- If a standalone book becomes a series, we can add *"Being part of the series ..."*
- If we receive media coverage, we can include *"Having been featured in ..."*
- If our book becomes a bestseller, we can say *"[NAME] is the best-selling author ..."*
- If we publish multiple books, add *"As the author of more than a dozen books, ..."*

Realizing that I could have multiple versions of my author bio was incredibly freeing. I regularly adjust my bio depending on where it appears. For example, my author bio for some of my children's books on Amazon is very different from my bio I share in my article on *Forbes*.

There is no need to agonize over perfection. We can always tweak, refine, and adjust over time.

When drafting each version, ask yourself:

- *Who is this bio for?*
- *What do I want it to convey?*

Based on your answers to these two questions, you can tweak and refine your author bio. Just as I include information that resonates with entrepreneurial readers, I would highlight different details for regular parents. Mentioning an appearance in *Business Insider*, for example, builds credibility with entrepreneurial parents, while other parents may not find that as meaningful. They may be far more interested in seeing that I appeared in a parenting magazine or that I am an award-winning children's author.

NINJA TIP:

Look at your book's primary buying audience and tailor your bio accordingly.

REMEMBER: It's about the reader and what matters to *them*, not about you as the author.

OUR AUTHOR BIO: *The Visual Part*

A professional, consistent author photo strengthens our brand just as much as our words.

When choosing an image, use the same profile photo across platforms whenever possible. This makes you easier to recognize, whether on Amazon, Instagram, or Facebook.

To make your image more memorable, consider wearing a bright color or choosing a vibrant background. Small visual choices like these help readers remember us.

Our author bio and image are not just supporting details. They are marketing tools. When crafted with intention, they help readers recognize us, trust us, and remember us. Every future marketing effort, from our book description to media features and outreach, builds on this foundation. The more clearly and confidently we show up as an author, the easier it becomes for the right readers to connect with us and our book.

Now that we have looked at some things we can do to start building our brand as an author even while we're still in the creation phase, let's take a look at what else we can do marketing wise.

YOUR TO DOs FOR THIS CHAPTER:

- ❏ Based on what you've just learned, draft or update your author bio
- ❏ Based on what you've just learned, choose or update your author image

Find all your templates and swipe files using this link below. You may want to bookmark this page, so you can refer to it as quickly and easily as possible.

⬆ *https://www.eevijones.com/marketing-downloads*

CHAPTER 4
Building An Email List That Matters

I have thought long and hard about whether or not to introduce you to this marketing strategy. It is primarily meant for authors who wish to go beyond simply selling a single book.

WHY COLLECT EMAILS?

You might be wondering why we, as authors, would be interested in collecting people's email addresses. Whether or not you choose to do so is entirely up to you. But the thinking behind collecting emails is this:

Unless someone purchases our book directly from us, we usually have no way of knowing who our buyers are. Marketplaces such as Amazon do not share that information with us when we publish through KDP. Amazon simply does not tell us who purchased our book.

By providing an "incentive" for readers to visit our home on the web (our website), where we can then offer access to additional materials in exchange for an email address, we create an opportunity to connect with those buyers directly.

That connection allows us to continue the conversation beyond a single purchase, in a way that feels intentional, respectful, and entirely optional for the reader.

This can be especially helpful if we plan to write more than one book. When we have our readers' email addresses, we can let them know whenever a new book is released. Without that connection, we lose the ability to reach them again.

Readers who willingly share their email already know us and our work, which they hopefully enjoyed. Having a direct way to communicate with them makes it much easier to turn readers into true fans, people who are excited to hear about and read our future books.

———— ◆ ————

FUN "INCENTIVES"

When I say "incentives," what do I mean?

These *fun extras*, as I like to call them, are usually shared toward the end of the book. They can take many forms and can be as simple or as elaborate as you'd like.

Some easy examples include printouts, activity sheets, coloring pages, and even lesson plans. But before I share some more creative ideas, let's look at two additional reasons why providing extra materials can be especially powerful for us children's authors:

1. Providing fun extras can make our story more interactive and engaging for little ones, especially when they feature familiar characters from the book.
2. Additional materials can also be incredibly helpful for parents, caregivers, and even teachers, who can use them to deepen a child's understanding of the book's message or topic.

"INCENTIVES" EXAMPLES:

You may have already come across examples like these, as more and more children's books now include fun extras toward the end of the book. What I love about these additions is that they help extend the experience of the story beyond the final page.

Wonderful examples include coloring pages featuring book characters and even companion videos.

This first example comes from one of my students. Nicole MacDonald created a beautiful website and designed a downloadable coloring page for each of her adorable books.

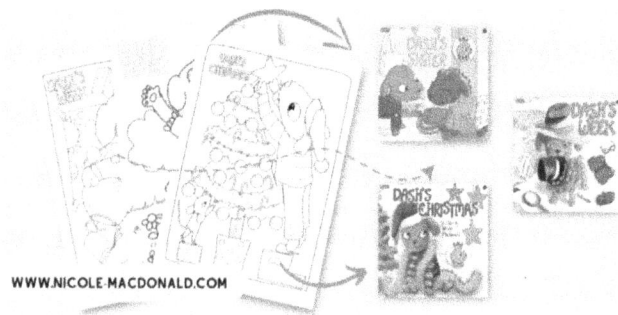

WWW.NICOLE-MACDONALD.COM

For her book *Dash's Christmas*, Nicole even created a printable cookie recipe. This ties in beautifully with the story, which features Dash baking Christmas cookies.

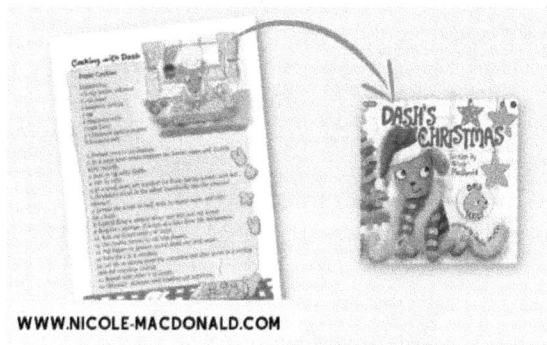

WWW.NICOLE-MACDONALD.COM

In Nicole's book, readers are prompted to visit her website to download these extras.

Another great example can be found in bestselling business author Mike Michalowicz's book *My Money Bunnies*, which I created with him.

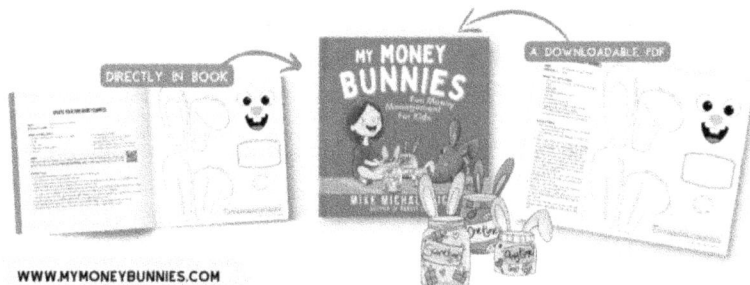

WWW.MYMONEYBUNNIES.COM

The book introduces children to a fun and approachable money-saving system using jars shaped like bunnies. To support that concept, we created instructions to help kids make their own bunny jars, along with cutouts for ears, labels, tails, and faces.

On the left, you can see how this appears directly in the back of the book, complete with instructions and cutouts. On the right, we created a downloadable printable that includes both the instructions and the cutouts, available on Mike's website.

If you have a read-along or sing-along video, sharing this as a fun extra is another wonderful option.

In one of my earlier books, I wrote rhymes to help children memorize important information such as their phone number and address. For a few of those rhymes, I created short videos that turned them into simple songs.

By making these videos publicly available on YouTube, I was able to offer a fun extra to readers who had already purchased my book, while also reaching new audiences who had not yet discovered it.

One of these videos now has over 31,000 views. If creating a video like this feels fun and aligned with your book, it can be a fantastic addition.

The key to a great fun extra is *relevance*. The more closely it ties into your book or characters, the more appealing it will be. Give it an enticing name, and it becomes an easy yes for readers to exchange their email address to access it.

Here are a few relevant and effective ideas for such fun extras:

1. **BEST-OF LIST:** If your book is about patience, create a resource such as "The 5 Best Patience-Building Exercises for Your Little Ones."
2. **AUDIO:** Record yourself reading the book aloud and offer it as a downloadable audio or video.
3. **COLORING PAGES:** Ask your illustrator for outlined versions of your illustrations to use as coloring pages.
4. **EXCLUSIVE PREVIEW:** Share a sneak peek of an upcoming book, cover, or character.
5. **HIDDEN MESSAGES:** Writing a chapter book with mystery elements? Hide secret messages that are revealed only to those who opt in.

The sky truly is the limit here. Ask yourself:

What would entice you, as a parent or caregiver, to visit an author's website?

A CALL-TO-ACTION PAGE

To let readers know about our fun extras, we will want to include a call-to-action page at the very end of our book.

The example below comes from Molly Mahoney's website for her book *Finding My Awesome*. By entering an email address, readers gain access to the book's video, audio version, action sheets, and additional printables.

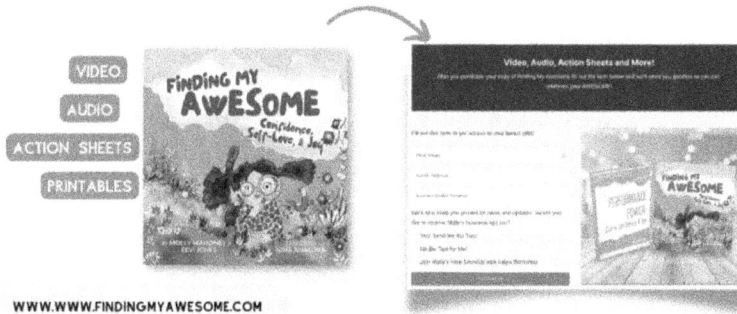

WWW.WWW.FINDINGMYAWESOME.COM

To guide readers there, we added a call-to-action, or CTA, at the end of Molly's book. These pages are called CTAs because they encourage the reader to take a specific action.

Molly's CTA reads:

"Want video, audio, action sheets, and more to help you find your Awesome and share it with the world? Go to: …"

We added a playful illustration and made sure the URL stood out clearly so it would be easy to spot.

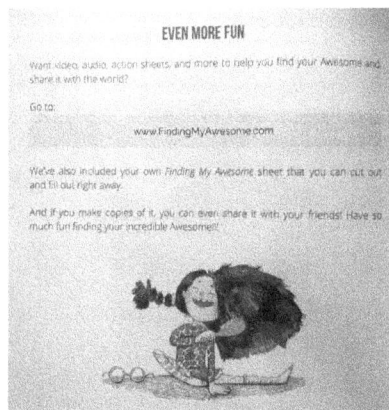

The best place to include a CTA is at the very back of the book. Whether or not you require readers to enter their email to access your extras is entirely your choice.

If you do decide to collect emails, you will need a system that automatically delivers the promised content. *Mailerlite.com* (↑) is a great option and is free for up to 500 collected emails.

To help you get started, I've created a short video tutorial (↑) that walks you through setting up your *Mailerlite.com* account.

NINJA TIP:

If your book is already published, or if this feels like too much to think about right now, know that this is not a must-have. It is a nice-to-have.

You can always add this later. You can either:

- update your book to include a CTA and website at a later time, or
- add downloads to your existing website and simply include the URL in your book. This way, you can introduce fun extras whenever you're ready, without having to make future changes to your book.

Creating fun, meaningful extras does more than delight our readers. It gives us a reason to stay connected.

When we offer something of value beyond our book, we are not just adding a nice bonus. We are creating a natural, respectful invitation for readers to raise their hand and say, "I'd love to hear from you again." That invitation is our email list.

An email list is one of the most powerful long-term marketing tools we have, because it allows us to connect directly with the people who already care about our work. It gives us a way to share updates, new releases, and behind-the-scenes moments without relying on algorithms, trends, or constant posting.

These fun extras are what make that connection feel easy and aligned. They turn a one-time book purchase into an ongoing relationship.

And that is where real marketing power lives - in building a space where readers choose to stay connected to us and our stories.

YOUR TO DOs FOR THIS CHAPTER:

❑ Create relevant *fun extras*
❑ Add a CTA (Call-To-Action) page at the end of your book
❑ Watch the short tutorial and set up your free *Mailerlite* account

Find all your templates and swipe files using this link below. You may want to bookmark this page, so you can refer to it as quickly and easily as possible.

↑ *https://www.eevijones.com/marketing-downloads*

LINKS SHARED:

• *https://www.mailerlite.com*

CHAPTER 5
Setting Amazon Up For Success Early

When it comes to selling books on Amazon, small creative decisions made early on can have a surprisingly big impact on visibility and sales. The way our book is titled, presented, and introduced to readers plays such a big role in whether it gets discovered at all. This chapter focuses on optimizing for Amazon early, so our book is positioned clearly, strategically, and in alignment with how readers actually search, browse, and buy.

TITLE & SUBTITLE (AND THE IMPORTANCE OF KEYWORDS - Part 1)

TITLE

For many of us, finding a title for our children's book is always one of the most exciting parts of the creation process.

And I write *finding* because it truly is a process of discovery. Remember, we want to keep marketing in mind throughout the entire creation process, and our title and subtitle present a perfect opportunity to do just that.

To make our title as marketable and strategic as possible, it's inevitable that we talk about keywords. We will dive much deeper into keywords in chapter 7. For now, let's look at how they relate specifically to our title and subtitle, and how to identify the best ones.

When it comes to your book's discoverability, having the right title is incredibly important. Yes, we want a clever and fun title. But just as important, if not more so, is making sure readers can actually find our book. That becomes very difficult if it isn't named strategically.

As I mentioned in *How to Self-Publish a Children's Book*, there is no single "correct" way to name a book. However, there is a right approach and a wrong approach. Unless buyers already know us, our book, and its title, most will search using keywords. In order for our book to be discovered more easily, we want to include the most descriptive and relevant keyword or keyphrase directly in the title whenever possible.

To illustrate this, here are a few examples from my own books:

KEYWORD	TITLE
Garbage trucks	The **Garbage Trucks** Are Here
(Lawn) mowers	The Little **Mower** That Could
Monster trucks	Lil Foot The **Monster Truck**

I absolutely love the titles of the garbage truck books *I Stink!* and *Smash! Mash! Crash! There Goes the Trash!* But I knew that in order to compete with these traditionally published books, I would need to be strategic.

My title, *The Garbage Trucks Are Here*, clearly communicates what the book is about. Including the keyword directly in the title also helps Amazon understand when and where to show the book to potential buyers.

For this keyword-based approach to work, we need to know what people are actually typing into Amazon when searching for books like ours.

You may be wondering, "Eevi, how do I figure out the best keywords for my children's book?"

There are several ways to approach keyword research. And it's important not to rely on just one method. Using a combination will give us a much clearer picture and help us make more informed decisions.

NINJA TIP:

Think of keywords not just as single words, but as keyword phrases. When brainstorming, always ask yourself:

"If I were looking for a book like this, how would I type it into Google or Amazon?"

For example, if I were searching for a children's book about monkeys, I wouldn't simply type "monkeys" into the search bar. That's far too broad. Instead, I might search for "monkey kids book" or "children's book about monkeys."

Keeping this in mind, let's look at a few ways we can go about our keyword research.

KEYWORD RESEARCH METHOD 1: *Similar Books*

Looking at similar books is always one of the first things I do. We can do this in bookstores or on any platform that sells books.

Focus on books that are performing well, and disregard those with very few or no reviews. Look at the keywords used in their titles, subtitles, and descriptions, and write them down. If you notice certain words appearing repeatedly, that's usually a strong indicator of a valuable keyword or keyphrase.

KEYWORD RESEARCH METHOD 2: *Amazon's Auto-Fill*

Amazon's auto-fill function is another excellent research tool. As you begin typing into Amazon's search bar, you'll see suggestions appear in a dropdown menu.

These are not random guesses. They are real phrases that Amazon users are actively searching for, which makes them incredibly valuable.

NINJA TIP:

Use incognito mode when researching keywords. This prevents Amazon from factoring in your previous search history.

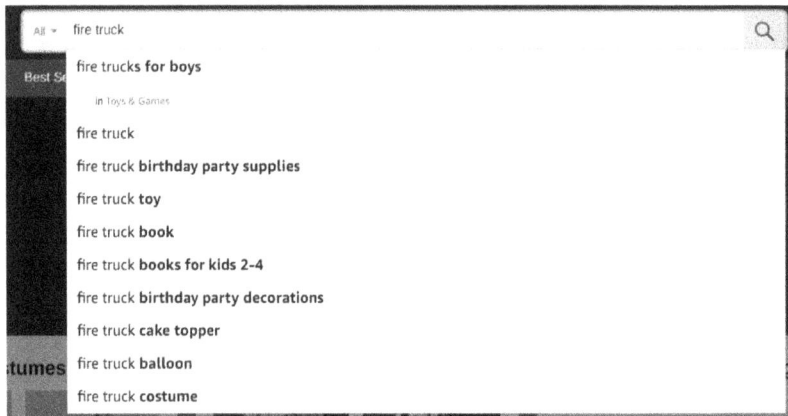

KEYWORD RESEARCH METHOD 3: *Thesaurus*

A thesaurus is another powerful but often overlooked tool. Look up synonyms for your main idea, then enter those words into Amazon's search bar to see what auto-fill suggestions appear and which books come up.

If relevant books show up, add those terms to your growing list of potential keywords and keyphrases.

KEYWORD RESEARCH METHOD 4: *Polling Friends & Family*

We can also involve friends and family in our research process. Most of our friends and family don't know about the importance of keywords, so instead of asking directly for keywords, try phrasing it like this:

"If you were looking for a children's book about [TOPIC], how would you search for it on Amazon?"

Phrasing it this way, you'll often be surprised by the responses. This is simple but effective market research, especially when asking people who regularly buy children's books.

KEYWORD RESEARCH METHOD 5: *Paid Research Tools*

The fifth method involves using a paid research tool. My personal favorite is *Publisher Rocket* (↑). You may have heard me mention it in my YouTube videos, as it truly is one of my secret weapons.

While it isn't free like the other methods, this is my favorite research tool, because it takes all the guesswork out of our research. We can simply type in a word that we think might be a great keyword, and *Publisher Rocket* will show us how often this word is searched for on Amazon.

Publisher Rocket removes much of the guesswork by showing how often specific keywords are searched for on Amazon. It also reveals which books appear for those searches and how well they are performing.

It *is* an investment, but especially if you are planning to write more than just one children's book, it's well worth the investment.

SUBTITLE

Something equally important, yet often overlooked, is the subtitle.

Even if you weren't planning to include one, I strongly encourage you to consider adding a subtitle to your children's book. Here are two key reasons why:

1. First, a subtitle gives you another opportunity to include alternative keywords or keyphrases. Not everyone searches using the same terms, so adding more relevant phrases increases discoverability.
2. Second, a subtitle can clarify your title. Many fellow authors struggle to let go of a title they've had in mind for a long time. While I don't always recommend sticking with an

unclear title, a subtitle can help remove confusion by clearly explaining what the book is about.

Here's an example from one of my books:

KEYWORDS	Children's book, writing, illustrating, publishing
TITLE	*How To Self-**Publish** A **Children's Book***
SUBTITLE	*Everything You Need To Know To **Write, Illustrate, Publish**, And Market Your Paperback And Ebook*

Adding a subtitle gave me more space to include keywords that didn't naturally fit into the title itself.

Most children's books even in the traditional publishing world do not use subtitles very often. In other genres, however, especially in nonfiction, subtitles are used heavily because they can really help potential readers see right away what the book is about, even without having to read the description.

So to help our book get this extra bit of an advantage and increase its discoverability, I always recommend adding a subtitle.

ALREADY PUBLISHED?

Looking back, I wish I had used subtitles for my early children's books. At the time, no one told me, and resources like this book simply didn't exist.

Some details can still be changed after publication, but there are limitations.

For ebooks, most details can be updated as long as they match the content and cover.

For paperbacks and hardcovers, however, certain elements are tied to the ISBN and cannot be changed after publication. These include the title, subtitle, and author name.

This means keyword-focused subtitles can only be added to ebooks after publication. Still, because all formats appear on the same Amazon sales page, this addition benefits *all* versions. A buyer who finds the ebook will also see our paperback and hardcover options.

WHAT TO STAY AWAY FROM

While keywords are important, we also need to be mindful of readability and aesthetics. Therefore, avoid awkward wording, unusual spelling, or unnecessary punctuation such as hyphens, colons, or brackets.

I learned this lesson the hard way with the title of my very first book:

KEYWORDS	Military families, soldiers
TITLE	*Closing the Gap: Understanding Your Service(wo)man*

The keywords are missing from the title, and it includes punctuation no one would ever search for. Would you type "Service(wo)man" into Amazon's search bar? Probably not. Lesson learned!

When it comes to weaving keywords into our title and subtitle, ...

NINJA TIP:

... think about your main character. Who or what are they? A dog, a monkey, a mail carrier, a garbage truck? Use this as a keyword or part of a keyphrase.

NINJA TIP:

... also think about what your story teaches. If it's about patience, kindness, or friendship, those should be keywords as well. These can be woven into your title, subtitle, and description.

Subtitles are especially helpful here, as they allow you to clearly communicate your book's theme the moment it appears in search results.

Our title and subtitle work together to set expectations, spark curiosity, and help the right readers find our book. When we choose them thoughtfully, they do more than name our story - they support discoverability, clarify who the book is for, and make our future marketing efforts much more effective.

———————————— •◆• ————————————

COVER

One of the very first things a buyer sees is our cover. Whether we choose a square, vertical, or landscape format, few things influence first impressions as much as our cover.

Our cover appears everywhere, on Amazon, our website, and social media. From a marketing perspective, it needs to be eye-catching, visually appealing, and instantly communicate what the book is about.

You worked hard to write your book. Make sure it has a cover that reflects that effort.

EMULATE THOSE THAT ARE DOING WELL

Familiarity matters. Especially as a new author, fitting into established genre expectations helps readers quickly identify your book's age group.

Take time to study similar books, either in bookstores or on Amazon. Notice which covers catch your attention.

For my book *Robot Bots*, I drew inspiration from Michael Yu's cover of *How to Catch a Monster*.

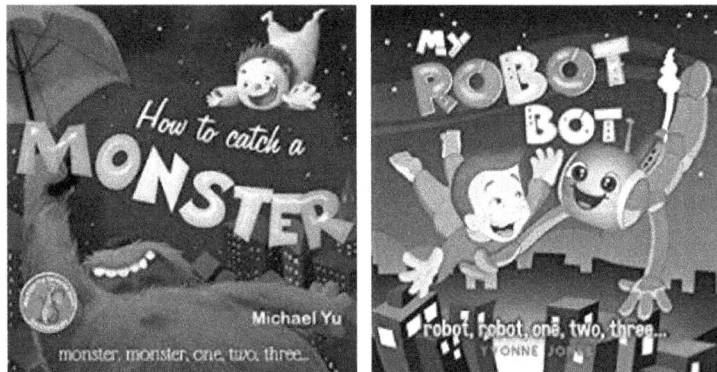

Besides the actual image on the cover, you can play with different fonts, the placement of the title (and subtitle), and the author name.

You can also experiment with fonts, title placement, and author name positioning. Resources such as dafont.com and fonts.google.com are great places to explore fonts, just be sure they are approved for commercial use.

One of my favorite tools I'd love to share with you is a font-finder. Font-finder tools like *fontsquirrel.com/matcherator* (↑) or *myfonts.com/WhatTheFont* (↑) allow us to upload an image and identify similar fonts.

INFUSING OUR COVER WITH MY *METHOD-OF-MULTIPLES*

One of my favorite ways to make a cover stand out is through my proprietary *Method-of-Multiples*.

The *Method of Multiples* is something that until now, I've only shared with my private 1-on-1 students. This concept focuses on showcasing diversity to subconsciously appeal to a broader audience.

To illustrate, let's look at some wonderful ways we can showcase diversity on our book cover:

1. **GENDER:** If you are planning to have children on your cover, consider showing more than one gender. When children and caregivers see both girls and boys represented, it becomes easier for a wider range of readers to imagine themselves inside the story.
2. **RACE & ETHNICITY:** Represent multiple backgrounds whenever possible. And to make this even more powerful, consider showing diversity across both race and gender. This helps more families feel seen at first glance and signals that the story is welcoming to many different readers.
3. **SPECIES:** Not every child's favorite dinosaur is a T-Rex. So if your book is about dinosaurs, consider featuring a variety of types. Different species spark curiosity and increase the chances that a child spots "their favorite" right on the cover.
4. **TYPES / MODELS:** Show variety within a category, such as different monster trucks, construction vehicles, or animals. When children recognize something they already love, even in a slightly different form, it strengthens that instant connection and makes the cover feel more dynamic and playful.

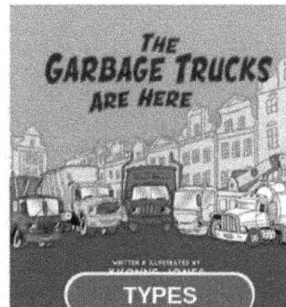

Parents may not consciously recognize why one cover resonates more than another, but this approach helps our book feel more inclusive and inviting.

I applied this method to the book *The Garbage Trucks Are Here* by showcasing multiple types of garbage trucks on the cover. It's the only book in its category to do so, and many reviews mention how much children loved seeing the variety.

There are many more things we can do to optimize the cover of our book, as I've shared in many of my YouTube videos (⬆). The main point I want to highlight here is that a thoughtfully optimized cover quietly supports every marketing effort we take on once our book is published. By considering these elements early and with intention, we give our book a stronger foundation and set ourselves up for smoother, more effective marketing down the road.

———— • ✦ • ————

THE FIRST VIEWABLE 10 PERCENT

Have you ever used Amazon's Look Inside feature? If so, you may have wondered what exactly decides what is being displayed in this digital preview. And the answer is actually pretty simple and straightforward. Amazon displays the first 10 percent of our book.

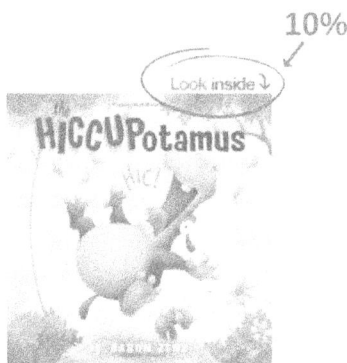

For a 37-page book, that usually means only three or four pages beyond the cover.

Knowing this allows us to choose intentionally what readers see first.

Use this space wisely by showcasing:

- *A beautiful title page*
- *Our first illustrations*
- *The beginning of our story*

Knowing that potential buyers only see the first few pages of our book, we want to make sure they are immediately introduced to the heart of the story. Avoid using these valuable pages for lengthy instructions or disclaimers; those can always be placed at the end of the book. Instead, use this space to showcase your vibrant illustrations and your beautiful story.

Optimizing for Amazon early gives our book the best possible chance to be discovered by the readers it was written for. When our title, cover, keywords, and first pages work together, marketing becomes easier, more effective, and more sustainable. These thoughtful decisions, made early on, create a strong foundation that will support every marketing effort that follows.

YOUR TO DOs FOR THIS CHAPTER:

- ❏ Research relevant keywords you can use for your title and subtitle
- ❏ Based on what you've just learned, carefully select your title and subtitle
- ❏ Based on what you've just learned, choose or update your cover
- ❏ Based on what you've just learned, arrange or rearrange the first pages of your book

Find all your templates and swipe files using this link below. You may want to bookmark this page, so you can refer to it as quickly and easily as possible.

⬆ *https://www.eevijones.com/marketing-downloads*

LINKS SHARED:

- *https://www.thesaurus.com*
- *https://www.fontsquirrel.com/matcherator*
- *https://www.myfonts.com/whatthefont*
- *https://www.eevijones.com/the-best-tool-for-childrens-book-authors*

CHAPTER 6
Activating Your Inner Circle With Intention

Marketing a children's book is not just about platforms, tactics, or launch-day checklists. It's also about people. The relationships we nurture while our book is being created play a major role in how supported, shared, and celebrated it will be later on. This chapter focuses on intentionally involving our inner circles early, not in a transactional way, but in a way that feels natural, generous, and aligned with who we are. These early connections become the foundation that makes our future marketing efforts easier, more authentic, and far more effective.

BUILDING & NURTURING OUR SUPPORT SYSTEM EARLY

Every successful book launch, no matter the genre, requires a strategy or plan, and benefits greatly from what is often called a launch team: a group of people who help spread the word about our book far and wide.

But before we even get there, there is something that needs to happen first. This is what we will focus on in this part of the book, because it is something we want to put in place well before the actual launch of our book.

The Chinese philosopher Zhu Xi once said, "Dig your well before you're thirsty."

What does this mean?

"Dig your well before you're thirsty" means preparing in advance for what we might need in the future. And something especially important for new and aspiring authors is support. Digging our well before we're thirsty means creating our support system before we actually need it.

But who, exactly, makes up our support system?

This could include:

- family members
- friends we regularly talk to or spend time with
- friends we haven't seen or spoken to in a while

- acquaintances and colleagues
- fellow authors

Now you may be wondering,

Why is having a support system made up of these people so important? And how does this tie back to a successful launch of our beautiful children's book?

Before answering that, it's important to get clear on what success means to us.

Usually, a launch is considered successful if it hits certain milestones:

- **MILESTONE 1:** to have strong initial sales
- **MILESTONE 2:** to receive a healthy number of supportive reviews
- **MILESTONE 3:** to experience ongoing sales over time

As the author of our precious books, it is our responsibility to help initiate these milestones. We are the ones who need to drive those initial sales and encourage early reviews. When those two pieces are in place, our book is far more likely to experience continued success.

Contrary to what many aspiring authors believe, a book's success is not based on luck. It is based on the initial and ongoing actions we take. And to support those actions, we need a support system.

Which brings us back to our original saying. Ideally, we build this support system before we need it for our launch. That means reconnecting with family members, friends, acquaintances, colleagues, and fellow authors ahead of time. Because imagine *this*:

You're connected with someone on Facebook, Instagram, or LinkedIn. Maybe you went to school together. You like each other's posts occasionally, but you haven't had a real conversation in years.

Out of the blue, this person messages you. They tell you about their newly published children's book and ask if you'd like to buy it, read it, or leave a supportive review on Amazon. How would that feel?

Would you feel excited to help, or would it feel a bit awkward to be asked for such a favor out of the blue?

When the first interaction after a long silence is an ask, it often feels uncomfortable. Not just for the person being asked, but also for the person doing the asking.

But if we dig our well before we're thirsty, everything feels more natural and far less awkward.

So the question becomes: how do we dig that well? And the answer is surprisingly simple.

To start building our support system now, all we need to do is stay connected. Reaching out to someone we already interact with from time to time feels much easier and far less transactional.

This makes it easier for others to say yes when we eventually ask for support. And it makes it easier for us to ask.

You might be thinking:

But Eevi - I DON'T have time to stay connected with all these people.

Let's take a look at what staying connected can actually look like, because it doesn't have to take much time at all.

Below are seven simple ways to nurture the relationships you already have, spending just a few minutes a day, so that asking for support later feels natural.

CONNECTION STRATEGY 1:

One of the easiest ways to stay connected is to make use of Facebook's handy-dandy birthday reminder feature. People often make fun of it because it almost feels like cheating. Because more often than not, we would forget most people's birthdays if it weren't for this little daily notification.

But if we use it in more intentional and thoughtful ways, it really can make a difference and strengthen our relationships, instead of getting lost in the sea of other seemingly obligatory birthday wishes on someone's feed.

This right here, for example, is a birthday notification I received for my friend Wendy. Looking at her feed, I can see that lots of people have already posted a sweet little birthday note, mostly using one of the pre-generated messages displayed along the bottom.

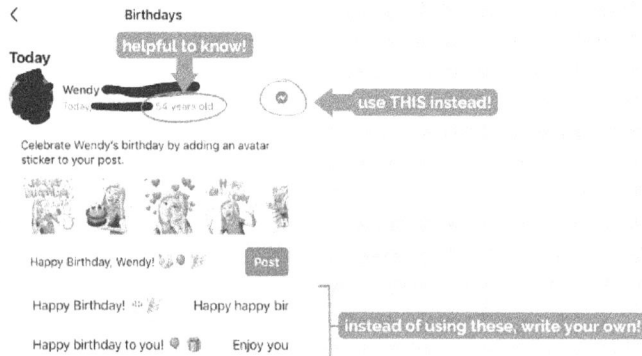

Simply posting one of those pre-generated birthday notes would already send us on our way toward nurturing our relationship with Wendy. I personally like to take it a tiny step further to help make others in my life feel a bit more special.

So instead of simply doing what everyone else is doing, I click on the Messenger button and share my birthday wish via a private message. Sometimes, I even go ahead and record a really quick 20-second voice message within Messenger, wishing them a happy birthday that way.

If you've ever received a birthday wish like this, you know how much more special it feels. We instantly know that this person went the extra mile to wish us a great day.

CONNECTION STRATEGY 2:

If I have their phone number, I send them a text message or a voice message instead. I love doing this, because now the recipient will often be really impressed that we remembered their birthday, since they no longer associate our message with Facebook's birthday notifications.

It's so easy to stay connected this way these days. I'm not big on calling people, but I absolutely love sending short yet thoughtful text messages or voice notes.

And even though this only takes a minute, people remember it. They remember because it makes them feel special, and because most people don't take these extra steps.

CONNECTION STRATEGY 3:

Another easy way to stay more connected with our friends and family is to pay attention to and interact with their posts.

For example, are they sharing about a recent move, or about having started a new job? Have they reached an exciting milestone in their career? Are they celebrating an anniversary?

We notice when someone gives our posts a thumbs-up. And we LOVE it when someone takes that literal extra second to hold down that "like" button and select the heart instead. So instead of just scrolling by, we can heart our friends' and family members' posts, as long as it feels genuine and right, of course.

CONNECTION STRATEGY 4:

To be even more supportive, we can add a heartfelt and thoughtful comment below their post. Whether it's to congratulate them, encourage them, or motivate them, any thoughtful comment we leave will help strengthen our relationship with that person.

CONNECTION STRATEGY 5:

Instead of commenting on their post, we can take this even further by writing them a private message or recording a quick voice message.

We don't have to do this with everyone. Reaching out to even just one person like this every day will make a difference. It will help us dig our well well before we are thirsty.

This is all about consistency. Taking just a few minutes each day is what helps us show up more regularly in people's lives.

CONNECTION STRATEGY 6:

Another easy way to stay connected with our friends and family is to pay attention to what they might currently need help with. And here, it's important to remember that being there for others doesn't have to cost money.

Maybe someone mentions that they're having a really hard time with something right now. Instead of just scrolling by, we can offer our moral support. Either in the comments or via a private message, we can let them know that we're thinking of them, that we're there for them, and that we're sending a virtual hug.

We so often underestimate how much our encouraging words and our kindness can affect others.

CONNECTION STRATEGY 7:

Or perhaps someone shares that they are trying to rent out their house. A really easy way to be supportive in this case is to simply share their post.

- It's really easy to do.
- It doesn't take much time at all.
- And it doesn't cost a dime.

Yet this simple gesture can really help someone else.

Sharing someone's post is such an easy thing to do, and yet most of us can probably count on two hands the number of times others have shared our posts. Because it doesn't happen very often, we remember it. We remember those supportive gestures.

These simple yet powerful ways of staying connected don't just pertain to Facebook. We can do the same on other platforms as well.

It's not the platform that matters. What matters most is that being there for others makes it so much easier for others to be there for us once we're reaching out for support during our launch.

Things are always easier with the support of others. And that's certainly true when it comes to launching a children's book.

To build a strong support system, it's incredibly helpful to nurture it before we actually need it. This doesn't require a huge time commitment. What it does require is intention and consistency. A little effort goes a very long way when we keep showing up.

———— • ◆ • ————

SHARE & UPDATE

Social shares and public updates are some of my favorite and most effective strategies for creating interest and curiosity even before the launch of our book.

This is such a fun thing to do for everyone involved. It's very likely that you're one of the only people among your friends and family who is writing a children's book. Sharing sneak peeks and updates about your project naturally creates excitement and curiosity, even before the book is finished.

This, for example, is an image I shared for one of my children's book projects. I created this sneak peek in Canva, and it only took me about five minutes. This is such a wonderful and engaging technique. And if you don't want to reveal your characters entirely, you can simply blur out parts of the illustration.

SNEAK PEEK

CHARACTER DEVELOPMENT

When sharing something like this on platforms such as Facebook or Instagram, be sure to talk about your excitement. You could write something like:

I'm beyond excited, guys!!!

I'm finally doing it. I'm finally fulfilling my dream of writing my very own children's book. The story is written, and now all my little characters are being created.

I'm really excited about this one, so I wanted to share a quick SNEAK PEEK with you guys!

More to come soon!

Make sure you break up the text so you don't post one big chunk. Short paragraphs increase engagement because people are more likely to read them. And don't forget to reply to every comment individually, so Facebook continues to show your post to more people.

My student Su Lee shared each of her book's milestones with her friends and family on Facebook, getting everyone curious and excited about her beautiful book *Old MacDonald's Lazy Farm*.

Scene & character development © Author Su Lee

We can share updates in many different ways.

In the end, it's not really about what we share, but that we share, so we take our friends and family along on this beautiful journey with us.

———— • ✦ • ————

ASK FOR FEEDBACK

Another way to involve others early and make them feel like part of our creative team is by asking for feedback.

Now, this can be a tricky one, because it can easily take us down a rabbit hole. So before we dive in, it's important to remember that this is meant as a strategy to get others excited, not necessarily to guide our decisions.

When asking for feedback, you'll receive all kinds of advice, some helpful and some not so much. Keep in mind:

1. Most of our friends aren't familiar with marketing and promoting children's books.
2. We all have different opinions.
3. Not everyone will agree with us.
4. **This strategy isn't really meant to ask for advice as much as it is meant to create awareness, curiosity, and interest in your upcoming book.**

Ideally, when asking for feedback, we already have a favorite option in mind and feel confident in the choices we've made.

To keep things manageable, always provide a set number of options, no more than three. Avoid open-ended questions, which can lead to overwhelming feedback. Be sure to clearly label each option so it's easy to respond.

For my oldest son's very first book, for example, I shared the following post with friends and family on Facebook:

We'd love your help!

Caen has been working all summer on his very first book! He is so excited and can't wait to become an author ☺ *We just completed his cover design and would love to hear what color choices would speak to you most.*

Please let us know what cover you'd prefer (1, 2, or 3). We can't wait to see what you guys think!

Caen is beyond excited about his summer project! Thank you SOOO much! xo

(P.S. More to come soon!)

You can also use Facebook's poll feature for things like title and subtitle choices.

Just remember, most people don't know about the keyword research and thought you've already put into your title and subtitle. The option you've chosen is likely already the strongest one. The poll simply helps spark interest and engagement.

I created this poll for the title and subtitle of my book *How to Self-Publish a Children's Book.*

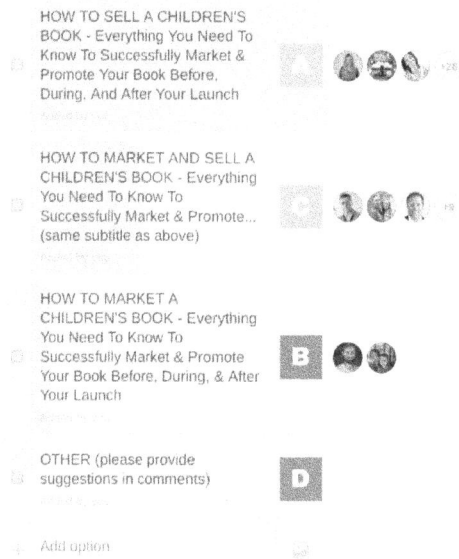

You could write something like:

*** BOOK TITLE, PLEASE ***

I'm getting ready for my very first children's book, and I'd love your feedback on my TITLE + SUBTITLE.

I so appreciate you brainstorming with me and am so very grateful for any of your thoughts and feedback.

xo ~ Eevi

By letting others be part of the creation process, most people will naturally support us and cheer us on throughout the journey.

———————— • ◆ • ————————

SHARE (LIVE) VIDEOS

If you want to go beyond static posts, you can also share short videos, either as Facebook Lives or pre-recorded videos. People love connecting with you directly, and videos are a wonderful way to do that.

The ideal length is under one minute, just long enough to keep people updated.

One of my students, Hanit, recorded herself unwrapping the proof copy of her children's book and shared it with friends and family on Facebook.

Within days, she received more than 400 likes, 249 comments, and over 3,000 views. She truly got her circle excited and ready to learn more. When you openly share your excitement, others naturally join in.

TEAMING UP WITH OUR ILLUSTRATOR

Teaming up with our illustrator and keeping them involved along the way is something very few authors think about. Illustrators are proud of their work, and by making them part of our marketing process, we can organically spread interest and excitement for our book even further.

This doesn't have to be anything formal or complicated. Sometimes it's as simple as tagging our illustrator when we share an image, celebrating their work publicly, or letting them know how excited we are about a particular illustration. That generosity and inclusion go a long way and often encourages them to share our project with their own community as well.

When illustrators feel included, appreciated, and excited about the project, they often become some of our biggest cheerleaders, which can make a meaningful difference when it comes to spreading the word about our book.

At the heart of all of these strategies is connection. Marketing a children's book doesn't have to feel loud or forced when it's built on genuine relationships. By involving our inner circles during this creation phase, sharing our progress, and inviting others behind the scenes, we are laying the groundwork for trust, awareness, and momentum long before our book is ready to launch.

With this foundation in place, we're ready to shift into the next phase, where that trust and momentum begin to work together in more visible, intentional ways.

YOUR TO DOs FOR THIS CHAPTER:

- ❏ Regularly interact with friends & family
- ❏ Share & update friends & family on social media

Find all your templates and swipe files using this link below. You may want to bookmark this page, so you can refer to it as quickly and easily as possible.

↑ *https://www.eevijones.com/marketing-downloads*

PART III
MARKETING WHILE
PREPARING FOR LAUNCH

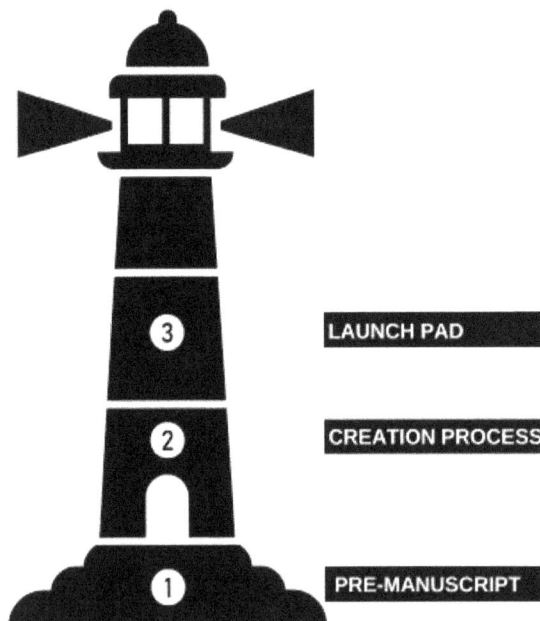

LAUNCH PAD

CREATION PROCESS

PRE-MANUSCRIPT

CHAPTER 7
Refining The Page That Sells Your Book

The launch pad phase is where everything we have been building starts to work together.

This is the phase where our book is no longer just a project in progress, but a finished story that deserves to be seen, understood, and chosen. Instead of focusing on who knows about our book, we now turn our attention to *how* our book shows up in the places where families are already looking.

And there is no more important place to start than Amazon.

Before we think about promotion, ads, or outreach, we need to make sure our book's home base is working for us.

Because every share, every recommendation, and every marketing effort will eventually lead people to the same place: our Amazon sales page. So let's begin this phase by optimizing the page that quietly supports all of our marketing, every single day.

Our Amazon sales page is not just a listing. It's a handshake. It's our book's first impression. And for many parents, grandparents, and teachers, it's the moment they decide, in a matter of seconds, whether our story feels worth their time, their trust, and their money.

Marketing isn't only about promotion or launch-day excitement. It's also about clarity, confidence, and removing unnecessary obstacles between our book and the families who are already looking for it. Our Amazon sales page is one of the most powerful pieces of marketing we have, because it works for us quietly and continuously, even long after our launch is over.

When we talk about optimizing our Amazon page, we're talking about thoughtful, intentional marketing - the kind that helps the right readers find us, understand our book quickly, and feel good about clicking that buy button.

We can have written the most magical children's book, but if the page surrounding it feels unclear, incomplete, or difficult to read, many of the readers who would have loved it may never stop to explore further.

This chapter is here to make sure our marketing does its job, so our story can do what it was always meant to do. With all of that in mind, let's take a closer look at the things we can tweak and optimize on our Amazon sales page:

KEYWORDS KNOW-HOW (Part 2)

A keyword, in its simplest terms, is a word used to describe something. In the author world, keywords help describe our book by indicating its topic, so it's easier to categorize and easier to find.

Nowadays, for better or for worse, we make many of our purchases online. We also do most of our research online before we even decide what to buy. And in the world of book marketing, being discoverable is half the battle. Keywords help make sure our children's book actually shows up where our readers are already looking. And because of that, it's very important to present our book in such a way that a search engine can find it.

Thinking of Amazon as a search engine gives us such an advantage, because we now understand that the information we provide about our book during setup will be used by Amazon to help its algorithm decide whether or not to put our book in front of potential buyers when they type something into Amazon's search bar.

We want to make sure to optimize our beautiful children's book to increase its searchability and make it easier to be found. Because visibility always begins with discoverability, which is exactly what thoughtful keywords help us achieve.

USAGE

We already talked about the importance of keywords during the *Title and Subtitle* section of this book, and how to go about finding the best ones in PART II. So by now, we should already have a great list of keywords and keyphrases from that earlier research.

This part of the book focuses on the keywords and keyphrases we can enter during the setup and uploading of your book on KDP. Adding keywords is optional. However, I highly encourage you to use this feature.

Every author gets seven keyword boxes, and each box allows up to 50 characters.

Your Keywords (Optional)

Naturally, this leaves many authors wondering:

Should we fill every box to the max? Or is it better to focus on one very specific phrase, even if we don't use all 50 characters?

No one knows for certain how Amazon's algorithm truly works. So instead of choosing just one strategy, I believe a thoughtful combination of different strategies across the seven keyword fields works best.

Choose 1 to 3 Highly Specific Keyword Phrases

Our first 1 to 3 keywords should be highly specific keyword phrases that:

- are deeply relevant to our story
- people actually search for on Amazon
- are not so competitive that we'll never show up for them

These should be the exact phrases our ideal reader (or their grown-up) would type into Amazon when looking for our type of children's book.

Some children's book specific examples would be:

- *bedtime story for toddlers*
- *kindness book for preschoolers*
- *picture book about sharing*
- *silly rhyming book for ages 3 to 5*
- *first day of kindergarten story*

Here, we can either use the *Amazon Auto Fill* research method I shared in the *Title and Subtitle* section, or we can use tools like *Publisher Rocket* (↑). Tools like that can be incredibly helpful because they tell us how often a keyphrase is searched and how competitive it is.

Once we've identified our top 1 to 3 highly specific phrases, we'll want to give each phrase its own keyword box.

Choose 1 to 2 Category-Affirming Keywords

Amazon always reserves the right to take books out of categories it feels they don't belong to - something that has happened to me multiple times. To help prevent that, we'll want to use one or two keyword boxes to reinforce our category choices.

To do this, we pick one or two of our most relevant categories and come up with a list of words that describe that category. Then we combine those words and place them in 1 to 2 of our keyword boxes.

For example, if our main category is **Books > Children's Books > Animals > Dinosaurs**, then descriptive category-affirming words could include:

Prehistoric, Fossil, Jurassic, Paleontology, T-rex, Triceratops, Stegosaurus, Velociraptor, Pterodactyl, Allosaurus, Brachiosaurus, Herbivore, Carnivore, Fossils, Extinct, Adventure, Discovery, Ancient, Paleontologist, Paleoart, Dino, Tyrannosaurus

Finding and combining some of these words in 1 to 2 keyword boxes signals to Amazon that our book truly belongs in that category.

Choose 1 to 2 Niche Terms and Phrases

For our remaining keyword boxes, we want to use as many of those 50 characters as possible with words and short phrases that clearly describe our book and its niche.

These can be broader terms - things that may not be typed exactly into Amazon, but still help Amazon understand and index our book correctly.

Think about words that describe:

- **Your main character**
  (e.g. unicorn, puppy, little dinosaur, brave girl, firefighter)
- **Your setting**
  (e.g. preschool, beach day, bedtime, jungle, classroom)
- **Your theme or issue**
  (e.g. big feelings, being brave, making friends, confidence, empathy)
- **Synonyms of the above**
  (e.g. courage / bravery, school / classroom)

You'll be surprised how quickly these 50-character boxes fill up when you take this approach.

NINJA TIP:

Amazon specifically tells us not to use quotation marks around our keywords or keyphrases, because that would limit us to the exact phrase.

For example, if we were to enter:

"Firetruck Rescue Adventure"

then our book would only be indexed for that exact phrase. However, if we enter it as:

Firetruck Rescue Adventure

our book will also be indexed for

- rescue firetruck adventure
- firetruck adventure
- rescue adventure
- adventure

… and every other rearranged version.

NINJA TIP:

There's no need to add plural versions of our nouns. For example, there's no need to enter both:

- *unicorn*
- *unicorns*

Amazon treats them as one and the same.

Thoughtful Combination of the Different Strategies

Here's the key:

- The **more words** we add to a box, the **more total phrases** we will index for.
- But the **more targeted** our phrase is, the stronger our ranking can be for that exact phrase.

This is why a combination of our above keyword strategies works best. Use some boxes for very specific, highly relevant keyphrases, and use others to fill those 50 characters with helpful descriptive terms.

Doing so will help us set our beautiful children's book up for stronger visibility and stronger keyword performance across Amazon.

Now, if this left your head spinning, don't worry! These keywords can be changed inside KDP's dashboard as often as you'd like, at any time. That makes keyword testing and adjusting a timeless strategy. And being smart with our keywords should always be part of our marketing plan.

NINJA TIP:

People's behavior changes, and so does their search behavior. That's why it's so important to remember that we can always update our book description and our seven keywords or keyphrases - even long after publishing.

Amazon offers so many products. So in order to cater to its shoppers properly, Amazon wants to put the right products in front of the right buyers. And it relies heavily on keywords and keyphrases to do that.

So using keywords smartly will help with the discoverability of our children's book. And this doesn't just hold true for Amazon. It's the same on Barnes and Noble, Target, and anywhere else with a search bar. If a marketplace has a search function, the items offered and sold rely on the proper use of keywords.

———— ·◆· ————

BOOK DESCRIPTION

Whether we write a picture book or a middle-grade chapter book, a well-written children's book description is an incredibly important marketing tool.

Unfortunately, many authors don't plan ahead and throw something together at the very last minute, right before hitting publish. The truth is, a planned-out description can set our book miles apart from others.

Oftentimes, it's this description that helps potential buyers decide whether our book is the one they've been searching for. A great blurb should do at least two things:

1. ***Hook readers right away so they want to read the blurb in its entirety.***

2. **Help readers quickly see whether this is the book that will address and fill their needs.**

While the title and subtitle help with discoverability and grab attention, it's often the words in the description that make a reader decide to buy - or not.

A book blurb is a short description (ideally no more than 250 words). If written well, it can be one of our most powerful marketing tools because it hooks readers and nudges them toward that buy button.

As you now already know, when deciding what to show to potential buyers, Amazon uses an algorithm. Because Amazon is a system and not a person, it evaluates every bit of information we provide, including:

- our book title
- our subtitle
- the age group we set
- the keywords and categories we choose
- and what we include in our description

All of this influences Amazon's algorithm, which then decides which books are shown to which shoppers. So we want to make sure these parts are **congruent,** and that we make the absolute most of them.

To get a feel for what makes a great blurb, I like looking at similar books and paying attention to length, word choice, and style. That's a great way to see what our audience expects.

The best descriptions follow four important guidelines.

GUIDELINE 1: *Begin with an Enticing Hook*

Most people stop reading after the first few lines. That's why the most important line of our description should be above the fold.

"Above the fold" is an old newspaper term where editors made sure the headline and most important part of the front page stayed visible above the fold. For us, it means making sure the reader can see the most compelling line without having to click "Read more."

In *How To Self-Publish A Children's Book*, Y. Eevi Jones outlines

⌄ Read more

We want to reduce friction and hook the reader right away. And showing the best part above the fold is one of the easiest ways to do that.

This "best part" can be:

- *a question*
- *part of a rhyme (if it's a rhyming book)*
- *a fun statement about the main character*
- *an unusual statement about a certain situation*

Here are some strong opening lines that keep us wanting to read more:

1. **It's a dream vacation for Jack and Annie - or is it?** *(The Magic Tree House - Shadow of the Shark)*
2. **A simple act of kindness can transform an invisible boy into a friend...** *(The Invisible Boy)*
3. **Gerald the giraffe longs to dance, but his legs are too skinny and his neck is too long** *(Giraffes Can't Dance)*

GUIDELINE 2: *Tie in Keywords & Synonyms*

Including keywords, keyphrases, and synonyms matters because Amazon evaluates every bit of information we provide.

Amazon's ultimate goal is to make a sale. So it tries to match each buyer with the product they're most likely to purchase. Including relevant keywords in our description helps with discoverability, especially if they align with our title and subtitle. This can raise our relevancy score for our chosen keywords.

So if buyers search for a monkey book, the books that consistently include "monkey" throughout their metadata (including the description) will often perform better than those that don't.

GUIDELINE 3: *Make the Description Easy to Read*

People's attention span is so short, so we want our description to look easy on the eyes, not tiring. We can do that by breaking text into short, digestible paragraphs and occasionally using bullet points.

Not everything might go our way sometimes - and that's okay! Showing little ones the true power of their own thoughts, USA Today bestselling and award-winning author Eevi Jones dives into a world of everyday scenarios kids encounter every single day. Feeling different emotions can be really hard at times, especially for 2 to 5-year-olds. Sometimes It Rains helps kids understand that … It's okay to want something, and then NOT get it. It's okay to NOT know something, and then ask. It's okay wanting to be happy, but feeling a bit sad sometimes instead. Boys and girls will learn that it is okay to feel all sorts of different …

Not everything might go our way sometimes - and that's okay!

Showing little ones the true power of their own thoughts, USA Today bestselling and award-winning author Eevi Jones dives into a world of everyday scenarios kids encounter every single day.

Feeling different emotions can be really hard at times, especially for 2 to 5-year-olds.

Sometimes It Rains helps kids understand that …
- It's okay to want something, and then NOT get it.
- It's okay to NOT know something, and then ask.
- It's okay wanting to be happy, but feeling a bit sad sometimes instead.

Boys and girls will learn that it is okay to feel all sorts of different …

NINJA TIP:

Awards can truly set us apart. And while we want to mention them, we want to do so concisely - ideally by weaving them into an existing sentence.

Here are two great examples:

- *"**Award-winning** author and illustrator Ashley Spires has created a charming picture book about an unnamed girl and her very best friend, who happens to be a dog."*
- *"**A New York Times Best Seller** and **award-winning book**, this story is for anyone who's ever had a big idea."*

These credibility markers are easy to spot but don't take up extra space. This is very similar to the *Weaving Technique* we used in the author bio chapter.

NINJA TIP:

If your book is part of a series, weave that into your description too. It signals to buyers that you have more to offer and helps cross-promote your other books.

This can be done very succinctly:

- *"Rich with author Aaron Blabey's signature rhyming text, Pig the Stinker is a laugh-out-loud story that teaches Pig - and listeners - an important (and hilarious) lesson, just like **in the five previous books in the series**."*

- *"This book is a great first introduction to Mouse, the star of the **If You Give... series** and a perennial favorite among children.*

GUIDELINE 4: *Make Use of the Lead-With-The-Heart Method*

Remember my *Lead-With-The-Heart Method* from an earlier chapter? Our description is an excellent place to appeal to little readers as well as the grown-ups who purchase the book.

Let's look at one of my book descriptions as an example:

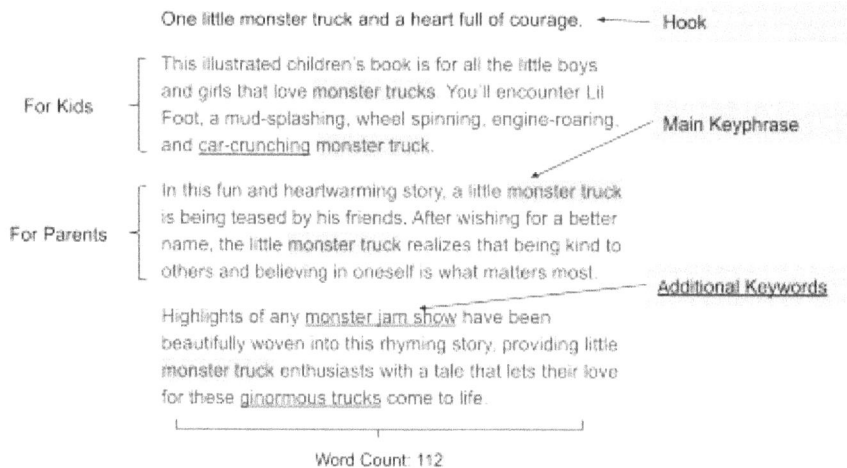

One little monster truck and a heart full of courage. ←——— Hook

For Kids

This illustrated children's book is for all the little boys and girls that love monster trucks. You'll encounter Lil Foot, a mud-splashing, wheel spinning, engine-roaring, and car-crunching monster truck. ——→ Main Keyphrase

For Parents

In this fun and heartwarming story, a little monster truck is being teased by his friends. After wishing for a better name, the little monster truck realizes that being kind to others and believing in oneself is what matters most.

——— Additional Keywords

Highlights of any monster jam show have been beautifully woven into this rhyming story, providing little monster truck enthusiasts with a tale that lets their love for these ginormous trucks come to life.

Word Count: 112

This description grabs attention right away. It opens with a hook and then defines (or gently hints at) the audience so the reader knows what to expect.

This blurb is relatively short (112 words) and still manages to bring the important points across.

Longer is not always better, especially when buyers are still deciding. We want to grab attention quickly, highlight the juicy parts, and end on a strong note. There's no room for the reader to tune out. Every word in these short paragraphs has been carefully chosen, and every word serves a purpose. There's no fluff and no filler - and that's exactly what we want.

The *Lead-With-The-Heart Method* is woven into the first two paragraphs, where the first part speaks to the monster-truck loving child, while the second part (with its lessons and values) speaks to the parent.

Throughout the description, we're also making extensive use of the main keywords. With five mentions of the main keyword, the density is quite high, and we also see alternative keywords sprinkled throughout.

Also note how it includes other details so readers know what to expect:

1. **BOOK TYPE:** illustrated children's book
2. **GENDER:** for both boys and girls
3. **FORMAT:** rhyming story

NINJA TIP:

Whether it's the description on the back of our book or on our Amazon sales page, remember: we can tweak, change, and optimize it any time.

CATEGORY-SMARTS

Besides our seven keywords, Amazon allows us to choose three categories for our children's book. From a buyer's perspective, categories help readers find the right book more easily.

From an author's perspective, categories are simply another marketing tool.

Here is my personal (perhaps a bit controversial) take on categories:

We don't sell more books because we rank higher in a category. Instead, we rank higher because we are selling more books.

In other words, ranking isn't the cause of sales. Ranking is a by-product of marketing.

The more books we sell, the higher we rank - not the other way around.

So if higher ranking isn't necessarily what causes more sales, why do categories still matter?

The main reason is this: the categories we choose affect whether our book can become an *Amazon Bestseller*. And being able to call our book a *bestseller* is a humongous credibility marker we can use across our marketing - in our author bio, our book description, on social media, and more.

No matter how long our book was on a bestseller list, we can use that title in perpetuity.

So if we want to get the most out of each marketing effort, we want to position our book so that every sale brings us closer to that bestseller status.

Amazon currently has over 11,000 categories. More than 450 categories are for children's books, and over 260 categories are for children's ebooks. That's a lot of opportunities.

But if we choose a category that's too competitive, it may be very difficult to outperform the books already ranking.

So we want categories that:

- *are highly **RELEVANT** to our book topic*
- *are not too **COMPETITIVE***
- *give us a realistic shot at earning the bestseller badge*

Amazon updates category ranking *hourly*, so there are plenty of opportunities.

HOW TO SEE HOW COMPETITIVE A CATEGORY IS:

To gauge how competitive a category is, we can look at the current sales of the book that is ranking number one in that category.

STEP 1:

First, we need to identify Amazon's available categories and subcategories and decide which ones might be a great fit for our book. Since Amazon doesn't provide a complete list, we first have to "uncover" them ourselves.

METHOD 1: Navigating on Amazon

- Go to Amazon.com and click "Books" or "Kindle Store."
- Look for something like "Bestsellers & More."
- Select "Children's Books" in the left-hand menu.
- Click subcategories to reveal deeper layers.

METHOD 2: Researching Similar Books

- Search for books similar to yours using relevant keywords.
- Click on a search result.
- Scroll to the book's "Product details" to find the categories it is listed in.

STEP 2:

Once we have found a category we think is a good fit, we want to see how many books we'd need to sell to beat the current #1 bestseller in that category.

To do that, find the book's **Amazon Best Seller Rank (ABSR)** in the Product Details section (right above the categories).

Product details

File Size: 2500 KB
Print Length: 46 pages
Publisher: Fat Moon Books (December 26, 2013)
Publication Date: December 26, 2013
Sold by: Amazon Digital Services LLC
Language: English
ASIN: B0095807LK
Text-to-Speech: Enabled
X-Ray: Enabled
Word Wise: Enabled
Lending: Enabled
Enhanced Typesetting: Not Enabled
Amazon Best Sellers Rank: #4,137 Paid in Kindle Store (See Top 100 Paid in Kindle Store)
  #1 in Kindle Store > Kindle eBooks > Children's eBooks > Mysteries & Detectives > **Detectives**
  #1 in Kindle Store > Kindle eBooks > Children's eBooks > Science Fiction, Fantasy & Scary Stories > Science Fiction > **Time Travel**
  #2 in Kindle Store > Kindle eBooks > Children's eBooks > Growing Up & Facts of Life > Family Life > **Parents**

STEP 3:

Next, use the *Kindlepreneur Sales Rank Calculator* (↑) and enter the ABSR to estimate how many copies it's selling.

In our example, the ebook is ranking #1 in

Kindle Store > Kindle eBooks > Children's eBooks > Mysteries & Detectives > Detectives

with an ABSR of 4,137.

Entering this number into the calculator shows it's selling about 50 ebooks per day. So to become #1 in that category, we'd need to sell about 50 ebooks per day.

Welcome to the Book and Ebook Sales Calculator, where you can input a book's best seller rank (BSR) & discover how much that book is making.

To see advanced data on audiobook sales and hidden categories, check out Publisher Rocket.

Enter the Kindle Best Seller Rank Below

4137

Book Type   **Marketplace**

Using this calculator is absolutely free, so it's the most cost-effective way to do our category research. Alternatively, *Publisher Rocket* can do much of this research for us.

REMEMBER: Categories help us position our book strategically during launch so we can earn that bestseller title and use it in current and future marketing. Categories alone won't necessarily make us sell more books.

NINJA TIP:

Consider using different categories for your paperback and ebook. That way, we can essentially double the number of categories our book can appear in.

For example, enroll your paperback in categories A, B, and C, and enroll your ebook in categories D, E, and F.

NINJA TIP:

We can change and update our categories any time, even after publishing, by going into our KDP dashboard, clicking the three dots next to the book, and selecting "Edit book details." After updating, we simply resubmit.

NINJA TIP:

Because Amazon re-evaluates performance metrics *hourly*, any banners we may earn are temporary. So take a screenshot of any banners your book receives, whether that's a "New Release" or "Bestselling" banner.

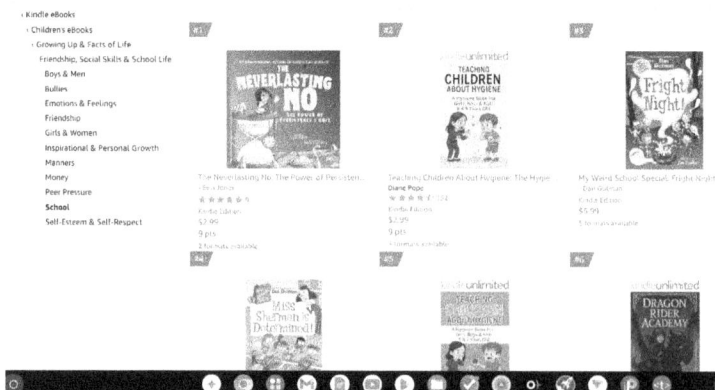

Any position on a bestseller list is worth celebrating, whether that's #1 or #50. Be sure to take a screenshot, share it proudly, and update your social media bios, your author biography, and your book description - because you are officially a bestselling author!

A PERSONAL NOTE:

Before moving on, I want to share a personal note with you.

Just because an author is able to call themselves a bestselling author doesn't necessarily mean their book is selling well long-term. It simply means that, at one brief point in time, they sold more copies than others in that specific category. So while that orange bestseller banner may be a big dream of yours, I want you to know that a banner alone does not define you or your book's success.

Personally, I would much rather focus on steady, continuous sales over time than chase a momentary bestseller badge.

————————— • ◆ • —————————

PRICING STRATEGICALLY

Pricing is one of the earliest marketing decisions we'll ever make for our children's book.

Pricing is not just a financial choice - it is a foundational marketing choice. The moment a reader sees our price, they're already forming an opinion about our book's value and whether it fits what they're looking for.

Most of my students and clients struggle with pricing. They've worked so hard writing the book, illustrating it, and getting it ready to be sold. In most cases, it's a passion project - something we truly can't put a price tag on.

So when it comes time to enter a price during setup, we often think in terms of time and money invested, which naturally leads to a higher price. Because that feels fair to us.

But here's the thing:

If we want to compete with books pushed by major publishing houses, we need to price accordingly. This is where pricing becomes a true marketing tool. By aligning with market expectations, we remove a major barrier between our ideal reader and that buy button.

Especially if this is our first book, we don't yet have much credibility or name recognition. So to give our book a real chance, we want to price it competitively.

By competitively, I mean: priced similarly to other children's books with similar topics.

Our book will pop up next to similar ones, and buyers will compare prices. And if our ebook is priced at $9.99 while every other ebook is significantly lower, the chances of our book being chosen are slim. Even the strongest marketing in the world can't overcome a price that instantly feels out of place.

So when deciding on price, look at comparable books and price yours accordingly. If most ebooks in your topic are around $2.99, price yours around that as well. If paperbacks are around $12.99, aim for that same neighborhood. If prices vary, go with the average.

As we're trying to get our foot in the door, we want to get our book into the hands of those who need it most. And in a competitive market, pricing accordingly helps us do just that.

To help you find a competitive price, I've created a printable pricing table (↑). Find about 10 comparable books, note their prices, and calculate the average.

By familiarizing ourselves with genre norms like pricing, we can use them as a guide and employ this information to our advantage when it comes time to market our beautiful work. Understanding pricing norms helps us position our children's book in a way that feels inviting rather than confusing - which is the essence of effective marketing.

————————— • ◆ • —————————

A+ CONTENT - ENHANCING OUR BOOK PAGE

One of the most exciting updates Amazon has given us in recent years is the ability for KDP authors to add *A+ Content* (↑) to our book sales pages. For the longest time, this feature was reserved for traditionally published books only. You may have noticed it before - that colorful "From the Publisher" section filled with extra visuals, interior pages, quotes, or even a carousel of books from the same series.

Here is why this matters for us as children's authors:

A+ Content is visual marketing.

It gives us a unique opportunity to enhance our book page with additional visuals and information that help readers connect with our work more quickly and more deeply. When someone lands on our Amazon page, we have only seconds to capture their attention. And that is exactly what these images, quotes, and visuals help us do.

Traditional publishers have known this for years. They don't add these sections just because they're pretty. They add them because they convert browsers into buyers.

A+ Content is simply Amazon's way of giving all authors the chance to do the same.

I always look for ideas and analyze what traditional publishers do, because they've done their homework. They know what is and isn't working. And we can use that knowledge to our advantage and emulate it. We get to take what they're already doing successfully and reimagine it for our own beautiful children's books.

With *A+ Content*, we can:

- add fun visuals that showcase our interior artwork
- highlight a key message or quote from our story
- display multiple books from our series in a polished, professional way
- create a cohesive, branded experience that makes our book feel instantly more credible

This is one of the easiest ways to elevate the look and feel of our Amazon page and make our book stand out in a crowded space. It reassures buyers, helps them understand our book quickly, and builds trust - which is especially important for newer authors.

Amazon has made the process simple. We create images (*Canva* works wonderfully (↑)), upload them in KDP, and apply them to our book. Within a few hours, our page can have that beautiful, traditionally published look.

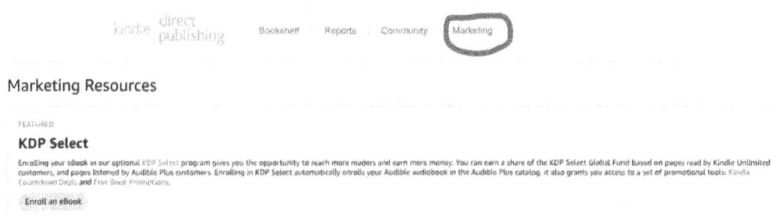

NINJA TIP:

If we want our *A+ Content* to appear across all of Amazon's international marketplaces, we need to set it up for each marketplace individually.

This is such a powerful visibility booster and a wonderful tool to use as part of our overall marketing strategy. Anything that helps readers feel more confident, more connected, and more ready to click "Buy Now" is worth exploring. And this one is both fun and impactful.

———— • ✦ • ————

EBOOK VERSION

So many of my clients, students, and readers tell me they're not interested in creating an ebook version of their children's book. And the main reason is this: they've always pictured their story being held by tiny hands. They imagine turning real pages, cuddling up, and holding the actual physical book.

And I completely understand that feeling, because I used to think the exact same way.

But over the years, I've come to see how powerful ebooks can be for us as children's authors, because ebooks can be one of our biggest marketing tools. Here are four reasons I always encourage fellow authors to consider offering an ebook version:

1. EASIER & MORE COST EFFECTIVE TO SHARE

While ebooks still aren't the primary way most people read to young children, usage continues to grow. And even though paperbacks make up most of my own sales, the ebook becomes invaluable the moment I begin promotions or request reviews.

Downloading an ebook is fast, simple, and far more cost effective than sending a physical copy - especially when we factor in shipping and packaging costs. If we plan to run outreach, get early reviews, or share our book with influencers or educators, having an ebook version is incredibly helpful and much gentler on our budget.

2. SPILL-OVER SALES

The second reason is spill-over sales.

I once enrolled one of my books in KDP Select to run a free ebook promotion. During and after that promotion, sales of my hardcover increased so much that it temporarily went out of stock. Even though I only promoted the ebook, interest spilled over to all other formats.

Why? Because once readers fall in love with the story, many want a physical copy. So offering an ebook doesn't compete with our paperback or hardcover - it often boosts them.

3. NO EXTRA COST

The third reason is that creating an ebook can cost nothing extra, especially if we format it ourselves.

Unlike paperbacks and hardcovers, ebooks don't require their own ISBN. And I share in various YouTube videos how to create an ebook version using free tools.

I like using the same images I used for the paperback. The only difference is that I use the double-spread illustration (the left and right page) as one single ebook page. I simply increase the text size so it's easy to read, no matter what device the book is being read on.

It's quick, it's simple, and it doesn't require purchasing anything new.

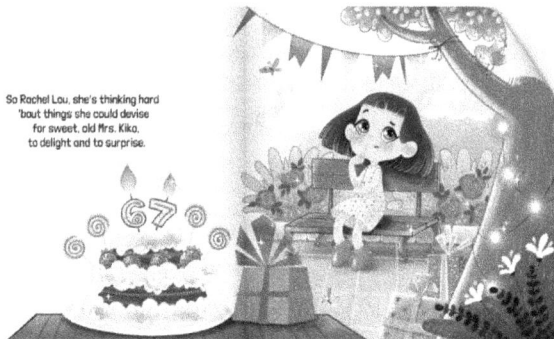

So Rachel Lou, she's thinking hard
'bout things she could devise
for sweet, old Mrs. Kiko,
to delight and to surprise.

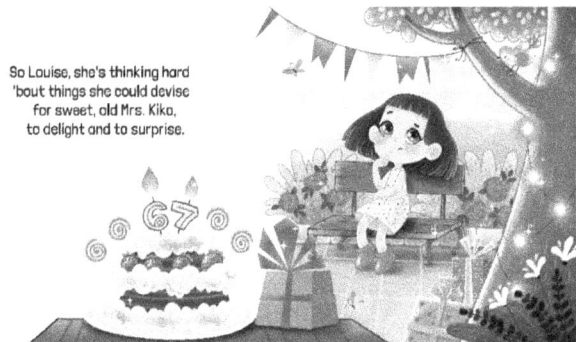

So Louise, she's thinking hard
'bout things she could devise
for sweet, old Mrs. Kiko,
to delight and to surprise.

4. *KDP SELECT* – AMAZON'S BUILT-IN MARKETING TOOL

KDP Select is Amazon's built-in marketing tool. It's a powerful way to get our book into more hands, increase visibility, and generate early momentum. And having an ebook allows us to take advantage of this tool.

Every time we enroll our ebook into *KDP Select*, it remains enrolled for 90 days. Within those 90 days, we can use it in two ways:

- *up to 5 days of a* **Free Book Promotion**
- *up to 7 days of a* **KDP Countdown Deal**

NINJA TIP:

We don't have to use all promotional days, and we don't have to use them on consecutive days.

On the buyer's end, enrolled ebooks display the *Kindle Unlimited* label. *Kindle Unlimited* subscribers can download our book for free during those 90 days.

A heartfelt and beautifully inclusive Baby Shower Gift, Welcome Gift & Mother's Day Gift for New Moms and Moms-To-Be by *USA TODAY* **BESTSELLING author Eevi Jones.**

Precious is a sweet tribute to new moms and moms-to-be, who, for the first time, venture out into the world of parenthood.

Often purchased as a baby shower gift or newborn welcome present. *Precious* marks and celebrates the beginnings of something

⌄ Read more

During that time, we can earn a share of the *KDP Select Global Fund* based on how many pages customers read. So we can still earn money even though the ebook is "free" to subscribers.

KDP SELECT - ADVANTAGES

Being able to offer the ebook version of our book for free or offering a countdown deal is huge. Here are five of the main reasons why:

ADVANTAGE 1: *Downloads and Sales Determine the Ranking of our Book.*

All sales count. Each sale bumps our book up in Amazon's algorithm, whether that's an ebook sale or a paperback sale. And even though we are offering our ebook for free or at a lower price for a short period of time, Amazon treats this free download like a regular sale in that it improves our book's ranking on Amazon. Every single download lets Amazon know that our book is in demand. And by doing so, we are increasing our chances of being put in front of other potential buyers.

ADVANTAGE 2: *Making it Free for our Launch Team.*

If we are planning to set up a launch team, enrolling our book into *KDP Select* would allow them to download it for free.

You might be wondering why we couldn't just send our launch team a free copy or a pdf of our book, instead of asking them to download our free ebook version. The reason why we want our launch team to download your book is two-fold:

1. It (again) improves our book's ranking on Amazon.

2. Amazon always distinguishes between **verified** and **unverified reviews**, by placing a little label shared right below each review. A review that has the verified label attached to it lets potential buyers know that the reviewer has actually purchased the book over on

Amazon. A review that doesn't have such a label means that the person that left the review did not purchase the book; at least not via Amazon. Amazon prefers verified reviews and will therefore often show these first. This verified purchase tag also shows up for reviews posted by those that downloaded the ebook for free. All that matters to get that verified purchase tag is that the ebook has indeed been downloaded, whether it was for free or not.

M. Meyer

★ ★ ★ ★ ★ Love this book!

Reviewed in the United States on April 2, 2022

Verified Purchase

Eevi has written a simple and concise book that has helped me tremendously. I would recommend this book and to anyone thinking about self publishing. She also has a YouTube channel that answers questions you may have about self publishing. Check it out! Thanks Eevi!

ADVANTAGE 3: *Promotional Sites.*

There are hundreds of sites that allow us to promote our free ebook, so by enrolling it into *KDP Select*, we will be able to promote our book on these sites.

This (again) may increase our ranking with each download, and may also lead to receiving reviews. This is of course not a given, but very possible, especially if we have a review request in the back of our book.

ADVANTAGE 4: *Making Use of KDP Countdown Deals.*

Besides the option of being able to offer our ebook for free, we can also make use of the *KDP Countdown Deal*. The pricing of our ebook very much depends on its file size. If our ebook file is very small, then we might be able to set our ebook price as low as $0.99.

But because the file size of children's books is usually fairly large due to our illustrations, the lowest we can often set our price is $2.99. If that is the case, enrolling our book into *KDP Select* would allow us to offer our book for a lower price for up to 7 days.

This is what our *KDP Countdown Deal* would look like on the front end. The Amazon buyer would see a bright banner, as well as our previous higher price that is now crossed out, right next to the temporarily lower price.

I Funny: A Middle School Story

Book 1 of 6: I Funny | by James Patterson, Chris Grabenstein, et al.

★ ★ ★ ★ ☆ · 1,304

Audible Audiobook   Ages: 9 - 12 years

1 Credit

Available instantly

Kindle

Limited time deal

$0⁹⁹ $8.99

Available instantly

NINJA TIP:

We can choose the *KDP Countdown Deal* option only after our book has already been published for at least 30 days. So we couldn't use this type of promotion during our initial launch.

ADVANTAGE 5: *Increased Discoverability*

Enrolling our book into *KDP Select* might help with our book's discoverability. The hope is that by enrolling our book into various ebook promotions, that we are being exposed to an audience we may have otherwise never reached on our own.

KDP SELECT - DISADVANTAGES

Personally, the only disadvantage I currently see of enrolling our children's book into *KDP Select* is the required exclusivity. But it really only is a disadvantage if we were planning to offer our ebook in other places as well, outside of Amazon.

So what does this exclusivity mean and refer to?

When enrolling our ebook into *KDP Select*, we are not allowed to offer that ebook anywhere else during the 90-day enrollment period. That rule only applies to the ebook version of our book, and not to your paperback or hardcover.

So for those 90 days, our ebook will have to be exclusive to Amazon.

HOW TO ENROLL INTO *KDP SELECT*

Enrolling is easy, and we can do so any time:

- *either when we initially set up our ebook and are presented with the option to enroll right away*
- *or any time thereafter by going to our KDP dashboard and clicking the three dots next to our ebook*

	Kindle eBook	$0.99 USD	KINI
	LIVE	View on Amazon	
	Submitted on September 8, 2021	ASIN: B09FP847LG	
Book in life's biggest moments	Paperback	$12.99 USD	PAP
Sisterly: To My Best Friend	LIVE	View on Amazon	
By Eevi Jones	Submitted on September 8, 2021	ASIN: 1952517079	

Edit eBook details
Edit eBook Content
Edit eBook pricing
Enroll in KDP Select
Promote and Advertise

Manage series
Unpublish eBook
Unlink Books

After confirming enrollment, we can select:

1. *KDP Countdown Deals*
2. *Free Book Promotion*

WHEN TO ENROLL INTO *KDP SELECT*

I would recommend considering *KDP Select* in 3 scenarios:

- If our ebook consists of a large file size that requires our lowest sales price to be set at $2.99 or higher. Enrolling it into *KDP Select* would allow us to offer it for a lower price (or for free).
- We might also want to consider it if we wish to provide our launch team members with a free copy, so they don't have to pay for it, and so that their review shows up as a verified review.
- And we might want to consider enrolling into *KDP Select* if we want to run promotions on different promo sites, as most of these sites will require a reduced price, or our book to be free.

Besides giving us a new way to earn royalties and use new promotional tools, *KDP Select* also enables us to reach new audiences - be it Amazon's *Kindle Unlimited* subscribers, or the promotions we will be able to set up for our book.

NINJA TIP:

Once we've run our promotions, make sure to un-enroll from *KDP Select* before the 90 days are up. Otherwise, it will automatically re-enroll for another 90 days.

To change the default settings, click "Manage KDP Select Enrollment," uncheck the "automatically renew" box, and click Save.

KDP Select Information   ×

Term start date: April 11, 2022 PDT
Term end date: July 9, 2022 PDT

- -

☐ **Automatically renew this book's enrollment in KDP Select for another 90 days.**
For your convenience, we will automatically renew this book's enrollment in KDP Select once the current term ends. If you wish, you can cancel automatic renewal by un-checking the box. Please note that cancelling automatic renewal does not affect the book's enrollment in KDP Select for the current term.

Save   Cancel

⅄ About KDP Select

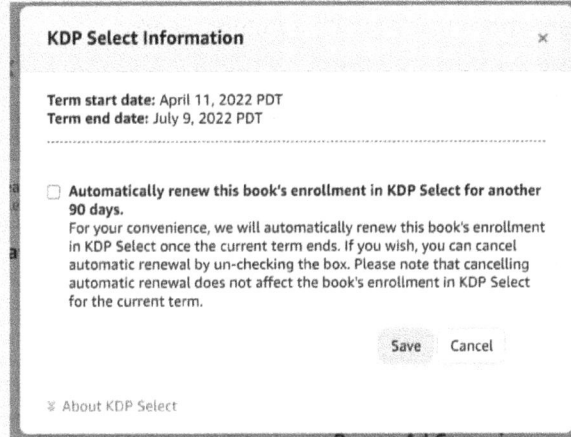

When it comes to marketing, having an ebook truly is a gift. It's flexible, accessible, and one of the easiest promotional tools available to us.

Even though I personally prefer little ones to experience my books in physical form, I also want to give buyers the choice. And from a marketing standpoint, there are so many benefits to having an ebook available.

Whether it's making our book more financially accessible, making it easier and faster for our launch team to review, or enrolling it in promotions and *KDP Select*, an ebook can be a wonderful and very effective marketing tool.

And best of all, it helps more people discover, enjoy, and fall in love with our beautiful children's book.

<hr>

EDITORIAL REVIEWS - Part 1 (<u>PRE</u>-Launch)

Traditionally, editorial reviews are professional, expert evaluations of our book from sources like newspapers, magazines, book review sites, or respected authors. Authors and publishers use them everywhere - on book covers, inside marketing materials, and across sales pages.

Oftentimes, editorial reviews serve as a form of social proof that carries more critical weight than customer reviews written by the general public. And that's because the writers of editorial reviews have reputations to uphold. Their name, their expertise, and their professional standing are on the line, which is why readers view these reviews as more authoritative and trustworthy.

On Amazon, editorial reviews appear in a designated "Editorial Reviews" section on the product page, typically right above the "About the Author" section.

Editorial Reviews

Review

Another winning picture book from the talented Katy Hudson! --"Imagination Soup"

Hudson (Bear and Duck) handily juggles profuse visual humor and a passel of life lessons, including taking only what you need, sharing what you have, and not taking advantage of friends. . . .Simultaneously sassy and sweet, Hudson's illustrations place her cast of cuddly, expressive animals in a variety of slapstick situations. . . .When life gives you carrots, Hudson suggests, make carrot cake (and juice and soup and cupcakes). --"Publishers Weekly"

Hudson's watercolor and ink illustrations are sprinkled with fun details. . . .The critters' faces are as expressive as they are cute, adding feeling to the dialogue-heavy storytelling. Children will empathize with Rabbit's need to collect and keep his favorite things near him at all times. They may even think a bit about sharing, the ultimate message of the book. This entertaining addition is suitable for sharing one-on-one or in a group. --"School Library Journal"

While we can seek out editorial reviews at any time, they are especially helpful for newly published books that have not yet accumulated many customer reviews. So if we're planning to use them for our launch, the key is to proactively seek them out before our book is published.

Editorial reviews come in many forms, and I like dividing them into two main groups.

TRADITIONAL EDITORIAL REVIEWS:

When most authors think of editorial reviews, their minds immediately go to classic, well-known professional reviewers and established publications that have long shaped the book industry. These outlets are respected and widely recognized, and they can add wonderful authority to our book's presentation. Here are some of the most common traditional reviewers authors tend to consider first:

- Professional trade publications (e.g.: *Publishers Weekly, Kirkus Reviews, School Library Journal*)
- Major newspaper & literary magazines (e.g.: *The New York Times Book Review, regional newspapers, local magazines*)
- Professional review services (e.g.: *BookLife*)

These are excellent options, but they represent only a fraction of what's available to us.

BROADER EDITORIAL REVIEWS (often overlooked, but incredibly powerful):

Traditional reviewers are just one part of the editorial landscape available to us as children's authors. There is a whole world of professionals, experts, educators, community leaders, and niche voices who can speak directly to the heart of our book's topic. These broader reviewers are often far more approachable, and their insights add what I like to call *contextual authority* - credibility rooted in the exact field or experience our book touches.

Some powerful examples include:

Professionals who work directly with children:

- Librarians, Early childhood educators, Reading specialists, Speech therapists, School counselors, Montessori or Waldorf teachers

Professionals connected to our book's specific theme or topic (this adds instant authority and relevance):

- A firefighter or fire chief for a fire truck story, a pediatrician or child psychologist for an emotions book, a park ranger for a nature story, a veterinarian for an animal-care book, a music teacher for a musical-themed story, a STEM educator for a science-themed book, a swim instructor for a water-safety story

Local experts or community leaders:

- Museum curators, Zoo educators, Owners of children's boutiques or toy shops, Directors of local nonprofits that align with our book's message, Environmental or sustainability leaders (for eco-themed books)

Service providers connected to childhood experiences:

- Pediatric occupational therapists, Child life specialists (especially great for hospital-themed stories), Grief counselors (for books about loss), Adoption agency counselors (for adoption-themed stories)

Local community heroes:

- Police officers, Military personnel or veterans (if thematically relevant), City officials who support literacy and education initiatives

Fellow Authors and illustrators in our niche:

- (Perfect for editorial reviews, not customer reviews.)

Organizations aligned with your book's message:

- Anti-bullying organizations, Environmental groups, Parenting advocacy groups, Literacy nonprofits, Animal rescue organizations

These broader editorial reviews matter because they bring something uniquely valuable to our book: real-world, experience-based credibility.

> A librarian speaks from the lens of literacy.
> A firefighter speaks from the lens of safety.

A grief counselor speaks from the lens of emotional support.

Their voices help validate our book in ways that parents, educators, and caregivers instantly understand and trust.

By choosing reviewers who align with our message, we elevate our book's credibility, strengthen our marketing, and make it easier for potential buyers to feel confident that our book genuinely serves the children who will read it.

HOW TO REACH OUT

It's always best to make our outreach message as personal and relevant as possible, where:

- we explain *why* we chose this specific person
- we share something personal about ourselves and our book
- we keep our ask short and respectful
- we make it easy for them to say yes

To help you get started, I've added an example script you can use and personalize.

OUTREACH SCRIPT: *BEFORE or AFTER Publication*

SUBJECT LINE:

- *Hoping to partner with [Organization Name]*
- *A small request from a local children's author*

Hi [Name],

I hope you're doing so well today. My name is [Your Name], and I'm a local children's book author here in [Your City]. I've followed [Organization Name] for a long time, and I'm such a fan of the work you do to help puppies find loving, forever homes.

I recently wrote a new children's book about pet adoption and responsible puppy care. It gently walks little readers through what to expect, how to prepare, and why adopting a puppy is a commitment filled with love and responsibility. My goal is the same as yours - to make sure every puppy finds the right home, and stays there for good.

If you'd be open to it, I would be incredibly grateful for a short sentence or two sharing why you think a book like this could be helpful for young families learning about adoption. Nothing formal at all - just your honest impression after taking a quick peek at the story.

I truly believe your voice would help parents see how meaningful and practical this book can be, and it would mean the world to me to have your perspective included.

I'd love to send you a digital copy so you can take a look - just let me know the best email address to send it to.

Thank you so much for the heart-centered work you do every single day. I would be honored to collaborate with you in even this small way.

With gratitude,
[Your Name]

NINJA TIP:

Notice how I make it clear that this does not require a big time commitment, how I avoid terminology like "editorial review," and how I focus on our shared mission. That's what makes this ask feel natural, meaningful, and so much easier to say yes to.

WHERE TO ADD OUR EDITORIAL REVIEWS ON AMAZON:

Editorial reviews are placed inside the dedicated *Editorial Reviews* section on our Amazon book page. This is where we can showcase reviews from professionals, influencers, niche experts, teachers, librarians, and more - essentially anyone who cannot post a regular Amazon customer review.

To add them:

1. Log into **Author Central** at *author.amazon.com* (⬆)
2. Go to the "book" tab
3. Select your book
4. Click "Edit Book Details"
5. Add your review text, bold key lines if desired, and include the reviewer's name and title

NINJA TIP:

If your book is available in multiple formats, you may need to add the review to each version individually. Usually, Amazon publishes these updates within a few hours.

NINJA TIP:

When showcasing editorial reviews, include not only the reviewer's name, but also their professional title. Titles add credibility and context, helping potential buyers understand *why* this person's opinion matters. A review from "Sarah Lopez, Librarian" carries a very different kind of weight than "Sarah Lopez."

Example:

> *"A beautifully written story that supports early readers in building emotional resilience."*
> **~ Jasmine Reed, Early Childhood Literacy Specialist**

This small detail elevates social proof more than almost anything else.

NINJA TIP:

Once the review is received, a heartfelt thank-you (whether through a handwritten note, a small gesture, or something memorable like a bouquet of flowers) not only expresses gratitude, but can also open the door to a lasting relationship. Many wonderful ongoing opportunities grow from small, thoughtful moments like these.

USING OUR EDITORIAL REVIEWS SECTION CREATIVELY:

Now, what if we don't have any editorial reviews just yet? Then we want to use our limited space on Amazon as efficiently and effectively as possible.

So here are 11 additional things we can add today to lend our book more credibility, more authority, and more connection - even if we don't have editorial reviews just yet. Each example is designed to lend our beautiful book more credibility, more authority, and more connection with the readers who need it most.

1. HIGHLIGHTING A SERIES:

Use this when your book is part of a series - especially if your newest release hasn't received its own reviews yet. Highlighting praise from earlier books helps build instant credibility.

EXAMPLE:

PRAISE FOR THE SERIES:

"A heartwarming collection that helps little readers navigate big moments with confidence and kindness." ~ **Early Childhood Literacy Review**

"Jones's stories always strike the perfect balance between comfort and real-world learning." ~ **Parent Insight Journal**

****

2. HIGHLIGHTING INSIGHTS FROM A TOPIC EXPERT:

Perfect for books that teach, guide, or explain real-life topics. A short note from a relevant professional adds authority and reassures parents that the book reflects sound, thoughtful expertise.

EXAMPLE:

INSIGHTS FROM A PUPPY ADOPTION SPECIALIST:

"Introducing a new puppy to a family is an exciting milestone, but it also comes with big responsibilities. This story offers children a gentle, realistic look at what it truly means to provide a forever home. I wish every adopting family had a resource like this."

~ **Maya Weston, Certified Canine Behavior Counselor, Northern Virginia Pet Rescue**

****

3. HIGHLIGHTING THE EDUCATIONAL VALUES OF THE BOOK:

Ideal when your story aligns with classroom themes or social-emotional learning. This section shows teachers and homeschoolers exactly how your book supports meaningful discussions.

EXAMPLE:

WHAT EDUCATORS LOVE ABOUT THIS BOOK:

- Encourages empathy, responsibility, and decision-making
- Offers conversation-ready moments for parent-child or teacher-student discussions
- Ideal for classroom units on animals, kindness, and community helpers

****

4. HIGHLIGHTING THE BOOK'S VALUES TO PARENTS:

A great way to spotlight the practical benefits your story offers families - especially if parents are looking for guidance, reassurance, or help navigating a specific situation.

EXAMPLE:

WHAT PARENTS WILL FIND INSIDE:

- A child-friendly introduction to the realities of pet adoption
- Gentle guidance on preparing a home (and a heart) for a new puppy
- Sweet, reassuring moments that help little ones understand what "forever home" truly means

****

5. HIGHLIGHTING AWARDS & RECOGNITIONS:

If you or your previous books have received any honors, this section helps readers see your broader track record and strengthens their trust in your work.

EXAMPLE:

AWARDS & RECOGNITIONS:

From the bestselling children's author behind multiple award-recognized titles celebrated for helping young readers navigate real-life experiences with compassion and clarity.

****

6. HIGHLIGHTING BOOKSELLERS & LIBRARIANS:

Use this to reflect general feedback from industry professionals, even without direct quotes. It signals that your book is valued in settings where quality and usefulness truly matter.

EXAMPLE:

WHAT BOOKSELLERS & LIBRARIANS SAY:

"A natural pick for storytime, especially for families preparing to welcome a pet."

"Parents often ask for books that help explain responsibility in a gentle way - this one does it beautifully."

****

7. EARLY READER REACTIONS:

Perfect for sharing heartwarming responses from launch teams, beta readers, event attendees, and even those who aren't able to leave official Amazon reviews - such as family members or anyone with a financial stake in the book. This section allows you to highlight their genuine reactions in a thoughtful, and Amazon-Review-Rules compliant way.

EXAMPLE:

EARLY READER REACTIONS:

"My daughter asked, 'Can we adopt a puppy like in the book?' Such a sweet, meaningful read."

"Perfect for helping our kids understand that adopting a pet is more than just bringing home something cute."

****

8. EDUCATOR NOTES:

Great for nonfiction-leaning or lesson-friendly stories. This section quickly communicates how your book fits into curriculum goals or themed units.

EXAMPLE:

EDUCATOR NOTES:

This story pairs wonderfully with lessons on:

- *Responsibility and caretaking*
- *Emotional awareness*
- *Animal welfare*
- *Community helpers and rescue organizations*

****

9. SHARING WHAT'S BEHIND THE STORY:

A simple, powerful way to connect with readers by sharing the real inspiration behind your book - helping them understand the heart and intention shaping your story.

EXAMPLE:

BEHIND THE STORY:

Inspired by real experiences volunteering with local rescue organizations, this book was created to help families prepare children for one of the most joyful commitments they'll ever make - loving and caring for a new puppy.

****

10. A SPECIAL MESSAGE:

Use this to highlight a meaningful line or sentiment that captures the essence of your story and draws readers in emotionally.

EXAMPLE:

A MESSAGE FROM THE HEART OF THE BOOK :

"Every puppy deserves a forever home - and every child deserves to understand how to help make that forever truly last."

****

11. READERS' FAVORITE HIGHLIGHTS:

Use this section to spotlight a few standout quotes from your regular Amazon customer reviews, especially those that beautifully capture what makes your book special. This draws attention to your strongest feedback and helps shoppers quickly grasp the impact your book has had on real families.

EXAMPLE:'

READERS' FAVORITE HIGHLIGHTS:

"My 5-year-old was glued to every page. This book made our upcoming puppy adoption feel so much more real and exciting."

"Beautiful illustrations and such a meaningful message. I wish we had this before adopting our first dog."

"A gentle way to teach responsibility. My kids understood instantly what it means to care for a new pet."

NINJA TIP:

The secret is in the *framing*. **By giving each part a clear, compelling header**, you show shoppers what they're about to discover - whether it's expert insights, educator notes, early reader reactions, or a meaningful message. This simple shift turns your editorial section into an engaging, trust-building showcase for your book.

So feel free to mix and match the different sections, and make sure to include the headers.

At the end of the day, our Amazon sales page isn't just a place where our book sits - it's one of our most important marketing assets. It's where discoverability turns into confidence, and where curiosity turns into clicks.

When we take the time to fine-tune things like keywords, description, categories, pricing, and those little credibility builders that make a reader trust us, we are making it easier for the right families to find the right book.

And that's the heart of marketing. Not convincing people to buy something they don't need - but helping the people who do need our story actually discover it, understand it, and feel excited to bring it home.

—————— · ✦ · ——————

YOUR TO DOs FOR THIS CHAPTER:

- ❏ Optimize your Amazon sales page by fine-tune things like keywords, description, categories, pricing, and adding A+ content
- ❏ Create the ebook version of your book
- ❏ Make use of Amazon's editorial reviews section

Find all your templates and swipe files using this link below. You may want to bookmark this page, so you can refer to it as quickly and easily as possible.

⬆ *https://www.eevijones.com/marketing-downloads*

LINKS SHARED:

- *https://www.eevijones.com/KindleCalculator*
- *https://author.amazon.com*
- *https://www.eevijones.com/the-best-tool-for-childrens-book-authors*
- *https://kdp.amazon.com/marketing/manager*
- *https://www.canva.com*

CHAPTER 8
Building Momentum Before The Big Day

By the time we reach this point, our beautiful children's book is no longer just an idea. It exists. It has a title, illustrations, heart, and purpose. And now, it deserves to be seen.

This chapter is about creating curiosity and building excitement. Marketing during this phase means giving families and friends an opportunity to support us, so when our book steps into the world, it doesn't do so quietly.

BOOK TRAILER WORTHY

Did you know that most big traditional publishers create book trailers for their children's books? And what's really interesting is that while the creation of book trailers for most other genres has drastically decreased over the years, the creation of book trailers for kids' books has not.

With the growth of platforms like TikTok, book trailers have made an incredible comeback, especially for authors who are taking marketing matters into their own hands.

So if you've been wanting to add a book trailer to your marketing strategy for your children's book, then these next few pages are for you.

Many moons ago, I used to own a small motion graphics studio that specialized in creating book trailers for all genres. I created trailers for authors like *New York Times* bestselling author Nicholas Sansbury Smith, and *USA Today* bestselling authors Debra Webb and James Hankins. During that time, I also created lots and lots of book trailers for publishers and fellow children's book authors.

Seeing the renewed growth of book trailers for children's books is really exciting for me, because book trailers truly work - if they are done well.

Below, for example, is the trailer for my book *The Impatient Little Vacuum* (↑). I've included the video on the template page, so you can view it if you'd like. It has been viewed nearly 14,000 times, generating buzz on social networks and engaging new audiences in an exciting way.

WHAT ARE BOOK TRAILERS?

Book trailers can be a wonderful addition to our marketing strategy. They are 60-second (or less) snippets of our children's book that function much like mini commercials.

Another industry that uses trailers very successfully is the movie industry. We see those everywhere, especially right before a movie is released.

And the main goals for both book trailers and movie trailers are the same:

GOAL 1: Trailers are meant to inform potential viewers about the existence of the movie - or in our case, our children's book.

GOAL 2: And they are meant to help potential viewers or readers decide whether or not the movie or book is something they might be interested in watching or reading.

Trailers work especially well for children's books because we already have all the visual assets - the illustrations.

WHY SHOULD WE CONSIDER USING BOOK TRAILERS AS A MARKETING TOOL?

Being able to reach potential readers directly is the holy grail for us children's authors. And the number one place we can do this is during school visits and book fairs. But to reach little ones on an even *bigger* scale, we can - and should - make use of the web.

Nowadays, children are all over YouTube. In my book *How To Self-Publish a Children's Book*, I mentioned that between 35 and 45 percent of kids in the UK between the ages of 4 and 7 use YouTube every week. From age 8 upward, that jumps to 60 percent, increasing to around 80 percent by age 11.

And a Smarty Pants brand popularity survey of 6- to 12-year-olds here in the U.S. found that YouTube beat other brands like Disney, Netflix for Kids, and Nickelodeon.

And this is where book trailers come in.

WHERE CAN WE USE OUR BOOK TRAILER?

Book trailers can be a wonderful addition to our marketing strategy because they can be shared nearly everywhere. We can use them in places such as:

- *Amazon Author Page*
- *Social Media (Facebook, Instagram, TikTok)*
- *Goodreads*
- *LinkedIn*
- *YouTube*
- *Our own Website*
- *Our Newsletter*

I love having trailers for some of my children's books and listing them directly below my books on my Amazon Author Page.

My student Hanit had a beautiful book trailer made, which she shared with her family and friends during her book launch. This trailer was viewed more than 2,000 times on Facebook alone. People absolutely loved it and couldn't wait to read their own copy.

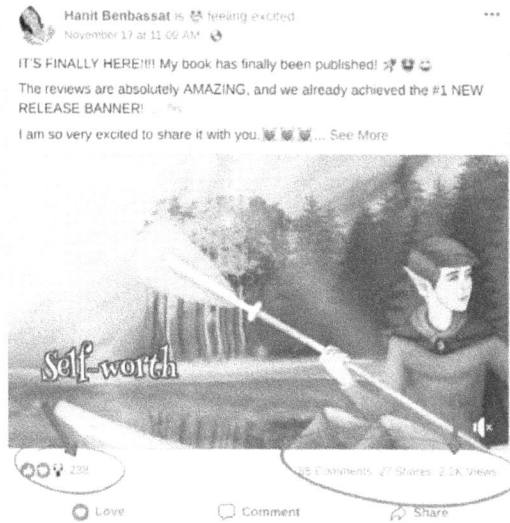

With this simple, yet very strategic share, Hanit was able to pique her friends' and family's interest in such a fun and creative way.

OUR BOOK TRAILER KNOW-HOWS:

As a former director of a small motion graphics studio, I've created hundreds and hundreds of book trailers for authors as well as publishing houses. What follows are my seven most valuable tips when it comes to creating your very own amazing trailer, whether you want to try creating one yourself or plan to hire someone to do it for you.

That way, you'll know what makes a great trailer - and what can make one less effective.

1. Keep it short. Really short.
People's attention spans (ours included) are very short. We want to hook and intrigue viewers as quickly as possible. Forty-five to sixty seconds is more than enough time.

2. Keep text bursts short and simple.
When people commit to watching a video, they want to *watch*, not read paragraphs. Avoid text bursts longer than one line. Use the shortest possible phrases, dropping unnecessary words. If needed, break ideas into separate scenes.

3. Minimize the number of text bursts.
One text burst per scene is a great guideline. You shouldn't need more than eight or nine total. More than that makes the trailer feel wordy and takes attention away from your illustrations. Like a good haiku, an effective trailer uses short, descriptive bursts to pique interest.

4. Use your book's illustrations as full-screen backdrops.
To avoid a slideshow look, have illustrations fill the entire frame. You can add gentle movement by panning or slowly zooming in or out.

5. Give each scene enough time.
Aim for about 6-7 seconds per scene. That allows viewers enough time to read the text comfortably without dragging the trailer out.

6. If using narration, keep it short.
Aim for 80 words or fewer. If you include narration, minimize on-screen text or remove it altogether, since reading and listening at the same time can be difficult.

7. End with clarity.
Your final scene should show your book cover, title, author name, and where to buy it. Something like "Available on Amazon" is plenty.

NINJA TIP:

Be clear on the message you want your trailer to convey before you begin. That clarity will guide every creative decision.

To help you prepare, I've included the book trailer intake form (↑) I used with my former clients. **Please note that we no longer take on new clients.**

If you decide to outsource your trailer, you can explore platforms such as:

- *Fiverr.com* (↑)
- *Freelancer.com* (↑)
- *Upwork.com* (↑)

NINJA TIP:

Avoid opening your trailer with your book title or author name unless you're already well known. That precious time is better spent hooking viewers immediately.

If a marketing strategy works for big publishing houses, it can work for us too. Book trailers for children's books have been around for a long time, and they're still going strong for a reason. They help others discover our stories and offer a fun, engaging way to share what our book is all about.

— ◆ —

USING READ-ALOUDS AS A FREE MARKETING TOOL

What are read-aloud or read-along videos, and why might they be a valuable marketing strategy?

Let's start by looking at what they are *not*.

Read-along videos of our books are not book trailers. Book trailers are very much like movie trailers. They are short snippets or teasers that we share to get people interested in our book.

Read-aloud videos, on the other hand, are videos where a book is read in its entirety.

Read-alouds had a big moment during the pandemic, when many people recorded themselves reading children's books and shared them on platforms like YouTube.

These types of videos work especially well with picture books, and less so with middle-grade chapter books. That's because picture books have lots of illustrations to focus on during the read-aloud, and because picture books are relatively short. Most can be read out loud in under five minutes, which is perfect for little readers.

Now you may be asking, *"But Eevi! Why would I want to share my entire children's book this way? Wouldn't that take away the need to buy my book?"*

So let's look at the three main reasons why creating a read-aloud video can be incredibly beneficial.

REASON 1: *Using a Read-Aloud as a FREE Marketing Tool*

Very similar to a book trailer, we can share our read-aloud video on large platforms like YouTube.

YouTube, just like Google, is a massive search engine. So with a read-aloud video, we essentially get to attract potential eyeballs absolutely free.

If you're worried that this might hurt your sales, consider this:

When someone finds and watches your read-aloud video on YouTube, chances are very high that they've never heard of you before. Before that video, they likely didn't even know your book existed.

So it is usually *because* of your video that they discover your book in the first place.

After watching the read-aloud, they can then decide whether they liked it enough to go and buy it.

I'm a prime example that this "test-driving" method really works, because I've discovered and purchased so many children's books this way. *The Great Realization*, *The Very Hungry Caterpillar*, *Dragons Love Tacos*, and *Otis and the Tornado* are just a few of them.

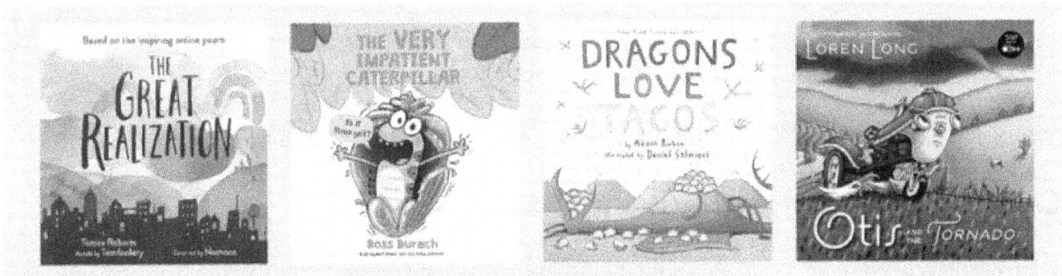

Watching those read-aloud videos didn't prevent me from buying the books. Instead, they helped me discover them and fall in love with them enough to go out and purchase my own copies.

Sharing our book this way is very similar to libraries, in a sense. Just on a much greater scale, with a much higher chance of being discovered. And that's exactly why so many authors want their books in libraries in the first place.

REASON 2: *Using Read-Alouds as Part of Your Book Launch Strategy*

Another way I love using read-aloud videos is as part of a launch strategy.

For many of my own launches, I create a read-aloud video and then share it directly with my launch team.

For example, this is a webpage I shared with my launch team for my book *Sometimes It Rains*. It includes a short note, a three-minute read-aloud video, a link to the Amazon sales page, and a direct link to the review page.

Sharing the book this way makes it incredibly easy (and fun) for launch team members to "read" the book in under five minutes so they can then leave a review.

And the easier we make it for others, the better - especially considering how busy everyone is.

REASON 3: *Using Read-Alouds as an Additional Resource*

When my boys were little, they loved being read to. And sometimes, when I was busy doing something else, I would give them one of their books and play the audio version or a read-aloud video on repeat.

That way, they could turn the pages of their physical book while listening along. And they loved doing that.

But we don't have to share a read-aloud publicly if we don't want to. As authors, we can create a read-aloud version of our book and offer it as a bonus to those who have already purchased the book.

HOW TO CREATE OUR READ-ALOUD

There are many ways to create a read-aloud video. One method I really like is using a realistic page-turn effect. It feels much more like reading an actual book and less like watching a slideshow.

To create a video like this, we'll use two tools. At the time of writing, both tools are absolutely free for the way we'll be using them. If that ever changes, simply search for free alternatives.

TOOL 1: *Heyzine.com* (⬆)

Heyzine helps us add the page-turning effect. The basic plan currently allows up to five flipbooks with unlimited pages and is free.

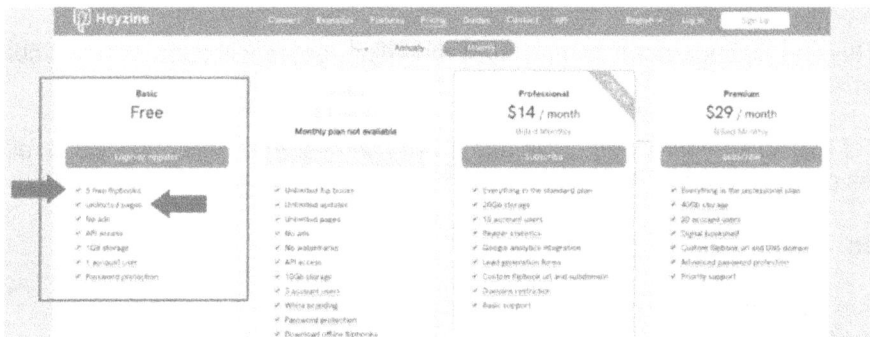

Simply upload your formatted interior file, and Heyzine will convert it into a flipbook.

NINJA TIP:

Most formatted interior files do not include the cover. If you want your flipbook to show the cover, temporarily add it to your interior file before uploading.

TOOL 2: *Loom.com* (⬆)

Loom allows us to record our screen while reading the book out loud.

At the time of writing, the free plan allows up to 25 videos, each up to five minutes long - more than enough for our needs.

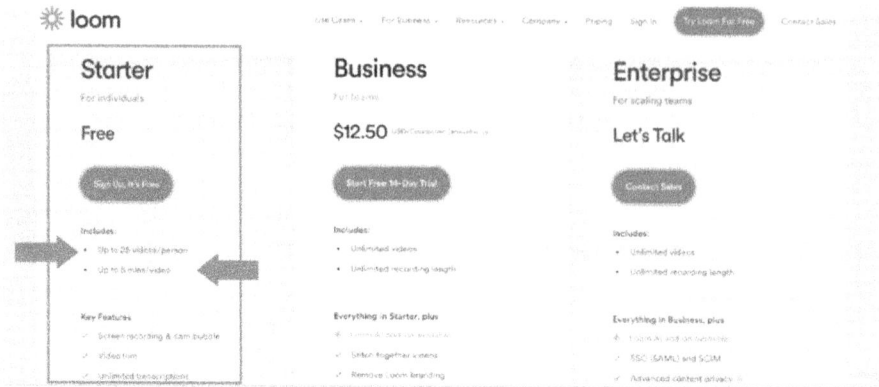

Once signed up, Loom walks you through recording your first video.

With your Heyzine flipbook open, simply start recording. Loom will capture both your voice and the page turns.

Be mindful of pacing so your video stays under five minutes. After recording, Loom allows you to trim mistakes easily.

You can then:

- *Share the video via a Loom link*
- *Download it and upload it to YouTube*
- *Embed it directly on your website*

To see an example of how I use read-aloud videos, visit: ***https://eevijones.com/tough*** (↑).

Kids love read-aloud videos. If you search "read aloud books for children" on Google or YouTube, you'll find countless examples with tens of thousands of views.

It's such a powerful marketing tool - and best of all, it's completely free.

———————————— ● ✦ ● ————————————

LAUNCH TEAM - THE POWER OF A LAUNCH TEAM

By the time we reach this point in the process, most of the hard work is already done.

> We've shared our journey publicly.
> We've talked about our book while it was still being created.
> We've invited feedback, conversation, and curiosity along the way.

In other words, we've already dug our well before we were thirsty.

Creating a launch team now isn't about cold asks or convincing strangers. It's about organizing and activating the support that already exists.

WHY LAUNCH TEAMS ARE SO POWERFUL FOR CHILDREN'S BOOKS

Social proof matters - especially when it comes to children's books.

Social proof is the idea that consumers adapt their behavior based on what others are doing. More often than not, people follow the crowd.

Parents, in particular, are intentional about the books they introduce to their children. Reviews, recommendations, and feedback play a significant role in their buying decisions.

According to research by ConversionXL, 66 percent of consumers trust online customer reviews. Most of us read reviews before making a purchase, and we tend to hesitate when there are none.

This is true for books as well.

If we're choosing between two otherwise similar books, we'll usually pick the one with more positive reviews. And this is exactly where a launch team becomes incredibly valuable.

WHAT A LAUNCH TEAM IS (AND ISN'T)

A launch team is a group of people who are genuinely interested in our book and willing to support its release. This can include friends, family members, acquaintances, colleagues, and members of our wider community.

Organizing a launch team does take intention and follow-up, but it is one of the most impactful early marketing strategies we have.

A launch team:

1. *is completely free*
2. *allows friends and family to support us*
3. *provides early social proof through reviews*
4. *helps trigger Amazon's algorithm*
5. *supports visibility and ranking*

WHO TO INVITE (AND WHY THIS FEELS EASIER THAN YOU THINK)

When creating a launch team, we want to reach out to people who are a genuine fit.

Ask yourself:

- *Who is likely to enjoy this book?*
- *Who has already shown interest or support?*

This is where all your previous work comes into play. Because you've shared your journey, you already have warm connections - people who liked, commented, and cheered you on.

These are the perfect people to invite.

HOW TO MAKE THE ASK

There are two effective ways to invite people to join our launch team:

- *A more private, one-on-one request*
- *A more public request shared with your wider audience*

Both work beautifully when done with clarity and warmth.

A. A MORE PRIVATE LAUNCH-TEAM REQUEST

If you prefer a personal approach, reaching out individually is a wonderful option. A private message allows for a genuine, thoughtful connection, and it often results in a higher level of commitment.

To help you get started, I've included one of my own messages below. Personalization is key, so feel free to adjust it to sound like you.

Hi {Name},

I really wanted to thank you for the wonderful comment you posted when I shared about my upcoming children's book {Title of Book}. Your support means so much to me!

I'm so very excited about this and can't wait to share it with the world. And that's why I wanted to ask you if you would like to be part of my launch team.

Being a member of my launch team simply means that you would be one of the very first people to read the book, and then post a 1 to 2 sentence review onto Amazon as soon as it has been publicly released.

The first initial reviews of any book are crucial to its success. You've been so very supportive, and I would love for you to join.

{Title of Book} can be read in less than 5 minutes and is:

- Less than 200 words
- 17 beautiful double-spread illustrations (34 pages)
- For 2-5 year olds

I poured my heart into this, so I know you'll love it.

Whether you read it with or without a little one, this is a fun and adorable book, teaching 2 to 5 year olds that THEY'RE PERFECT JUST THE WAY THEY ARE {your purpose/value of your book}.

I can't wait to hear from you, {Name}! I'm so very excited about this and would love for you to be part of this.

Happy {day of the week}

Love,

{Your Name}

There are a few things that make this request so powerful, so we'll want to make sure to include these in our outreach message:

1. **Use the person's name,** not just at the beginning, but throughout. That's what truly makes our message feel personal.
2. **Mention a specific moment where they already showed interest**, like a comment they left or a post they reacted to. That way, it doesn't feel like it's coming out of the blue.
3. **Let your excitement show.** If we're excited and this is clearly important to us, others will feel that too.
4. **Explain what a launch team is.** Most friends and family won't know what it means, so they may assume it's time-consuming. We want to keep it simple, light, and clear.
5. **Keep the ask small and specific.** A 1 to 2 sentence review is enough. And because reviews are time-sensitive, we want to gently communicate that timing matters.
6. **Mention how quick it is to read.** This removes a huge barrier. People are busy, and "less than 5 minutes" feels doable.
7. **Include the "with or without kids" line.** This is important. Without it, people may respond saying they'd love to help, but they don't have little ones. This single sentence prevents a lot of unnecessary no's.
8. **Describe the value of the book in one simple sentence.** We may be tempted to write more, but one clear sentence is stronger here.
9. **Keep paragraphs short.** People are far more likely to read a message that feels easy on the eyes.

As we send out these messages, we'll want to stay organized, tracking who we contacted, and when and whether they responded. If we don't hear back after a day or two, it's perfectly okay to follow up.

B. A MORE PUBLIC LAUNCH-TEAM REQUEST

If you prefer a public request, sharing it on a platform like Facebook can work beautifully.

Here, I recommend adding a visual element, like your book cover, or even better, a short 1 to 2 minute video of yourself personally making the invitation. This helps people feel your excitement and understand the ask more clearly.

In your post or video, make sure to cover the same key points:

- *What the book is about*
- *What being on the launch team means*
- *How simple and time-friendly the support is*

And just like we did before, reply to every comment individually and tag the person's name. This keeps the conversation going and helps the post stay visible in people's feeds.

NINJA TIP:

Not everyone who joins our launch team will follow through. A general rule of thumb is that about 30 percent of our launch team members will support our book by leaving a review.

That means if our goal is 30 reviews, we will want a launch team of around 100 people.

And here's the encouraging part: when we stay organized, communicate clearly, and follow up thoughtfully, our follow-through rate can be much higher.

Marketing a children's book is about creating moments of connection that invite others to care. Everything we covered in this chapter is designed to help our book be seen, remembered, and supported in a way that feels natural and aligned with who we are.

By using tools like book trailers, read-alouds, and a launch team, we are not just promoting a book. We are giving people a reason to engage, to share in our excitement, and to help our story reach the families it was written for. And that kind of marketing doesn't fade after launch. It builds momentum that carries our book forward long after it first enters the world.

———————— • ✦ • ————————

YOUR TO DOs FOR THIS CHAPTER:

- ❏ Share your excitement by making use of tools like a book trailer and/ or a read-aloud video
- ❏ Watch my book trailer example and view my read-aloud example page
- ❏ Reach out to create excitement to join your launch team

Find all your templates and swipe files using this link below. You may want to bookmark this page, so you can refer to it as quickly and easily as possible.

↑ *https://www.eevijones.com/marketing-downloads*

LINKS SHARED:

- *https://www.fiverr.com*
- *https://www.freelancer.com*
- *https://www.upwork.com*
- *https://heyzine.com*
- *https://www.loom.com*
- *https://eevijones.com/tough* **(read-aloud example)**
- *https://www.eevijones.com/TrailerExample* **(book trailer example)**
- *https://www.eevijones.com/briefingform* **(book trailer preparation form)**

PART IV
MARKETING DURING OUR LAUNCH WINDOW

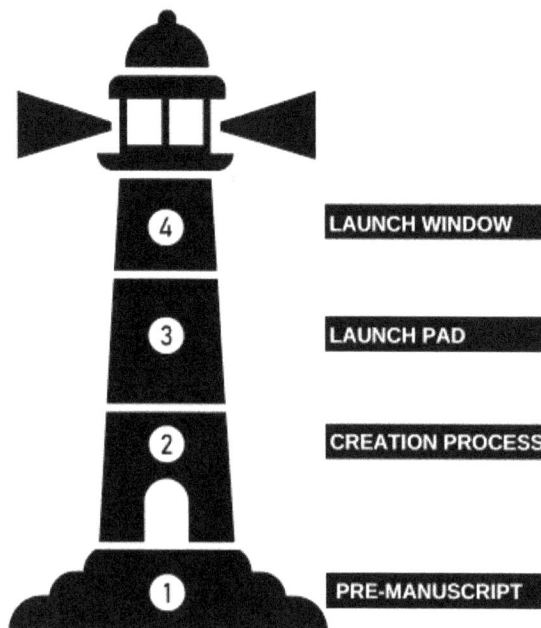

4 — LAUNCH WINDOW

3 — LAUNCH PAD

2 — CREATION PROCESS

1 — PRE-MANUSCRIPT

INTERLUDE
Our Launch Philosophy

Before we step into the launch phase, I want us to pause for just a moment. By the time we reach this point of the book, a lot of meaningful work has already been done.

We have clarified our author identity, shaped how we show up, and laid a strong foundation for our precious children's book. We have thoughtfully optimized our Amazon page, involved our inner circle, gathered early feedback, and prepared our book to be discovered by the readers it was written for.

That matters greatly and will make such a humongous difference. Because a launch is *not* where marketing begins. Instead, …

… it is where all our preparation gets its first opportunity to work together.

In its simplest form, our book launch is a short, focused window of *activation*. It's the moment when we invite our support system to step in, introduce our book to the world, and create early signals of interest and engagement.

For children's books especially, a launch is not about hype or pressure. It is neither a guarantee of instant success nor an indicator of how successful a book may be later on. Its purpose is much more grounded than that.

A thoughtful launch simply helps us:

- *Create initial visibility*
- *Gather early reviews and feedback*
- *Build confidence as an author*
- *Give our book a gentle push into the marketplace*

Nothing more, and nothing less.

This interlude is here to remind us that there is no "perfect" launch. There is only an *intentional* one. And when we approach our launch with clarity instead of pressure, it becomes exactly what it is meant to be:

A natural next step in a much longer, sustainable marketing journey.

With this empowering mindset and launch philosophy in place, we are ready to move forward and step into our next marketing phase.

CHAPTER 9
Activating Your Launch Team

Now that we're clear on our launch philosophy, this is where that mindset turns into action.

We're ready to intentionally activate the support system we have already built, helping our book enter the marketplace with clarity and confidence. This is where our launch team becomes one of our strongest and most effective marketing tools.

When launch team members download, review, and interact with our book in a coordinated way, they create data points Amazon pays attention to, including:

- *Search behavior*
- *Clicks*
- *Purchases and downloads*
- *Review language and keywords*

Together, these signals help Amazon better understand our book and who it should be shown to next.

Below are best practices to help us activate our launch team in a way that supports our launch goals and contributes to our book's long-term discoverability.

PRACTICE #1: *Intentional Sharing of Our Book On Amazon*

When it's time for our launch team to access our book, we have two options.

OPTION 1: *SEARCH-BASED DISCOVERY*

Instead of sending a direct link, we can ask our launch team members to search for our book directly on Amazon using a specific keyword or keyphrase in the search bar, together with our author name.

Relevant Keyphrase + Author Name

Here, we can choose one pertinent keyphrase and ask everyone to use the same one. Ideally, this is one of the keyphrases we already selected during our book setup.

This tells Amazon:

- *Our book is relevant for that search term*
- *Real users are actively looking for our book*

If enough people search for our book using the same phrase, Amazon is more likely to show our book to future shoppers using those terms.

OPTION 2: *DIRECT LINKS (USE "CLEAN" LINKS ONLY)*

Alternatively, we can also share a direct Amazon link. In this case, we want to make sure it's a *clean* link.

A clean link does not include any tracking information. This helps prevent Amazon from tracing the purchase or review back to us as the author.

A clean link is **not**:

- *A link copied after searching for our book on Amazon*
- *A shortened link (such as Bitly)*
- *An affiliate link*
- *The link generated by Amazon's share button*

Because our KDP account is often tied to the same entity as our personal Amazon account, these links could potentially be traced back to us. To avoid that, we'll want to make sure our URLs are stripped of any identifying remnants before sharing them.

To make this as easy as possible, I've created a tool that cleans Amazon links for all major marketplaces for us:

https://www.eevijones.com/clean-link-builder

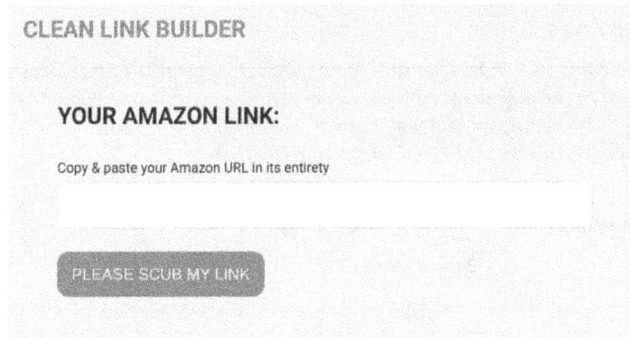

CLEAN LINK BUILDER

YOUR AMAZON LINK:

Copy & paste your Amazon URL in its entirety

PLEASE SCUB MY LINK

PRACTICE #2: *Verified Reviews*

Amazon allows customers to leave reviews even if they did not purchase the book on Amazon. However, when possible, we may want to ask our launch team members to purchase and download the ebook before reviewing.

This has two advantages:

- *The purchase counts toward our sales ranking*
- *The review is marked as a "verified purchase," which is often displayed more prominently*

We want to use our judgment here, based on our relationship with our launch team members.

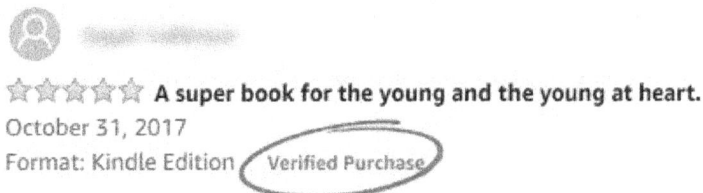

☆☆☆☆☆ **A super book for the young and the young at heart.**
October 31, 2017
Format: Kindle Edition   Verified Purchase

PRACTICE #3: *Providing Buzzwords & Keyphrases*

Reviews are an important marketing signal. Amazon analyzes the language used in reviews and highlights commonly mentioned terms above the review section.

By providing a short list of buzzwords or phrases, we help guide the language Amazon associates with our book, increasing its relevance for those terms.

Customers say

Customers find this book to be a valuable teaching tool that helps children learn about choices and their consequences. The book features multiple stories in one, with engaging illustrations that keep children entertained. Customers appreciate that it can be read multiple times and is ideal for parents, with one customer noting how it helps children reflect on their actions.

ai, Generated from the text of customer reviews

Select to learn more

✓ Teaching tool (445) ✓ Book for kids (320) ✓ Fun to read (283) ✓ Story variety (283)

✓ Making choices (188) ✓ Readability (155) ✓ Thought provoking (133) ✓ Illustrations (101)

PRACTICE #4: *Providing Short Review Templates*

Many people hesitate leaving a review simply because they don't know what to write. A simple one to two sentence template removes friction and reassures them that a short review is more than enough.

This makes it easier for them and more effective for us.

- "As a [YOUR PROFESSION], I really found chapter [#] so helpful, because [XYZ]."
- I love the story that [AUTHOR] shared in chapter [#] about [XYZ], because of [ABC]."

PRACTICE #5: *Asking for Video Reviews or Reviews with Images*

If our launch team members ask how else they can help, we can provide them with even more impactful options.

Video reviews stand out. Very few reviewers include them, which makes them incredibly eye-catching for potential buyers.

Here, we could ask one or two reviewers to record a short video of themselves reading the book with a child, or sharing their reaction. We can make this easier by offering prompts such as:

- *What did your child love most about this book?*
- *What stood out to you as a parent or caregiver?*
- *What made you feel this book was a good fit for your child?*

Photos of children reading our book are just as powerful and add instant emotional connection and credibility. Even a single image can make a review far more compelling.

Here is one of the images that was submitted for one of my books. Note that I actually don't know the reviewer. Wouldn't a review like this catch your eye?

The Garbage Trucks Are Here

★★★★★ **Wonderful book....**
By M. E. Hagenberg on Jan 02, 2018

I just read Garbage Trucks are here to my 5 year old grandson who got the book in his stocking. He loves the book and all things garbage trucks. His dad wanted to make him a truck bed for his 4th birthday but Dylan decided it had to be a garbage truck. This thing occupies most of his room. He sleeps on top and underneath is a play space that lights up and has books along the walls. Yes, he loves his bed and your book is now his favorite.
I know writing is hard work but remember that somewhere a child is nestled in with one of your creations loving every word.
Thank you,
Mary H. Grandmother to two boys. 2 and 5...

Images in this review

PRACTICE #6: *Following Up (this is part of marketing too)*

People are busy. Even those who genuinely want to support us may forget.

If a launch team member hasn't posted a review within about a week, a kind, personalized reminder is appropriate and often appreciated.

If you're anything like me, you might feel a bit funny sending a third or even fourth reminder. We don't want to be a bother to our family and friends. But here are three things that may help shift your mindset around follow-ups:

- Many of us check our messages while standing in line at the grocery store and then forget about them entirely.
- We're often overwhelmed by the sheer amount of noise competing for our attention.
- We're usually grateful, not annoyed, when someone reminds us in a kind, guilt-free way.

To make the review process even easier for your launch team members, you can create a direct Amazon review link of your book, using this tool I have put together for you right here:

https://www.eevijones.com/review-link-builder

YOUR AMAZON LINK:

Copy & paste your Amazon URL in its entirety

PLEASE CREATE MY REVIEW LINK

PRACTICE #7: *Saying Thank You & Extending the Momentum*

Once someone posts a review, we want to thank them individually. Gratitude strengthens our relationships and reinforces positive engagement.

We can also invite our launch team to share our book publicly on social media. To support them, we may want to provide ready-made images they can post. *Canva.com* is a wonderful free tool for this.

NINJA TIP:

Make sure posts and images are set to "public" so they can be shared easily. Include a clear call to action either in the image itself or in the accompanying post, so viewers know exactly what to do next.

And don't forget to include the *clean* Amazon link to your book.

Activating our launch team is about coordination. When our launch team acts in a coordinated and intentional way, they create the early activity and data points that help our book gain visibility, credibility, and momentum.

When done thoughtfully, this short window of action amplifies everything we've already prepared and gives our book a confident, visible start in the marketplace.

Now that we've successfully introduced our book to the world, we can shift our focus to what comes next: ongoing, intentional marketing that continues to support our book well beyond its launch.

———— • ◆ • ————

YOUR TO DOs FOR THIS CHAPTER:

- ❏ Create your book's clean & shareable link
- ❏ Activate your launch team and guide them through how they can best support you during your launch

Find all your templates and swipe files using this link below. You may want to bookmark this page, so you can refer to it as quickly and easily as possible.

⬆ *https://www.eevijones.com/marketing-downloads*

LINKS SHARED:

- *https://www.canva.com*
- *https://www.eevijones.com/clean-link-builder*
- *https://www.eevijones.com/review-link-builder*

CHAPTER 10
Promotions With Purpose

Book promotions are one of the most commonly discussed marketing strategies in the publishing world. They revolve around a simple idea: announcing that our book is temporarily free or available at a reduced price, and letting promotion sites share that deal with their email subscribers.

These subscribers are readers who actively seek out new books and love discovering fresh titles at a lower cost. Some promotional sites are entirely free to use, while others charge a fee to send our deal to their list. A few higher-priced services may even promise a minimum number of downloads, while others make no such guarantees.

Used strategically, book promotions can be a powerful visibility tool.

WHY AUTHORS USE BOOK PROMOTIONS

During a launch, promotions can help signal early activity to Amazon's algorithm. A spike in downloads or sales can, in turn, encourage Amazon to show our book to more shoppers, creating momentum in those crucial early weeks.

That said, it's important to understand a few limitations before deciding whether this strategy is right for us.

Limitation 1:

Some promotion sites require our book to be completely free in order to feature it. That means these promotions are only available to authors enrolled in *KDP Select*, which we discussed earlier in this book. If we choose not to enroll, we won't be eligible for those particular sites.

Limitation 2:

Because most promotion sites require us to submit our Amazon URL during the booking process, these promotions can only be scheduled after the book has already been published.

BEST USE

If we are planning to enroll our book in *KDP Select* in order to make it available for free to our launch team members, this is where book promotions can fit in beautifully.

We could combine both efforts by scheduling book promotions during the same window our book is free for our launch team. That way, we are doubling our reach: supporting our launch team members while also placing our book in front of readers who actively browse deal newsletters.

A REALISTIC LOOK AT CHILDREN'S BOOK PROMOTIONS

Here's where I want to be especially honest when it comes to promoting children's books.

Book promotion sites tend to work exceptionally well for genres like romance, fiction, and young adult. Readers in these categories devour books quickly and are constantly searching for their next read, which is why so many of them subscribe to deal lists.

Readers of children's books, however, often behave differently.

Parents, educators, and gift buyers are not typically browsing deal emails looking for children's books in the same way adult readers are hunting for their next novel. As a result, paid promotions often do not convert as strongly for children's authors as they do in other genres.

This does not mean promotions are useless for us. It simply means we should approach them with the right expectations.

PRICING CONSIDERATIONS

There is also a practical limitation we often run into as children's authors: pricing.

Many promotion sites that accept discounted books focus on $0.99 deals. Because children's books typically have larger file sizes due to illustrations, we are often unable to price our ebooks that low. In many cases, $2.99 is the lowest list price available to us, which makes those $0.99-only promotions inaccessible.

That leaves us with two realistic alternatives if we want to run a promotion at a reduced price:

- Enrolling our book in *KDP Select*, so we can offer our ebook for free for up to five days during each 90-day enrollment period, or
- Waiting at least one month after publication, which then makes us eligible to run a *KDP Countdown Deal* that allows us to offer our book at a reduced price

Think of children's book promotions as an additional visibility and discovery tool we can employ if we are already planning to enroll our book in *KDP Select* for our launch.

NINJA TIP:

It's worth remembering that only paid sales count toward your sales ranking. If your goal is to earn a bestseller badge, charging the size-permitting minimum list price is often a better option than offering your book for free.

MAKING THIS EASIER FOR YOU

There are hundreds of book promotion sites out there, each with different rules, prices, timelines, and genre preferences. Some require submissions weeks in advance, while others allow bookings with less than 24 hours' notice.

To save you time and help you get started, I've created a curated list of promotional sites that specifically offer children's book categories (↑).

Some of these sites are free, others charge a fee. Some require our book to be free, while others allow a discounted price. We get to choose the option that aligns best with our goals and our budget.

Several sites, however, require a minimum number of reviews before they will promote our book to their audience. This is yet another reason why gathering early reviews is such an important part of our launch strategy.

NINJA TIP:

If you are considering a *KDP Countdown Deal*, keep Amazon's timing requirement in mind:

We can only choose the *KDP Countdown Deal* option after our book has been published for at least 30 days. This means it is not available during our initial launch period and should be planned as a post-launch strategy instead.

Book promotions are not magic, and they are not a shortcut. But when used thoughtfully, they can play a supportive role in our overall marketing plan.

If we go into them informed, realistic, and intentional, they can absolutely be worth experimenting with. And if we decide to skip them altogether, that's perfectly okay too. Marketing is not about doing everything. It's about doing what makes sense for our book.

YOUR TO DOs FOR THIS CHAPTER:

- ❏ Download your curated list of promotional sites and see which ones would be a great fit

Find all your templates and swipe files using this link below. You may want to bookmark this page, so you can refer to it as quickly and easily as possible.

⬆ *https://www.eevijones.com/marketing-downloads*

CHAPTER 11
Celebration As Strategy

We have spent months, maybe years, bringing our beautiful book into the world. That work often happens quietly. Late nights. Early mornings. Notes scribbled between family responsibilities. Decisions no one else sees.

A launch party is our moment to pause and say: "This matters. This happened. And we did it."

But it is also something else entirely. A book launch party does three powerful things at the same time:

- It gives us space to openly recognize, honor, and celebrate our accomplishment.
- It provides us with an opportunity to thank everyone who has helped shepherd the book up to this point.
- It lets people outside our launch team know that our book is officially available, triggering a fresh wave of awareness, interest, and purchases.

That combination is magic. And the best part? There is no single "right" way to do this.

Our launch party can be:

- *A cozy, inexpensive gathering with our biggest supporters*
- *A joyful get-together at a local bookstore or restaurant*
- *A themed celebration tied to our book's topic*
- *A virtual party for friends and family near and far*
- *Or something wonderfully simple and entirely our own*

The only requirement is this: it should feel good to you. This is not about perfection, but about presence, connection, and joy.

WHY A BOOK LAUNCH PARTY WORKS

We invest an enormous amount of ourselves into our books, yet that investment is largely invisible to the outside world.

A launch party makes our work tangible.

It gives us a legitimate, newsworthy reason to gather people, share our story, and talk about what went into the book behind the scenes. It also creates something far more memorable than a single social media post that disappears after a few hours.

One of the smartest things we can do is create our own events.

Events are easy for local media to cover. They give people a reason to show up. And they create natural opportunities for photos, stories, and word of mouth.

Even if people may not be able to attend, the invitation alone can spark more interest than weeks of casual posting and social media announcements. A party feels real. It feels exciting. It signals that something important is happening.

CHOOSING THE RIGHT LOCATION

The venue we choose for our book launch party sets the tone, but it does not need to be fancy.

Some beautiful options include:

A bookstore:
Local independent bookstores or Barnes & Noble lend instant literary credibility. Media outlets are often more inclined to cover events tied to established booksellers, and bookstores already know how to host author events.

A venue related to our book's topic:
If our story involves animals, for example, a local pet shelter or rescue could be perfect. If it centers on nature, we could consider a park or community center.

Our home:
Hosting at home can feel intimate and deeply meaningful. We have full control over the atmosphere, the decorations, and the flow. It can also be more affordable and far less stressful.

There is no wrong choice. We choose the space where we will feel most present and supported.

PREPARING FOR THE PARTY

STEP 1: *Spreading the Word*

We can spread the joyful occasion by creating an invite post on our Facebook, Instagram, and LinkedIn profiles. We can share it in groups we are already part of, like book clubs, church groups, school communities, neighborhood circles, our kids' swim teams, or scout groups. We can mention it to colleagues, neighbors, and friends.

STEP 2: *Securing the Venue*

If we decide to host our party outside our home, we want to come prepared when approaching a venue. We can share our media kit (see chapter 15) and explain why this event will benefit them and their establishment. We can let them know how we plan to promote the party and how many guests we expect. A clear plan builds confidence and makes a *yes* far more likely.

STEP 3: *Ordering Books Early*

We will want to make sure to order our paperback books weeks in advance, with plenty of buffer. Delays happen, and the peace of mind this gives us is priceless.

STEP 4: *Enlisting Help*

Not everything has to be done by ourselves. We can ask friends or family to help with:

- *Food and drinks*
- *Greeting guests*
- *Managing book sales*
- *Taking photos or videos*

People love being part of this moment, so we want to give them an opportunity to support us.

STEP 5: *Inviting the Press*

This is our one true launch for this book. We will never have another first release. So let's go big.

We can reach out to local newspapers, weekly publications, community newsletters, radio stations, and online event calendars, ideally at least two months in advance. We will want to send a concise, exciting press kit and keep track of who we contacted and when.

THE PARTY ITSELF

Here is an example timeline we can follow:

Doors open
We arrive early. We greet guests warmly. Helpers handle snacks and drinks.

Official welcome
A bookstore owner, event coordinator, partner, or friend welcomes everyone and introduces us as the author to help build anticipation.

Our moment
We share a few words. We thank people. We offer a short reading or reveal. We raise a glass. We record this moment if we can.

Conversation and Q&A
This is often where the magic happens. A reading allows folks who know us well to see a different side of us. They get curious and tend to ask questions because they genuinely want to talk about the book and the writing process.

Signing and photos
If we decide to sell our book at the event (which we should), we will want to display our prices clearly. We can use QR codes for easy payment options like PayPal, Venmo, or Zelle.

Photos are a valuable marketing tool for later posts on social media, so we will want to make it a point to take a photo with each guest holding their purchased and signed book.

Thanks and goodbyes.
We thank folks for attending.

AFTER THE PARTY

The way we follow up matters. This is where so much of the long-term value lives.

- *A heartfelt message goes a long way, so we will want to send a thank-you email or note to every guest who took the time to celebrate with us.*
- *Relationships matter, so we will also want to make sure to thank the venue.*

A launch party is meant to be fun. Something we do to celebrate our beautiful accomplishment with others who wish to support us.

We can host it on our actual launch day, months later, or not at all. It can be private or public. There is no one right way. However we choose to celebrate ourselves and our book is the right way for us.

We deserve to be celebrated. And so does our beautiful book.

Now that we have successfully introduced our book to the world, we can shift our focus to the post-launch phase. This is where marketing becomes about support and follow-through, making sure our book is positioned clearly, professionally, and consistently as new readers continue to discover it in the days and weeks after launch.

——— · ◆ · ———

YOUR TO DOs FOR THIS CHAPTER:

- ❏ Host a beautiful book launch party where your guests can celebrate your author journey with you and have the opportunity to purchase your precious book in person

Find all your templates and swipe files using this link below. You may want to bookmark this page, so you can refer to it as quickly and easily as possible.

↑ *https://www.eevijones.com/marketing-downloads*

LINKS SHARED:

- *https://www.eevijones.com/pinterest-party*

PART V
MARKETING AFTER
THE CONFETTI SETTLES

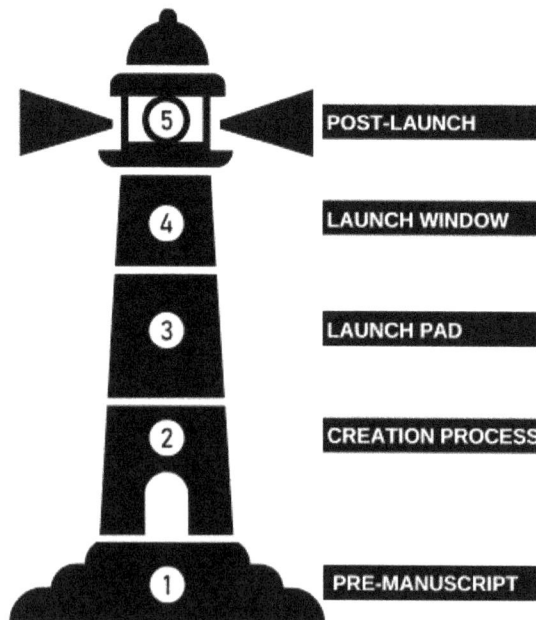

POST-LAUNCH

LAUNCH WINDOW

LAUNCH PAD

CREATION PROCESS

PRE-MANUSCRIPT

CHAPTER 12
What To Watch For After Launch

With the marketing strategies outlined in the previous chapters, we have now accomplished two incredible things:

1. You've given your book a strong, intentional launch that helped it gain early visibility and momentum.
2. You now have meaningful social proof in the form of wonderful reviews for your beautiful book

What we are trying to accomplish in this post-launch period is to spread the word even further and share your work with the world.

So far, only your launch team and those who purchased your book through your various promotions know about your children's book. Now it's time to share it more widely, with a big, bright bang.

In this chapter, I'm going to walk you through several very important things to be aware of during this phase. These insights will help you protect your time, your energy, and your budget as you move forward with marketing your book in a thoughtful and sustainable way.

———————— • ◆ • ————————

BEWARE OF SCAMMERS

As soon as you hit that proverbial launch button, you may find yourself bombarded with book marketing services. Sadly, many of them are scams.

Please do not skip this section, because this *will* affect you.

Every new author is understandably excited to share their newly published book. That excitement is easy to spot, and it can make us an easy target for those who prey on newly published authors.

That's why proper vetting of publicists and marketing services is so important, especially if you have been approached by one of them.

The number one reason I wanted to include this section in this book is because more and more of my students and readers have told me they were approached by publicists or marketers and weren't sure whether investing in those services would be worth it.

Please trust me on this. I have been there. I have spent thousands of dollars because I didn't know any better. So in this part of the book, we're going to look at how to decide whether or not investing in a book publicist or marketing service might actually make sense.

We will focus on three main marketing services:

1. *Book Publicists*
2. *Book Review Services*
3. *Buying Amazon Reviews*

———————— · ◆ · ————————

BOOK PUBLICISTS

In this section, we will explore:

1. **WHAT** a children's book publicist actually is
2. **HOW** to vet a publicist *before* investing
3. **WHICH** services might be worth it
4. **WHICH** services are not worth the investment
5. **ALTERNATIVES** that may serve you just as well

! NOTE OF CAUTION:

Always be extra careful if it is the agency or service provider who reached out to *you*, rather than the other way around.

WHAT A PUBLICIST IS

A publicist can be helpful in two main ways.

1. A publicist can save us time.

Publicists often handle the research of potential media outlets, as well as the outreach, coordination, and scheduling of interviews.

2. A publicist can connect us with people and outlets we may not have access to on our own.

The real value of a seasoned publicist often lies in their existing relationships with media outlets. They know who to contact and how to pitch your book effectively. Building those connections takes time and energy, which is why this experience often comes with a steep price tag.

New authors are eager to get their message out into the world, which makes the demand for marketing services very high. That demand is exactly why so many "professional" book publicists have popped up over the years.

Before signing with anyone, we want to be sure they actually have the kind of connections we are looking for. Getting booked on a podcast with ten monthly listeners, for example, is far less valuable than getting booked on one with thousands. And realistically, almost anyone could secure the former.

That's where vetting becomes essential.

HOW TO VET A PUBLICIST BEFORE INVESTING

Whether or not a publicist is worth investing in depends entirely on our goals for ourselves and our book. Before committing to any service, we need clarity around what we hope to achieve.

For example, our primary goal might be:

1. *Increasing exposure for our newly published children's book*
2. *Practicing and honing our interview skills*
3. *Gaining social authority we can later share on our website and social media*

Once we're clear on our goals, we can ask ourselves:

1. *How experienced is this publicist with children's books specifically?*
2. *What exact services will they provide?*
3. *Which of those services could I realistically do myself?*
4. *Does the value justify the investment?*

5. *Can this publicist reach audiences or outlets I could not access on my own?*

Before signing anything, we want to dive deeply into their website and testimonials, and look closely at the actual results they've achieved for other clients.

If you want to go even further, you could reach out to past clients and ask about their experience.

Also take time to review their social media presence. Look at:

1. *Comments and engagement on their posts*
2. *Views and likes*
3. *Overall interaction levels*
4. *Whether the account is active and current*

NINJA TIP:

If an account actively hides its likes or views, consider this a major red flag.

Anyone can create a profile and post content. The real value lies in interaction.

Here the golden rule is that…

The more engagement a post receives, the more reach it tends to have, and the more valuable it becomes to us as authors.

Brands understand this well. They care far more about engagement than follower counts. We should do the same when vetting a publicist.

WHAT SERVICES MIGHT BE WORTH IT?

I always recommend looking at a publicist's offerings one service at a time.

SERVICE 1: *Connecting You with Bookstores*

A publicist may help place your book in physical bookstores or arrange book signings. These are often local efforts, such as approaching Barnes & Noble or independent bookstores on your behalf.

If this is something you want but do not have the time to pursue yourself, this service may be worth considering.

ALTERNATIVE:

You can also approach bookstores yourself. Starting locally is often easier than expected. Calling your local Barnes & Noble or independent bookstore can go a long way.

My *How to Get Your Children's Book Into Any Store* workbook can help you create a repeatable outreach plan for this (↑).

SERVICE 2: *Connecting You with Media Outlets*

This may include:

- Podcasts
- Magazines
- TV Shows
- Radio Stations

If a publicist can connect you with *meaningful* outlets, this can be valuable. But quality matters.

For podcasts, always ask about average downloads per episode. With so many podcasts launching every month, many have very small audiences. Interviews on those shows may not justify the investment.

Look carefully at the publicist's media network, review their testimonials, and explore actual interviews they've secured for past clients.

ALTERNATIVE:

You can research where other children's authors have been featured. Those outlets have already demonstrated interest in children's books and may be more accessible than you think.

WHAT SERVICES AREN'T WORTH IT?

What follows are a number of typical services offered by book publicists that I have personally tried with some of my earliest books when I first started out as a children's author. Most of these services were not worth it, even though they cost me thousands of dollars, simply because I didn't know any better at the time.

SERVICE 3: *Author Spotlights (also called Author Interviews) by a Publicist*

If this is a service that is meant to be shared on the publicity provider's website itself, then I wouldn't recommend it. The problem here is twofold.

1. First, having your interview published on the publicity site itself means it heavily relies on you, the author, to drive traffic to the interview. So it doesn't do much in terms of reaching *new* people.
2. Second, it's important to remember who usually visits these publicity sites. More often than not, it's other newly published authors who, just like you, are looking for publicity. They are not your target audience. They won't be very interested in reading or sharing your interview, let alone purchasing your newly published book.

This right here is one of my earliest books, from a time when I was still very eager to try everything to get my message out into the world.

INTERVIEW
FEAT AUTHOR
JONES

Jones Discusses Lil Foot the Monster Truck

Always drawing inspiration from her own two children, Jones loves to write. Here she discusses

24 Comments

And while I enjoyed the interview itself, the only people who saw it and commented on it were those I personally sent to the interview. The publicist didn't create any new exposure for me or my book. Instead, I helped that website rack up more views.

So having our interview shared on a publicist's own assets, whether that's their website, Facebook page, or Instagram, usually won't be very helpful when it comes to increasing our exposure.

To determine whether or not this service might be worth it, always look at the publicist's previous shares and posts, and pay close attention to the interaction, such as likes and comments, especially on social media.

ALTERNATIVE:

A much better alternative here would be to reach out to influencers yourself (more on this in chapter 18). If you can connect with an influencer whose audience actually matches your target readers, that can be far more valuable than having an interview sit quietly on a publicist's website.

SERVICE 4: *Book Spotlights by a Publicist*

This service is very similar to author interviews and comes with the same limitations.

These spotlights are usually reviews or features that live on the publicist's website. Just like with author interviews, they rely heavily on you to bring the traffic. And if you are the one bringing readers to the page, then you are not gaining new exposure.

I truly tried everything to gain exposure for my first couple of children's books. While I loved being able to share my book's message, it sat very lonely on this publicist's website, never to be commented on or interacted with, as you can see right here with the zero comments and zero views.

Lil Foot Written with a Big Heart and an Important Life Lesson

With more than 50 raving, 5-star reviews, Lil Foot the Monster Truck was catapulted in to Amazon's bestselling lists in...

0 Comments / 0 Views

ALTERNATIVE:

Instead of having your book highlighted on a publicist's website, a much stronger option would be to find content creators who already share children's books with their followers.

Platforms like Instagram are especially wonderful for this. Many parents, teachers, and caregivers have blogs and accounts where they regularly talk about children's books.

Just be sure to do your due diligence. Look at engagement below their posts, including likes, views, and comments, not just follower counts.

We will cover how to decide whom to reach out to in part chapter 18.

SERVICE 5: *Book Readings by a Children's Book Publicist*

Having someone read our book to children is, in itself, a beautiful thing. Some children's book publicists offer services where they read your book and share it on their YouTube channel.

However, unless that YouTube channel has a large following that includes actual parents and caregivers, this service often won't result in meaningful new exposure.

ALTERNATIVE:

Virtual storytimes have grown tremendously over the past few years. If you are interested in paid readings, consider reaching out directly to YouTube storytime channels that already have established audiences.

When evaluating these channels, look at:

- *Number of subscribers*
- *Views per video*
- *Likes on each video*

Even though YouTube disables comments on children's content, likes still give us a good sense of engagement.

This will usually be far more valuable than having your book read on a small channel that is primarily visited by other authors.

To find these channels, simply start typing "Children's Book" into YouTube's search bar and see what suggestions come up.

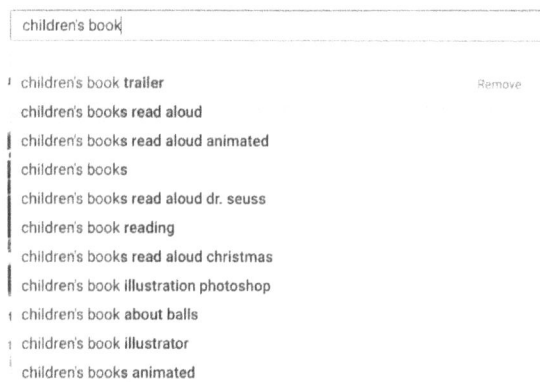

children's book

children's book **trailer**   Remove

children's books **read aloud**

children's books **read aloud animated**

children's books

children's books **read aloud dr. seuss**

children's book **reading**

children's books **read aloud christmas**

children's book **illustration photoshop**

children's book **about balls**

children's book **illustrator**

children's books **animated**

SERVICE 6: *Press Releases*

Unless you are using a high-end press release service that costs several hundred dollars, please do not invest in press release services.

I can't even begin to describe how silly I feel now, looking back at how much money I spent on press releases when I first started out.

My press releases were always "picked up" by hundreds of media outlets. At the time, it felt incredibly exciting. Until I realized that even though some of these outlets sounded impressive, they didn't actually mean anything.

My press release wasn't featured on their main pages. Instead, it was buried deep on a sub-sub-sub page that no regular person would ever find unless they had a direct link.

So while the distribution numbers looked impressive on paper, the exposure was essentially meaningless and didn't lead to real visibility for my book.

In the end, it is entirely up to you whether or not you want to invest in services provided by a publicist. The main reason I included this section is to help you make an informed decision when you are approached.

It's flattering to be contacted by someone who says they believe in our book and wants to help spread the word. But we all have limited budgets, and we want to invest in strategies that actually lead to results.

— ◆ —

BOOK REVIEW SERVICES

In this part, we will look at:

1. **WHAT** the two main types of review services are
2. **WHAT** to look out for when considering a review service
3. **WHAT** review service to definitely stay away from
4. An **ALTERNATIVE** that might be worth considering

! NOTE OF CAUTION:

Always be extra careful if it's the agency or service provider that reached out to you, rather than you reaching out to them.

This part of the book is meant to help you vet and verify the validity of these types of marketing services. So remember, if any of these services are approaching you instead of the other way around, your spidey sense should go off. More often than not, these services are not quite what they seem or promise to be.

This section focuses specifically on social media "influencers" who reach out asking whether or not we would like them to review our newly published book.

Generally speaking, there are two different types of review services we may be offered. Let's take a look at both.

REVIEWS SHARED ON SOCIAL MEDIA

The first type of review offer is for reviews that are meant to be shared on social media.

Here is a great example of the kind of message you might receive in your inbox or DMs:

"Hey Author Eevi, Good Day! I came to know about your amazing book and would love to share my view and ratings on various social media platforms. Confirm with me if you're interested, I would love to read and review your book. Warm regards, [NAME]."

Hey Author Eevi,

Good Day!

I came to know about your amazing book and would love to share my view and ratings on various social media platforms. Confirm with me if you're interested, I would love to read and review your book.

Warm Regards,

Now, these types of messages usually come with several red flags.

> **RED FLAG #1:** We are being approached instead of doing the outreach ourselves. These messages are completely unsolicited and often show up right after a book launch,

when we are posting heavily about our new book and using hashtags that these services monitor.

RED FLAG #2: There is no direct mention of our name. In this example, they used "Author Eevi," which is already unusual.

RED FLAG #3: There is no mention of the actual title of the book they claim to be interested in. This can be especially misleading for first-time authors who only have one book and assume the message must be genuine.

However, as someone who has published many books and still receives messages like this, it becomes very clear that this is a template sent to countless authors.

RED FLAG #4 : Sometimes these messages include awkward wording or typos.

What makes these messages especially tricky is that they usually do not mention payment upfront. Many authors assume the person is genuinely interested, only to find out several messages later that payment is expected.

There is nothing inherently wrong with paying for a review that will be shared on social media or a blog. The problem arises when these services pretend to be something they are not.

This is where vetting becomes essential.

Clicking through to this person's Instagram page, for example, we might see a beautifully curated feed with thousands of followers and lots of book photos. At first glance, this can look like a great opportunity.

But this is where I strongly encourage you to dig deeper.

When clicking into individual posts, we may notice that the number of likes is hidden. Instead of a number, we see "Liked by xyz and others."

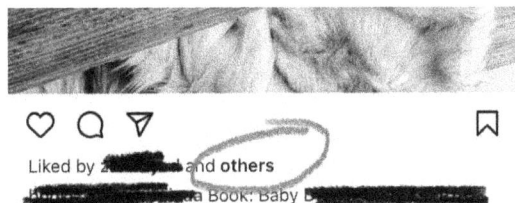

When this happens, it means the account holder has actively chosen to hide engagement numbers. With a following of nearly 19,000, there should be visible likes on posts.

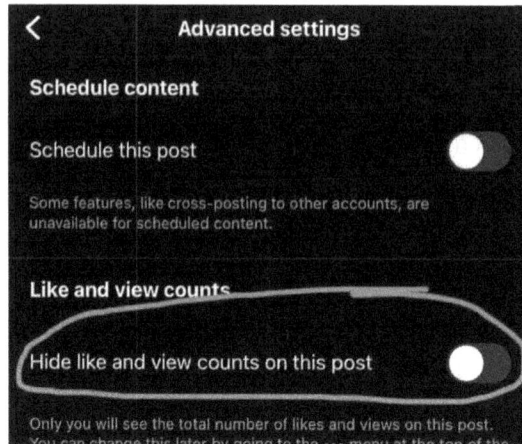

Hidden likes are a major red flag. More often than not, it indicates that a large portion of the followers are not real. Purchased followers do not engage, and hiding likes prevents that reality from becoming obvious.

NINJA TIP:

If a book review account has lots of followers but very few or hidden likes on their posts, don't use them. Spend your money elsewhere.

It is far more valuable to work with an account that has fewer followers but significantly higher engagement.

Engagement matters. Follower counts do not.

REVIEWS SHARED ON AMAZON

The second type of review offer we may receive is for reviews that are meant to be posted directly on Amazon.

Here is an example of such a message:

"Greetings, I'm [NAME] and I am pleased to inform you that I have critiqued over 500 literary works encompassing various genres. Considering this, I believe that you may be interested in availing my promotional services. My promotional services include: elaborative post and Instagram story, a review on Amazon, a review on Goodreads, an exclusive interview with the author. Please let me know if you are seeking any promotions for your book. Cordially, [NAME]."

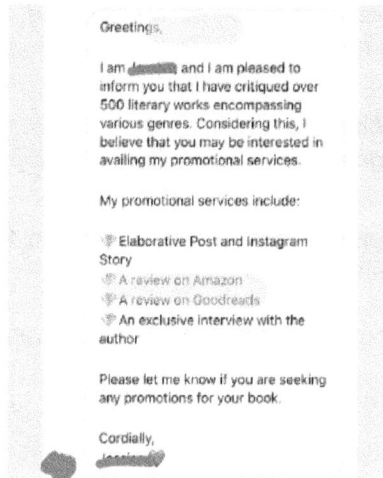

Greetings,

I am ▓▓▓▓▓ and I am pleased to inform you that I have critiqued over 500 literary works encompassing various genres. Considering this, I believe that you may be interested in availing my promotional services.

My promotional services include:

   ✏ Elaborative Post and Instagram Story
   ✏ A review on Amazon
   ✏ A review on Goodreads
   ✏ An exclusive interview with the author

Please let me know if you are seeking any promotions for your book.

Cordially,
▓▓▓▓▓

This message checks every red flag we've already discussed:

- They reached out to us
- There is no personalization
- There is no book title mentioned
- The wording is awkward

But in addition to all of that, it includes something far more serious: an Amazon review as part of a paid service. This is something we must absolutely stay away from.

NINJA TIP:

Per Amazon's review policy, Amazon does not allow reviews that are received in exchange for any form of compensation.

Amazon actively enforces this. Platforms like Fiverr constantly cycle through accounts offering paid Amazon reviews, and those accounts disappear just as quickly because they are flagged.

We do not want to take that risk. It is simply not worth it.

ALTERNATIVE: *Blogs*

Reviews matter. They signal credibility and social proof. Most people hesitate to purchase anything that has no reviews at all, and books are no exception.

Blogs can be a wonderful alternative.

Unlike social media vanity metrics, which can be manipulated, websites give us access to two numbers that are much harder to fake:

- *A website's domain authority*
- *A website's monthly page views*

Domain authority is a search engine ranking score from 1 to 100. The higher the number, the more likely the site is to appear in search results.

Monthly page views tell us how many visitors a website receives.

For example, Amazon's domain authority is 96, and its monthly traffic is in the billions.

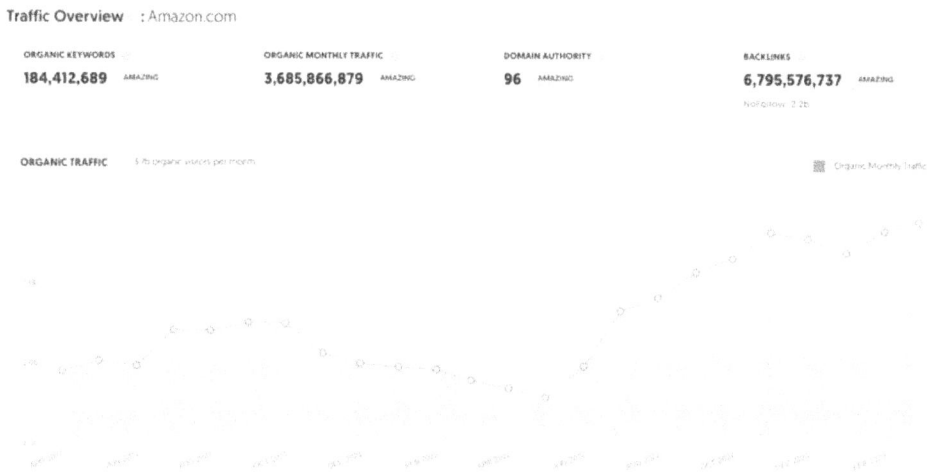

Traffic Overview : Amazon.com

ORGANIC KEYWORDS	ORGANIC MONTHLY TRAFFIC	DOMAIN AUTHORITY	BACKLINKS
184,412,689 AMAZING	3,685,866,879 AMAZING	96 AMAZING	6,795,576,737 AMAZING

These metrics give us a much clearer picture of whether a review is likely to be seen.

To help you get started, I have put together a list of children's book review blogs (↑), including their domain authority and estimated monthly visitors.

Some of these blogs are free. Others charge a fee.

!   **NOTE OF CAUTION:**

Even with this resource, it is still important to do your own due diligence.

So always look at

- *the blog's traffic*
- *their previously posted reviews*
- *their engagement with readers*

Then decide whether it feels like a good fit for you and your beautiful children's book.

You can find the curated list among the other resources for this book.

We can always dig a bit deeper to decide whether a review service is truly worth our time and hard-earned money, but this is a great and easy way to get started with blogs that specialize in reviewing books.

———————•◆•———————

BUYING AMAZON REVIEWS

Especially for newly published authors, it can take a while to gather our first couple of reviews. And because this is a known challenge, we see all sorts of services popping up that promise to "solve" this problem for us.

That is exactly why Amazon put review rules into place.

Amazon's main reason for having review guidelines is to ensure that reviews help customers genuinely learn more about a product, so they can decide whether or not to purchase it. Every review should be authentic and not misleading.

To protect that integrity, Amazon has very clear rules when it comes to reviews.

RULE #1: *We cannot buy reviews.*

Amazon does not allow reviews that are created, edited, or removed in exchange for compensation. And compensation goes beyond just cash. It also includes discounts, free products, gift cards, and refunds.

What does this mean?

1. *We cannot go to Fiverr.com, for example, and pay someone to leave a review.*
2. *We cannot pay any type of review service in exchange for a review.*
3. *We cannot offer a refund in exchange for a review.*

However, what *is* absolutely okay is providing someone with a free or discounted copy of our book, including Advanced Reader Copies, also known as ARCs.

But even then, we cannot *require* a review in exchange.

We can provide a free copy. We can ask for a review. But we cannot say, *"If I give you this book, you must leave a review."*

We also cannot try to influence or manipulate the review in any way. Again, we can ask for a review, but we cannot say, *"Your review must be positive."*

So while products may be provided for free or at a discount by enrolling our book into *KDP Select* (see chapter 7), and readers *may* choose to leave a review, any attempt to influence or require that review is prohibited.

REMEMBER:

Don't ever pay for a review in any way, shape, or form. Not directly. Not indirectly. Not through a service.

RULE #2: *We cannot require a review in exchange for something.*

This is another important one. There should be no "tit for tat," which is something I unfortunately see quite often.

A common example is when an author requires a reader to leave a review *before* granting them access to a webinar. Or when a review is required before someone receives a downloadable resource. That is not allowed.

NINJA TIP:

What *is* allowed is requiring the **purchase** of our book in exchange for access to something.

So if we want to offer bonus content, like coloring pages, activity sheets, special downloads, or read-aloud access, we can absolutely do that in exchange for the *purchase* of our book.

Then, *after* the purchase, we can simply ask for a review.

The key difference is this: Access can never be contingent on leaving a review. The review must always be optional. How we phrase things truly matters here.

RULE #3: *We cannot partake in any review swapping.*

Review swapping means, "If you review mine, I'll review yours." This often happens between authors and usually involves positive reviews exchanged as favors.

Amazon does not allow this.

That said, this does *not* mean that we as authors cannot review other books. Authors are readers too, and Amazon wants readers to leave reviews for books they read.

Ideally, we simply want to avoid reviewing the books of authors who have reviewed ours.

So the rule of thumb here is simple: Review books you genuinely read and enjoy, just not as part of a review exchange agreement.

RULE #4: *We cannot review our own book.*

This one almost goes without saying, but I wanted to include it because I see it happen more often than you might expect. Usually, Amazon won't even allow authors to access their own book's review page. But sometimes, for various reasons, it does.

Amazon removes reviews that are posted by someone with a financial interest in the product. And as the author, we clearly have a financial interest in our own book.

I know how tempting it can be, especially when you are waiting for those first reviews to come in.

But this is one we absolutely want to avoid.

Marketing is not just about what we do. It is also about what we choose not to do.

Knowing how to spot misleading offers, ineffective services, and outright scams protects not only our budget, but our book's credibility and long-term visibility. Every decision we make in this post-launch phase shapes how our book is perceived, discovered, and trusted.

Thoughtful marketing is informed marketing. And when we move forward with clarity, discernment, and intention, we give our book the strongest possible chance to grow in a way that is both ethical and sustainable.

———————— • ◆ • ————————

YOUR TO DOs FOR THIS CHAPTER:

❏ Access & download your curated list of children's book review blogs

Find all your templates and swipe files using this link below. You may want to bookmark this page, so you can refer to it as quickly and easily as possible.

⬆ *https://www.eevijones.com/marketing-downloads*

LINKS SHARED:

- *https://www.eevijones.com/workbook1*
- *https://www.eevijones.com/best-childrens-book-review-blogs*

CHAPTER 13
Your Digital Home - When A Website Matters

Marketing doesn't stop at discovery or purchase. It also includes where people go next when they want to learn more about us and our work. That's why this chapter focuses on building an online home that supports our book, our credibility, and our long-term visibility.

A WEBSITE - Our Home On The Web

Having a virtual home on the web is so important. So many fellow children's authors are hesitant or resistant when it comes to creating their own website. Yet, it is absolutely essential to our personal branding and our visibility *beyond* Amazon.

In these next few pages, we will look at:

1. *WHY* you may want to consider a website.
2. *WHEN* you should start thinking about a website.
3. *WHAT* to include on our website.
4. *WHAT* to name your website.

———— • ◆ • ————

WHY SHOULD WE CONSIDER A WEBSITE?

Amazon is wonderful. But it is rented space. We don't own it. Besides the tweaks we can make to our Amazon sales page, we can't customize it. And perhaps most importantly, it's filled with distractions that lead readers away from our books.

Our own website, on the other hand, is our home base.

It's the one place online that is completely ours, where readers can get to know us, where stores and libraries can learn how to order our book, and where we can share the deeper story behind why we wrote it.

Our website doesn't have to be complicated. It just has to be you.

A clean homepage, a place for your book or books, an "About the Author" section with a friendly photo, and a simple contact form are all we need to instantly establish a healthy level of credibility.

And to make this even more powerful, we can also add a "For Stores & Libraries" page that immediately positions us as a professional who is ready for opportunities.

When we have that hub in place, every other visibility effort we make, from a podcast mention to a promotional interview, has somewhere meaningful to send people.

———— • ◆ • ————

WHEN SHOULD WE START THINKING ABOUT OUR OWN WEBSITE?

The answer here very much depends on what you are planning to do and be once you write and publish your children's book.

Creating a professional-looking website takes time, especially if this is your very first one. So I want to make sure you're making the right decision for you and your circumstances.

To help you with that decision, I created a simple breakdown for you. A YAY side, with a big yes to creating your own website, and a NAY side, with a big no.

YAY

You'd want to give yourself a big thumbs-up regarding the creation of your own website if:

- *You wish to brand yourself and your book or books.*
- *You're planning to write more than one children's book.*
- *You want a dedicated place on the web to send potential readers.*
- *You're planning to have your own platform to share, offer, or sell your books.*

NAY

On the other hand, an author website might not be necessary if:

- *You're not planning to write more than one book.*
- *You're not planning to share or promote your children's book online.*
- *You have a publisher who creates a website for you.*

Oftentimes, we already feel overwhelmed when thinking about the creation of our very first children's book. And that's why I want you to know this:

It is absolutely okay not to start out with an author website.

You may decide to publish your book without one and add a website later. That is perfectly fine.

However, if you are planning to write more than one children's book, it will eventually make sense to create a website from a branding perspective.

———————————— • ♦ • ————————————

WHAT SHOULD WE INCLUDE?

Something I really want to emphasize is this: your website does not have to be grand. It only needs a few key elements to look professional and to truly benefit you and your beautiful children's book.

1. THE BOOK PAGE:

This is where you share your book. Showcase your beautiful cover and include a direct, clean link to Amazon or wherever you want people to purchase your book.

This page is also a wonderful place to share a book trailer, as well as your book blurb or description.

2. THE ABOUT PAGE:

This page is all about you, the author. Here, you will want to share a picture of yourself along with a short biography. This bio is usually a bit longer than the author bio we include on Amazon or inside the book.

If you'd like to see an example, I've included one of my own About pages here (↑):

https://www.bravingtheworldbooks.com/about

3. A MEDIA PAGE:

A media page showcases where your book has been mentioned or featured.

This page will always be a work in progress, because you will add to it over time. And that's perfectly okay. If you haven't had any media coverage yet, don't worry. This page can always be added later.

Here's an example of one of my own media pages (↑). Just remember, it took me years to fill this page.

https://www.eevijones.com/media

4. A CONTACT PAGE:

This page allows others to easily reach you, whether that's to learn more about you or your books, send a media request, or simply connect.

You can also list the social platforms you use, such as:

- *Facebook*
- *Instagram*
- *LinkedIn*
- *TikTok*

Your contact page can be its own page, or it can be part of your media page, where you simply list your preferred way to get in touch right above your media features.

The next element I want to mention is optional, but can be very powerful if you wish to grow your audience.

5. A CONTACT "COLLECTION" PAGE:

This page is used to collect email addresses from visitors so we can begin building our email list (see chapter 4).

This becomes especially important if we're planning to write multiple books or a series. Collecting readers' emails allows us to reach out whenever we're ready to share a new story.

6. AN AUTHOR VISIT PAGE:

If we are available for school visits or author presentations (see chapter 25), we want to make sure this is clearly communicated on our website.

This page can include:

- **A warm introduction** that explains we're available for visits and which age groups we typically speak to.
- **Photos of us**, ideally including at least one photo of us presenting to children. These images act as powerful social proof.
- **A clear description** of our sessions, activities, or workshops.
- **Our contact information**, such as a booking email and, if we choose, a phone number.
- **Testimonials** from teachers, librarians, or coordinators.
- **Our fees**, if we wish to list them publicly.
- **A list** of past schools or organizations we've visited.
- **Downloadable resources**, such as:

  - *a to-do list for coordinators*
  - *an editable poster announcing our visit*
  - *teacher guides or activity sheets*

This page acts as both an information hub and a quiet credibility builder. When schools see that care has gone into this page, they feel more confident reaching out.

———— • ✦ • ————

WHAT SHOULD WE NAME OUR WEBSITE?

The most common website-related questions I receive are:

- *What should the domain name be?*
- *Should I create a website for each of my books?*

When it comes to naming your website, you have three solid options:

1. *Use your author name*
2. *Use the name of your book or series*
3. *Use the name of your imprint*

All three are valid. There is no right or wrong.

That said, there are a few things to keep in mind:

1. First, make sure the domain is available. You can check availability through a provider like *GoDaddy.com* (↑).
2. Second, if possible, try to secure a .com domain. Or, if you are outside the US, your country's primary domain suffix. For example, German authors often use .de.
3. Third, make sure the domain name is easy to spell and type. Avoid hyphens, periods, underscores, or extra characters. I made this mistake with my first website, and it only made things unnecessarily complicated.

If you base your website on your own name, you are establishing yourself as the brand.

Two wonderful examples are:

- *LorenLong.com*
- *WillHillenbrand.com*

Some authors create websites for their series, especially once a series develops its own fanbase. Great examples include:

- *BerenstainBears.com*
- *MagicTreeHouse.com*

And finally, you can use your imprint name, which works especially well if you have multiple books that don't all belong to the same series:

- *Readonbooks.com*
- *BravingTheWorldBooks.com*

Whether you choose your name, your book or series title, or your imprint should always reflect your goals and the direction you want your author journey to take.

A website is not a requirement, and it does not need to happen all at once. But when you are ready, it can become one of the most steady and reliable pieces of your marketing. It gives your book a home beyond algorithms, a place where readers, educators, and partners can truly understand who you are and what your work is about. Used intentionally, it supports every other marketing effort you make and helps your book stay discoverable long after the launch excitement has passed.

———————— • ✦ • ————————

YOUR TO DOs FOR THIS CHAPTER:

- ❑ Consider whether a website would be a supportive and natural fit for you and your book(s)

Find all your templates and swipe files using this link below. You may want to bookmark this page, so you can refer to it as quickly and easily as possible.

⬆ *https://www.eevijones.com/marketing-downloads*

LINKS SHARED:

- *https://www.bravingtheworldbooks.com/about*
- *https://www.godaddy.com*
- *https://www.LorenLong.com*
- *https://www.WillHillenbrand.com*
- *https://www.BerenstainBears.com*
- *https://www.MagicTreeHouse.com*
- *https://www.Readonbooks.com*
- *https://www.BravingTheWorldBooks.com*

CHAPTER 14
One Link, Many Doors - A Simple Alternative

What if we don't want to invest the time in creating an entire website at this point in our author journey, yet still wish to present ourselves professionally to our launch team, schools, press, and retailers?

This is where the *One-Link* option comes in handy. It's a quick alternative to a more extensive, robust website. One single link that leads to multiple other links.

In the next few pages, we are going to look at:

1. **WHAT** this One-Link option is
2. **WHY** we might need such a link
3. **WHEN & WHERE** to use and share this type of link
4. **WHERE** to create your own One-Link page
    a. If you **DON'T** have your own website
    b. If you **DO** already have your own website.

WHAT IS A ONE-LINK OPTION?

Right about now, you might be wondering:

"Eevi, a link that leads to multiple other links? What in the world are you talking about?!"

Below is an example of one such link that leads to a page holding a number of other links of mine.

QUIZ: Do You Have What It Takes To Write A Children's Book?

FREE: Find Your BESTSELLING Story Idea TODAY - Video

FORBES Feature

EOFire Interview

BESTSELLING BOOK: How To Self-Publish A Children's Book

COURSE: Children's Book University

Each of these gray bars is a button that, when clicked, leads to a website.

For example:

- The first button leads to a fun quiz I created for my readers to see if they have what it takes to write a children's book.
- The second button leads to one of my free resources that helps aspiring children's authors find their own bestselling story idea.
- The third button leads to a *Forbes* article I was featured in.

By providing others with just one single link, I'm able to lead visitors to a page that holds a number of my other important links that I feel are relevant and helpful to them.

If you'd like a peek, here's the link to that page (↑):

https://linktr.ee/eevi_jones

The concept behind this is simple: If we could provide just one single link to others, which one would be most relevant or most beneficial, both to us as the author and to the visitor?

Perhaps you'd think a link to your website would be most helpful. Perhaps a link to your book's Amazon page. Or maybe a link to your most recent interview.

Instead of having to choose just one destination, this option allows us to share multiple links to the places on the web we deem most relevant and important. That way, visitors can decide for themselves what they'd like to explore next, whether that's our website, our book, or a recent interview.

———— • ✦ • ————

WHY WE MIGHT NEED THIS ONE-LINK OPTION

Let's look at the two main reasons why something like this can be so helpful, and how this concept came to be.

REASON 1: *Convenience*

Many online platforms only allow us to add just one single clickable link.

Because of that, we would constantly have to update that link to reflect whatever we are currently talking about in our most recent post. Platforms like Instagram, for example, don't allow clickable links directly in posts. We can only add them to our profile.

So one day, when we're sharing about our newest children's book, we'd want that one link in our bio to lead to our Amazon page. The next day, when we share a new interview, we'd want that same link to lead somewhere else.

Besides the hassle of constantly changing that link, there's another problem.

If someone comes across an older post a week later and clicks through to our profile, the link will already have been changed. There's no way for that link to stay both current *and* relevant to older posts at the same time.

That's exactly why one single link that leads to a page with multiple links is so beneficial and much more convenient.

REASON 2: *Having More Control*

Another great benefit of a One-Link page is that it gives us, as the author, more control over what visitors see about us.

We get to curate the experience.

If we simply share a link to our website, there are often many different things to look at. And if someone is searching for something specific, most people won't take the time to hunt for it.

Just like us, they want things to be quick and easy.

Clear buttons that state exactly where they lead make the experience simple and intuitive. Visitors immediately know where to click and what to expect.

————————— • ✦ • —————————

WHEN & WHERE WE CAN SHARE OUR ONE-LINK

Many platforms allow only one clickable link in a profile, such as TikTok.

Other platforms like Instagram, Facebook, and LinkedIn allow more than one clickable link. Even there, the One-Link method can still be incredibly useful, especially if we want to keep our profiles clean and uncluttered while sharing many different resources.

Here are a few examples of links we might want to include:

- *Our website*
- *Our book's Amazon sales page*
- *Printables or fun extras that come with our book*
- *An embedded book trailer*
- *A recent interview*
- *A public reading schedule or event calendar*
- *Links to our other social media platforms*
- *A sign-up page for our newsletter*

So really, if something has a link and you feel it would benefit others, it may be worth adding it to your One-Link page.

＊＊＊

USING A ONE-LINK FOR OUR LAUNCH TEAM

But the use of a One-Link page can go beyond social media.

Another way I love using a One-Link page is during a book launch, specifically for my launch team.

This right here is the One-Link page I created for my book *When Things Get Tough* (↑):

https://linktr.ee/eevijones

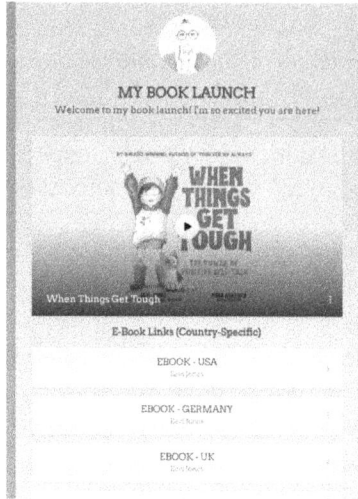

On this page, I shared items that were most relevant to my launch team:

- *A photo of myself*
- *A short welcome message*
- *A read-aloud video for the book*
- *Country-specific links to the ebook on Amazon*
- *Country-specific links to the Amazon review page*
- *A thank-you message*
- *A section with frequently asked questions*

In that FAQ section, I included questions like:

- *How helpful will my review really be, Eevi?*
- *Should I purchase your book?*
- *How else can I best support you, Eevi?*

Creating a One-Link page for our launch team allows us to keep everything in one clear, organized place, making it easier and more enjoyable for our team to support us during our book launch.

WHERE TO CREATE A ONE-LINK PAGE (IF WE DON'T HAVE A WEBSITE)

There's no shortage of services that allow us to create pages featuring multiple links. Here are a few popular options that offer free plans, with paid upgrades available (↑):

- *Linktr.ee*
- *Campsite.bio*
- *Lnk.bio*
- *Beacons.ai*

These services are especially helpful if we don't yet have our own website and need something quick for an upcoming event or promotion.

WHERE TO CREATE A ONE-LINK PAGE (IF WE ALREADY HAVE A WEBSITE)

That said, even if we *do* have our own website, creating a One-Link page is still incredibly valuable. In that case, instead of hosting it on a third-party platform, we can create our own link-sharing page directly on our website.

And this option comes with two major benefits.

BENEFIT 1: *SEO Benefits*

Even if SEO (Search Engine Optimization) feels overwhelming, here's the simple version: Traffic to *our* website is always a good thing.

So instead of sending visitors to a link-sharing platform and boosting *their* visibility, we can direct traffic to our own site and strengthen our own online presence.

BENEFIT 2: *Complete Design & Branding Freedom*

Hosting a One-Link page on our own site gives us full control over design and branding. We can add images, videos, and even downloadable resources.

This right here is the link I currently share in my Instagram profile (↑):

https://www.eevijones.com/VIP

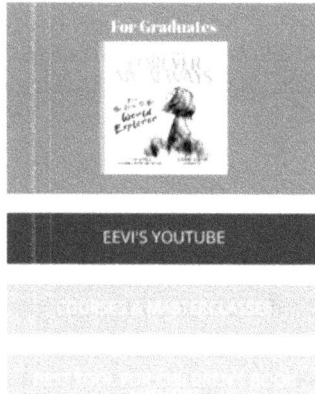

On that page, there are links to:

- *One of my newest books. Instead of using text, I uploaded an image of the book cover to make it visually engaging.*
- *My YouTube channel.*
- *My courses and free resources.*
- *My Illustration Template Generator, giving aspiring children's authors quick access to a free tool.*
- *My other books.*

At the very bottom, I also include a short bio and an invitation to sign up for my weekly Sunday email.

When we host a link-sharing page on our own website, there are truly no limits to what we can include.

By clicking just one single link, we give visitors access to a curated list of places we believe are most relevant and helpful, making it easier than ever for them to find exactly what they're looking for.

A One-Link page may seem simple, but it's a powerful marketing tool. It gives us a clear, intentional place to send people when they're curious about our work, and it removes friction at the exact moment interest is highest. Whether it lives on a platform like *Linktr.ee* or on our own website, this single link helps us guide attention, support discovery, and present our book professionally at every stage of our journey. And in marketing, making it easy for people to take the next step matters more than almost anything else.

YOUR TO DOs FOR THIS CHAPTER:

❏ Consider whether a One-Link would be a supportive and natural fit for you and your book(s)

Find all your templates and swipe files using this link below. You may want to bookmark this page, so you can refer to it as quickly and easily as possible.

⬆ *https://www.eevijones.com/marketing-downloads*

LINKS SHARED:

- *https://linktr.ee/eevi_jones*
- *https://linktr.ee/eevijones*
- *https://www.eevijones.com/VIP*
- *https://linktr.ee*
- *https://campsite.bio*
- *https://lnk.bio*
- *https://beacons.ai*

CHAPTER 15
Being Media-Ready

Before a journalist ever presses record or a blogger begins drafting a post, one quiet thing almost always happens first: they look us up.

A media kit is one of the most practical, behind-the-scenes marketing tools we have. It shapes first impressions, signals professionalism, and helps others quickly understand who we are, what our book is about, and why it matters to their audience.

As children's authors, much of our visibility happens long before an interviewer ever asks a question or a journalist types their first line. Before anyone decides to feature us - whether it's a magazine, a parenting blogger, a librarian, or the host of a local morning show - they will almost always peek at our media kit.

This little packet of information becomes our professional first impression. And when created with care, it instantly communicates who we are, what our book is about, and why sharing our story will matter to their audience.

Think of your media kit as your tiny, polished storefront. A place where the media can step inside, look around, and quickly understand the heart behind your beautiful children's book.

———————— • ✦ • ————————

Why Media Kits Matter

A thoughtfully assembled media kit makes a journalist's job easier. And anything that makes an interviewer's life easier will always work in our favor.

Instead of attaching multiple large files to our pitch emails, we can simply include one elegant link to our complete kit. Quick, clear, and incredibly professional.

You may come across companies charging $1,000 or more to design a media kit. While that may be helpful for some authors, you absolutely do not need to invest in that. You can create a lovely, organized, and compelling kit all on your own, and you'll learn exactly how right here.

Who Your Media Kit Is For

This is the number one mindset shift for many children's authors:

Our media kit is not for our little readers. It's for the grown-ups who may help spread our book into the world.

Think of our media kit more as a presentation for "investors" than a tool to grab a new reader.

Our audience for this kit includes:

- *Journalists*
- *Parenting and education bloggers*
- *Children's librarians*
- *Bookstore owners*
- *School administrators*
- *Reviewers*
- *Podcast hosts*
- *Event coordinators*

These are busy professionals, and they want to know very quickly why our book matters to their readers, viewers, listeners, or customers.

As we put together our media kit, we will want to think about a few angles that help us stand out. If any of these apply, they are worth mentioning:

- **Does the book have any local tie-ins?**
  Example: A book set in Virginia, written by a Northern Virginia author
- **Does the book contain timely or culturally relevant themes?**
  Example: kindness, neurodiversity, grief, emotional resilience
- **Can I, as the author, provide professional expertise?**
  Example: a teacher writing about classroom inclusion, a pediatric therapist writing about coping skills
- **Does this book contain a unique art style or storytelling approach?**
  Example: a mixed-media illustration style, a lyrical or rhythmic narrative, an interactive storytelling format

- **Does this book foster community involvement?**
  Example: school visits, literacy events, nonprofit collaborations

Whatever makes our book or author story unique, we will want to make sure to share it.

Where Our Media Kit Lives

We always want our media kit to be easy to find and easy to share. Ideally, it should be:

- On our author website; a dedicated "Press" or "Media Kit" page works beautifully
- Available as a downloadable PDF
- Linked in our digital business card or email signature
- Ready to send anytime someone requests more information

And if someone wants a printed version, we can have a clean, professionally printed copy ready to go.

What to Include in Our Media Kit

Our media kit should be polished but not overwhelming. Most journalists don't want a 30-page booklet, and a sparse two-page kit may feel incomplete. We are aiming for something curated, clean, and easy to skim.

Here are the essential elements.

1. Author Bio (100–200 words)

Now you may be thinking: *"Eevi, didn't I already write an author bio?"*

While our Amazon bio and our media kit bio can certainly share the same heart and message, a media kit bio serves a very different purpose. And because of that, it should be written differently.

Our Amazon bio is written for parents, grandparents, teachers, and the sweet grown-ups who buy children's books. Our media kit bio, however, is written for the media, which means it needs to do something completely different:

It needs to give journalists a clear angle.

Think of it this way:

- Our Amazon bio builds *trust and connection*.
- Our media kit bio builds *interest*.

It gives reporters, bloggers, podcasters, and producers an immediate sense of why featuring us and our beautiful book will matter to their audience.

A strong media kit bio still feels warm, but it leans more into:

- **Relevance:** *why our book matters right now in the world of children's reading and parenting*
- **Expertise:** *any background or experience that gives us authority (teaching, therapy, education, childhood development, or even lived family experiences)*
- **Timely or meaningful themes:** *big emotions, resilience, friendship, inclusion, kindness, grief, confidence*
- **Notable achievements:** *awards, endorsements, features, bestsellers, events*
- **Media-readiness:** our availability for interviews and the topics we can confidently speak about

Your media bio is still you, just with a clearer focus on why your voice is a valuable one for the media to amplify.

Making Our Media Bio More Intriguing

Journalists and bloggers often scan bios quickly, looking for a spark. These elements tend to catch their attention most:

- **A unique or surprising angle**
  Maybe your stories come from your work as a social worker, a speech therapist, a teacher, a military spouse, a child of immigrants, or a parent raising a neurodivergent child.

  "After working as a pediatric nurse for 12 years, she turned the coping tools she used with anxious young patients into stories children can embrace."

- **A timely topic**

  "Her book arrives at a cultural moment when emotional literacy and resilience have become top priorities for families and educators."

- **A compelling origin story**
  Not long. One sentence is enough.

"She began writing stories at her kitchen table after seeing her son struggle with bedtime fears."

- **A quotable mission**
  Journalists love pulling lines like:

  "I believe children's books can be tiny mirrors that help kids recognize their own bravery."

- **Authority or lived experience**
  Anything that connects your life with the message behind your book.

  "Drawing from her years as a kindergarten teacher, she writes stories that help children navigate friendships, emotions, and classroom dynamics."

- **Proof of impact**

  "Her school visits routinely draw 200+ students."
  "Her read-aloud videos have been viewed over 100,000 times."
  "Her debut sold out its first print run within two weeks."

- **A "moment of now"**
  Why your book and your voice matter today, in this season, for families, educators, and children.

  "As conversations around mental health and emotional regulation continue to grow, her stories offer age-appropriate tools for young readers navigating big feelings."

Journalists love bios that give them a *ready-made* introduction they can copy straight into an article or use to open an interview. Your bio becomes the bridge between your book and their audience.

In short, our 100–200 word media kit bio should be a polished, press-ready snapshot that gives journalists a complete angle they can run with.

2. Contact Information

We will want to make it as easy as possible for someone to reach us directly. This can be short and simple:

- *Full name*
- *Email address*
- *Website*

- *Social platforms we use professionally*

3. Sample Q&A or Tip Sheet

This is one of the most helpful things we can include. Not every journalist will read our book. Bloggers may skim it quickly. Producers may only have minutes to prep.

By including 7–10 thoughtful question prompts with sample answers, we make their job easier and help keep the conversation aligned with our message and mission.

I put together a few examples for you below. Make sure to tailor them to your own needs to ensure your interview stays aligned with your message and mission.

1. *Your story touches on themes parents and educators are talking about everywhere right now. Why do you think this moment is so important for children's literature?*

   WHY: Instantly ties our book to a timely cultural conversation.

2. *Every children's book begins with a spark. What was the moment (or child!) that first planted the seed for this story?*

   WHY: Interviewers love origin stories. They're relatable, emotional, and memorable.

3. *What real-world challenge did you witness that made you feel this story was truly needed?*

   WHY: Shows substance, empathy, firsthand understanding, and signals "this author has seen something worth talking about."

4. *You've described your mission in a beautifully memorable way. Can you share what drives that mission, and how it shapes the stories you tell?*

   WHY: Journalists crave quotable lines. Missions = instant soundbites.

5. *Why do you feel this book belongs in the world right now, at this particular moment in children's lives?*

   WHY: Gives interviewers a timely "why now" justification to feature you immediately.

6. *Is there a moment from your own childhood that found its way into this book in a way readers might not expect?*

   WHY: A unique, personal hook. This is the type of detail that ends up in print.

7. *What has surprised you most about the way families, schools, or libraries have used*

your book?

WHY: Proof of impact + unexpected results = instant story material.

8. *What role do you believe picture books play in helping children recognize their own bravery, kindness, or resilience?*

   WHY: Positions us as a thoughtful voice on emotional literacy. Media loves experts with heart.

9. *Which parts of your lived experience made their way directly into the pages of this book?*

   WHY: Lived experience is one of the strongest credibility markers for journalists.

10. *If children remember only one message from your book years from now, what would you hope that message is - and why?*

    WHY: Powerful, emotional, quotable. Journalists will pull this line almost every time.

4. Photographs

We never want journalists or bloggers to spend time searching the internet for images of us or our book. Instead, we can make their job wonderfully easy by providing everything they need directly inside our media kit.

Here, we will want to include high-quality, stand-alone JPGs of:

- *Your author photo*
- *Your book cover*
- *Optional lifestyle photos of you reading, signing, or sharing your book*

These images give media outlets immediate, ready-to-use visuals and help them feature us beautifully, accurately, and with confidence.

5. One-Sheet

We'll go over this more in chapter 16, but our One-Sheet is our book's polished elevator pitch on one tidy page.

6. Book Excerpt

If appropriate, we can also include a short excerpt. Usually the first spread or first few pages; just enough to showcase our voice and pique interest.

NINJA TIP:

Make sure to label all your files clearly. Journalists download files constantly, so we want to make it as easy as possible for them to find your files on their computer.

INSTEAD OF: "mediakitfinalFINAL.pdf"
TRY: Lastname_Firstname_MediaKit.pdf

NINJA TIP:

Review media kits from other children's authors. Look at authors who share your themes or audience to see what is helpful and common.

NINJA TIP:

Keep your media kit updated.

Your author journey will grow and shift over time. As you reach new milestones, remember to refresh your kit. This could include:

- Awards you have won
- Notable endorsements
- School visits or speaking engagements
- Media interviews
- Updated author photo
- New book release

Each of these additions strengthens your social proof and reassures the media that featuring you is a worthwhile use of their time.

At its core, a media kit is a marketing tool that works quietly in the background. It helps us show up prepared, credible, and easy to feature, long before we ever have a conversation with the media. When our kit is clear, thoughtful, and up to date, it removes friction and builds trust. And in marketing, being ready when opportunity knocks is half the work.

YOUR TO DOs FOR THIS CHAPTER:

- ❏ Prepare your very own media kit

Find all your templates and swipe files using this link below. You may want to bookmark this page, so you can refer to it as quickly and easily as possible.

⬆ *https://www.eevijones.com/marketing-downloads*

CHAPTER 16
A Decision Page That Gets A *Yes*

As we prepare to spread our marketing wings post-launch, it's time to create what is called a One-Sheet.

Think of a One-Sheet as a resume for our book.

It's one of those quiet marketing tools that does its work behind the scenes, helping others decide quickly whether our book is a good fit for their shelves, platforms, or audiences. In a single page, it presents the most relevant details about our book in a clear, intentional way, making it easy to understand at a glance and a natural addition to the media kit we just worked on.

TWO TOOLS, TWO PURPOSES:

The difference between a media kit and a one-sheet is largely who they are created for.

MEDIA KIT: designed for journalists and media outlets, helping them quickly decide whether your book and story are a good fit for coverage.

ONE-SHEET: created for stores, schools, libraries, and other decision-makers, helping them decide whether to carry your book or offer it to their audience.

One-Sheets are sometimes also referred to as:

- *Info Sheets*
- *Sell Sheets*
- *Pub Sheets*
- *Fact Sheets*

No matter what it's called, the key is that it's a one-page document, printed on both the front and back of a single sheet of paper, not two separate pages. This format saves on paper and ensures that all the important information stays together.

A well-crafted, thoughtfully designed One-Sheet can help our book stand out and position it confidently in a crowded market. As part of our media kit, we want it to look and feel as professional as possible.

WHAT TO INCLUDE

In a nutshell, our One-Sheet should include all the key details someone would need to make a decision about our book, whether that decision is about carrying it in a store, covering it in an article, or sharing it with an audience.

So let's break it down, starting with the front of the sheet. I'll use one of my own One-Sheets as an example.

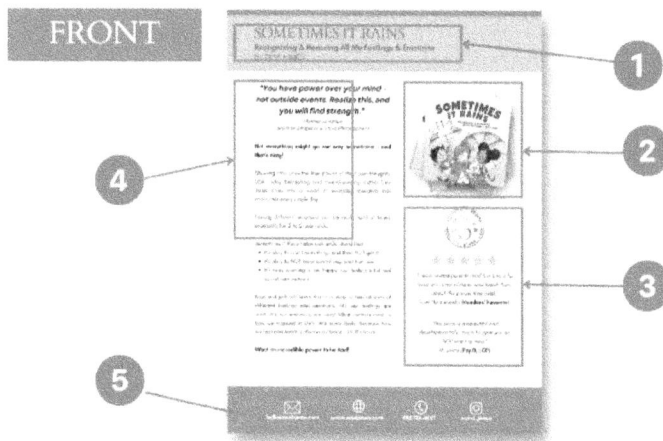

ELEMENT 1: *Title / Subtitle*

The first elements are the title of our book, the subtitle (if it has one), and the author name.

In my example, I have the title *SOMETIMES IT RAINS* in bold at the top, followed by the subtitle *Recognizing & Honoring All My Feelings & Emotions*, with *by Eevi Jones* just below it.

ELEMENT 2: *Cover Image*

Next, we'll want to include an image of our book cover. We can use a flat image, or, if we want to add a bit of visual interest, a 3D mockup. A little depth goes a long way.

ELEMENT 3: *Awards & Reviews*

The third element includes any awards our book has won, along with a few short review snippets we are especially proud of. Showcasing social proof here can be very powerful.

NINJA TIP:

When sharing reviews:

- **Keep it short and sweet.** To keep it concise, only include the juiciest part of the review. One strong sentence is all you need.
- **Choose relevant reviewers.** It's especially impactful to share reviews from people whose professional background directly relates to your book's subject. For example, reviews from teachers, pediatricians, or child psychologists are incredibly valuable when your book addresses emotions or child development. The more aligned a reviewer's role is with your topic, the more credibility it adds to your book.

For *Sometimes It Rains*, I included the *Readers' Favorite* five-star seal, along with a quote from a clinical psychologist who reviewed the book. Since the story focuses on emotions, that alignment mattered.

ELEMENT 4: *Book Description*

Next, we'll include a clear, concise book description. Personally, I like to use the same description that appears on my Amazon sales page or the back cover of the book. This copy is already optimized and crafted to:

- *speak directly to potential buyers*
- *clearly communicate the heart and purpose of the book*

ELEMENT 5: *Contact Information*

The final element on the front of our One-Sheet is contact information.

Our goal is to make it as easy as possible for others to reach us and learn more. Here, we can include:

- *Email address*
- *Website*
- *Phone number*
- *Social media handles*

That wraps up the front of our One-Sheet. Now, let's flip it over and dive into the back.

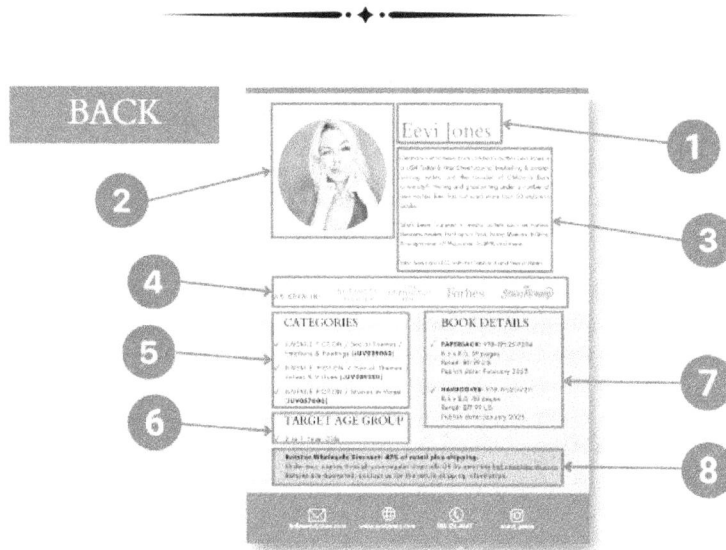

ELEMENTS 1 & 2: *Author Name & Profile Picture*

The first two elements on the back are our author name and profile picture.

We want our photo to be clear and sharp, ideally with a solid background. We want to avoid photos where other people are visible or ones that look like they were cropped from a vacation snapshot.

At the same time, remember this: we are children's authors. We get to show a bit of personality and playfulness here, something most authors don't get to do.

ELEMENT 3: *Author Bio*

Next, we'll include a short, relevant author bio. This should be concise and focused on why we wrote this book and why we are the right person to tell this story.

ELEMENT 4: *Credibility Markers*

This element is optional, but incredibly powerful. Credibility markers are logos or mentions of places where we or our book have been featured. These could include interviews, articles, media outlets, or notable platforms.

If we're newer authors, we may not have many of these yet, and that's completely okay. Building credibility takes time. It took me years to collect mine. Be patient with yourself.

We don't need dozens of logos. A handful of recognizable ones is enough.

On my One-Sheet, I include logos from *Forbes, Business Insider, Scary Mommy*, and the *Huffington Post*. These are publications many people instantly recognize.

ELEMENT 5: *BISAC Categories*

Next, we'll include our book's relevant BISAC categories.

This helps bookstores and retailers understand exactly where our book belongs on their shelves.

NINJA TIP:

Do not use Amazon categories here.

Amazon categories are not the same as industry-standard bookstore categories. The publishing industry uses BISAC codes, which stand for *Book Industry Standards and Communications*. Listing BISAC categories instantly makes your One-Sheet look more professional.

To find your book's BISAC categories (↑), you can use the official BISG page right here:

https://bisg.org/page/BISACEdition

On my own One-Sheet, I list three primary BISAC categories along with their codes.

ELEMENT 6: *Target Age Group*

Including the target age range helps readers quickly understand who the book is for. It's best to show a realistic age range. Something like "Ages 3–88" doesn't help decision-makers. Clear age ranges do.

ELEMENT 7: *Book Details*

The seventh element to include is the book's essential details - the information someone would need to place an order.

Here, we will want to share our:

- *ISBN*
- *Trim size and page count*
- *Retail price*
- *Publication date*

We will want to make sure to include this information for each version of our book, whether that's hardcover, paperback, or any other format we offer.

On my own One-Sheet, for example, I included all of these details for both the hardcover and paperback versions of my book *Sometimes It Rains*. This makes it incredibly easy for bookstores and libraries to quickly understand what formats are available and how to order them without having to ask follow-up questions.

ELEMENT 8: *Consignment Details*

If we are planning to use our One-Sheet when reaching out to stores, we will want to include information about consignment sales.

Here, we can share:

1. That consignment sales are welcome and appreciated
2. Our preferred way(s) of communicating (email, phone, etc.)
3. That a consignment agreement is available

These small details go a long way. They answer common questions up front and help make it easier for store owners to say yes, rather than needing to follow up for clarification.

These are the core elements to include in our One-Sheet. Together, they help make it as easy as possible for someone to take the next step.

————————— • ◆ • —————————

HOW TO USE YOUR ONE-SHEET

Our One-Sheet is like our book's business card. It's a simple and effective way to communicate all the key details about ourselves and our beautiful book.

If we're visiting a store in person, we'll want to bring a printed copy with us. And if we're reaching out via email, we'll want to attach our One-Sheet as a PDF.

NINJA TIP:

Remember - it's called a One-Sheet for a reason. When printing a hard copy, make sure to print it on both the front and back of a single sheet of paper, not two separate pages. This keeps everything together and reduces the chances of important details getting misplaced.

NINJA TIP:

When printing your One-Sheet, it's best to start small and print a limited number of copies. Your One-Sheet is a dynamic tool that should grow and evolve with you.

For example, when your children's book wins an award or you receive notable media coverage, you'll want to update your One-Sheet to reflect that. Just like a resume, it should stay current.

By starting with a smaller print run, you save both paper and money while ensuring you're always sharing the most relevant, up-to-date information.

NINJA TIP:

It's a great idea to always carry a few copies of your One-Sheet with you. Think of it as your book's business card - you never know when the perfect opportunity will come up.

Another fantastic place to share your One-Sheet is on your website. You can add it to your "About the Author" section, or, if you have a media section, make it available there as a downloadable PDF for anyone who wants it.

CREATING OUR OWN ONE-SHEET

Now that we've covered all the individual elements of our One-Sheet, it's time to create our very own.

With all the information we've gathered and the notes we've taken throughout these last few pages, putting your One-Sheet together will feel far less intimidating than it may have at first.

And to make it even easier, I've created a template (↑) for you that you can use, listed among the other resources for this book. All you have to do is plug in your own details, and you'll be ready to go.

Just as professional speakers use a speaker reel to showcase their expertise, and actors use self-tapes when submitting to casting directors, we authors can use a one-sheet to clearly and confidently present our book.

And just like that, we've upped our marketing game. Our One-Sheet will help us:

1. *Stand out from the crowd*
2. *Be prepared*
3. *Look and feel more professional*

With our media kit and One-Sheet in place, we are no longer marketing from a place of guesswork. We are prepared, clear, and equipped with tools that help others understand our book quickly and confidently.

These assets don't just support outreach. They are marketing. They make it easier for bookstores, media outlets, schools, and partners to say yes, and they ensure that every opportunity we step into is backed by clarity and professionalism.

Now that these foundational pieces are ready, it's time to extend our presence outward and meet readers where they already are. In the next chapter, we'll focus on strengthening our visibility across social media platforms and turning everyday online spaces into natural extensions of our marketing efforts.

———————— ◆ ————————

YOUR TO DOs FOR THIS CHAPTER:

- ❏ Access the One-Sheet template I've created for you and prepare your very own One-Sheet

Find all your templates and swipe files using this link below. You may want to bookmark this page, so you can refer to it as quickly and easily as possible.

⬆ *https://www.eevijones.com/marketing-downloads*

LINKS SHARED:

- *https://bisg.org/page/BISACEdition*

CHAPTER 17
Building A Social Presence That Feels Like You

Social media is one of the few marketing tools we have as children's authors that costs nothing but our time. When used intentionally, it can quietly and consistently help our book be discovered by the very people it was written for.

Being present on social media isn't about chasing trends or trying to go viral. It's about visibility, familiarity, and creating small, repeated touchpoints that help parents, educators, librarians, and fellow readers come across our book naturally.

With that in mind, social media can play a huge part in our marketing - if we let it.

This chapter is here to help us approach social media in a way that feels doable, sustainable, and even fun, so it can support our book without becoming another heavy task on our to-do list.

———————— · ◆ · ————————

OUR SOCIAL MEDIA PRESENCE

If you are on TikTok, you may already know that this platform in particular has been a real game-changer for romance writers. Romance writers, poets, and young adult fiction authors have seen their books blow up because of it. So whether or not we personally enjoy these platforms, or even use them regularly, they can still play an important role in promoting and marketing our children's books, so others can learn about them.

Something many people forget is that social media is one of the only ways we, as authors, can share our book completely for free.

And that is incredibly valuable, especially when we consider just how far-reaching social media can be. Going back to the TikTok example, it costs these authors nothing but time to create a 15-30 second video of or about their book. Yet, that one short video can potentially reach thousands, if not millions.

When creating our online presence, we want to make it as easy as possible for ourselves. Three things will help us do just that.

NUMBER 1: *Our Mindset*

Sharing our book on social media instantly becomes easier when we remember that it is absolutely free - and that it can, and should, be fun.

Remembering why we set out to write our precious book in the first place helps tremendously with this mindset shift. We didn't *have* to write it. We *got* to write it. And in the same way, we don't *have* to share our book. We *get* to share our book.

How lucky are we that we get to share something we created?

So instead of seeing social media as a chore, we can begin seeing it as something fun. And simply reframing it this way immediately lifts a lot of the pressure we may have felt before.

NUMBER 2: *Being Active*

Being active on social media doesn't just mean posting our own content. It also means interacting with others.

That could look like engaging with fellow authors, responding to people we follow, or interacting with content we genuinely enjoy. For example, if we see a friend's post on Facebook, we can like it, heart it, or leave a comment.

Doing this brings people back into our orbit.

Facebook notices. Our friend notices. And in turn, the platform's algorithm encourages this type of interaction by showing us more of their posts - while also showing more of *our* posts to them. That interaction often comes full circle when they then like or comment on our posts, increasing engagement on our content as well.

Interacting with others begets interaction with our own posts. Those two always go hand in hand.

And the same holds true across other social media platforms.

NUMBER 3: *Consistency*

Consistency matters, both when it comes to interacting with others and posting our own content.

The most successful authors on social media are those who show up, interact, and post regularly.

How often we post depends on many factors, such as our audience, our book, and our available time. But I generally recommend aiming for at least once a day.

I know that may sound completely unattainable at first. But what I've learned is that when we approach this with the right mindset and see it as something fun we get to do, it becomes surprisingly easy. Once we start and stay consistent, it turns into a habit. A habit that can take as little as 2–3 minutes a day.

If you ever need help coming up with ideas, you can use my Social Media Post Prompt Generator (↑). It creates daily content prompts for children's authors - 365 days a year - to help spark connection and conversation with fellow authors and future readers.

POST PROMPT WIZARD.™

Our posts don't have to be perfect. And most won't go viral. In fact, 99% of them won't. The first few weeks, or even months, may feel slow or discouraging. And that's okay, as long as we stick with it.

This is where we put our lab coat on and experiment.

We can repurpose the same content across platforms, sharing it on Facebook, Instagram, and even TikTok. We can try different captions, posting times, and hashtags to see what works best.

By being willing to experiment, we uncover what works for us and our book - all while having fun along the way.

NINJA TIP:

We don't need to be on every social media platform. Once we figure out which one works best for us and which we enjoy most, we can focus our energy there.

NINJA TIP:

Try to start creating a presence on social media even before your book is published. But also know that it's never too late to start having fun and experimenting with this. So even if your book has already been published, go ahead and create and use a social media account.

And if you don't have anything to share just yet, simply interact with others. Connect with fellow children's authors, and support and motivate one another.

NINJA TIP:

Don't get frustrated. Instead, have fun with this. Let go of any expectations you may have, and I promise things will feel so much easier. Even if a post flops in terms of engagement and doesn't get as many likes as we hoped, we can still learn something from it.

We don't ever fail. We either win, or we learn. And that's how we grow.

———— • ✦ • ————

BRANDING OURSELVES (Part 2): *Visual Consistency Is Key*

Now that we've laid the foundation for our social media presence, let's look at a few simple touches we can add to make our profiles more branded, memorable, and credible.

Social media platforms give us an incredible opportunity to share information about who we are and what we do. And while it can feel overwhelming to manage it all, there are a few easy ways to make our profiles work *for* us.

FACEBOOK

Facebook gives us five powerful branding opportunities we can use to market ourselves and our book.

COMPUTER   MOBILE

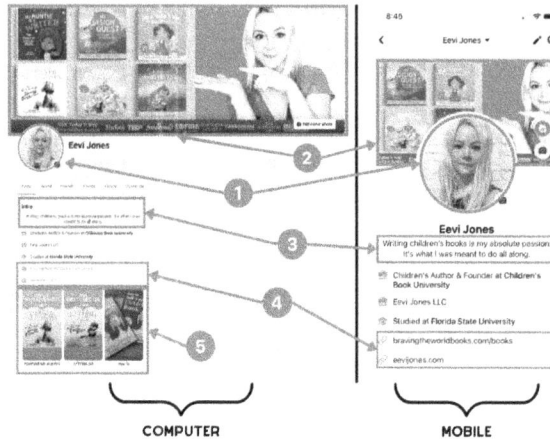

1. PROFILE IMAGE: We want to use the same profile photo across platforms whenever possible. This helps readers recognize us more easily. The same goes for our name and handle.

2. COVER IMAGE: Facebook's cover image is prime visual real estate. We can showcase our latest or upcoming book and include our website if we have one.

NINJA TIP:

Always check how your cover image looks on mobile as well, so nothing important gets cropped.

3. MINI BIO: We have 101 characters to describe ourselves and include a link. This text shows even on mobile, so let's use it intentionally.

4. CLICKABLE LINK: This could lead to our website, Amazon author page, or One-Link.

5. FEATURED IMAGES: These appear prominently on our profile. Fewer images mean larger displays, which makes them more impactful. Many children's book authors first discovered my book *How To Self-Publish a Children's Book* through this exact space.

NINJA TIP:

Because we rarely self-promote on personal Facebook profiles, many friends and family members may not know what we've been working on. These updates naturally show up in their feeds and can turn quiet supporters into fans.

INSTAGRAM

We can do the same on Instagram, LinkedIn, and any other social media platform we're planning to use in our marketing strategy. We want to make the most of the virtual real estate we've been given. Just like on Facebook, people can quickly see who we are and what we do simply by visiting our Instagram profile.

Instagram also allows for fun emojis, which gives us the chance to show a bit more personality and highlight what else is important to us.

I also like to use Instagram's highlights below the profile. This is something not many people take advantage of, but it can be very effective. Each highlight holds relevant information tied to different categories I've created and want to showcase.

My *programs* highlights, for example, share information about my programs, while my *shoutouts* highlights feature a number of testimonials. This would be the perfect place to permanently display some of the wonderful reviews our book has already received.

NINJA TIP:

Many authors treat their profiles as an afterthought. From now on, let's make intentional decisions about colors, images, and our voice.

We want to use this "branding" opportunity wherever we can. If there's a box to be filled out, fill it out. If there's a place to add an image of yourself, add one. If you have a website, share it. Don't leave anything blank.

Make it easy for your followers to find you. Use your name for your website's domain, your Facebook author page, your TikTok account, and your LinkedIn account. Whatever social media platform you're using, make it as easy as possible to be found.

OUR HASHTAG STRATEGY

Before diving in, here's a quick disclaimer: there is no secret hashtag rule that will magically make posts go viral.

Instead, we're going to learn how to think strategically and creatively, so our book can be found despite all the noise.

Hashtags depend on two things:

1. *The platform*
2. *The goal of the post*

And the only way to uncover what works is through experimentation.

METHOD 1: *Hashtag Sites*

Sites like *best-hashtags.com* (↑) work by using algorithms to analyze data from social media platforms in order to suggest relevant and effective hashtags. They typically categorize hashtags by popularity.

Because these sites mostly focus on finding hashtags with high usage volume rather than those with strong engagement rates or niche relevance, they tend to be quite broad and general. This can make it harder for our specific target audience to find us. That said, they are still a great way to kick off our hashtag research.

BEST #CHILDRENSBOOKS HASHTAGS

Most popular instagram **childrensbooks** hashtags

#childrensbooks #kidsbooks #books #reading #bookstagram #book #childrensbook #illustration #kidlit #rn #bj #l #childrensauthor #kids #art #read #picturebooks #kidsbook #children #bookworm #author #booksforkids #l #teddybear #barnbok #writer #illustrator #storytime #bok #bhfyp

METHOD 2: *Social Media Platforms' Auto-Fill Function*

The second way to help us find hashtags for our children's book is by using each social media platform's auto-fill function.

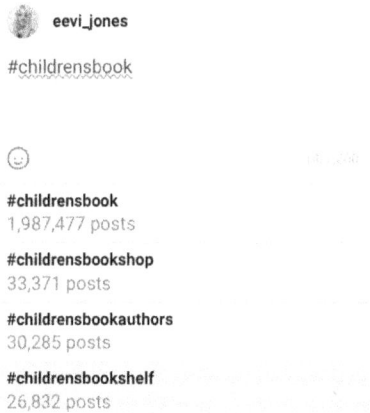

eevi_jones

#childrensbook

☺

#childrensbook
1,987,477 posts

#childrensbookshop
33,371 posts

#childrensbookauthors
30,285 posts

#childrensbookshelf
26,832 posts

Just like any search engine, a social media platform's search bar has an auto-fill function that generates a dropdown list of commonly used hashtags as soon as we start typing one in.

What makes this function so helpful is that it leverages the platform's internal, real-time data, which means it is instantly current with the latest trends and algorithmic shifts.

This dropdown list also shows us how often a hashtag has already been used. Based on that number, we can then decide whether or not it's worth using that particular hashtag.

NINJA TIP:

We want to find and use hashtags that are actively being used (so not too low of a number), but that are also not being overused. If a hashtag has been used billions of times, it means there is an extremely high posting rate, and our post will be competing with countless others. That makes it far less likely for our post to be seen.

Because this auto-fill function still requires us to come up with the initial idea for a hashtag, this method is only as good as the words or prompts we begin typing into the search bar.

Instead of adding a whole slew of hashtags, social media platforms like Instagram and X recommend using only a few highly relevant, niche-specific hashtags.

So in order to get the most out of this auto-fill approach, we need to come up with our own hashtag ideas first, or at least a general direction, so we can start typing meaningful prompts into that search bar.

To do so, we will want to think about two questions:

- *What platform is it for?*
- *What is the goal of the post?*

WHAT PLATFORM IS IT FOR?

Knowing which platform our hashtags are for is important, because each platform uses slightly different hashtags.

For example, #*authorsofinstagram* is used on Instagram, while #*authortok* is used on TikTok.

The number of characters we can use, as well as the number of hashtags we can include per post, also differs between platforms.

INSTAGRAM:	up to 2,200 characters; 30 hashtags per post
X (TWITTER):	up 280 characters; 2 hashtags per post
PINTEREST:	up to 500 characters; 20 hashtags per post
TIKTOK:	up to 2,200 characters; 5 hashtags per post
FACEBOOK:	up to 5,000 characters; 30 hashtags per post
LINKEDIN:	up to 3,000 characters; 3 hashtags per post

So depending on which platform we're using, we will want to plan our hashtag usage accordingly.

WHAT IS THE GOAL OF THE POST?

Just like we want to know what platform our hashtags are for, we also want to know the overarching goal we're trying to achieve with them.

For example:

1. *Is it to find and connect with potential readers?*
2. *Is the post meant to connect with other writers and the author community?*
3. *Is it meant to inform people about a special deal or sale?*

Making this distinction is important, because it directly influences which hashtags we choose.

For example, if we're trying to connect with potential readers for our children's book, we might use hashtags like *#childrensbook* or *#picturebook* on Instagram, and *#booktok* or *#readingtok* on TikTok.

If the main goal of the post is to share a special deal, we might use hashtags like *#bookpromotion* or *#freebooks*.

Each hashtag is used by different people, for different goals, and for different reasons. That's why we want to be specific and intentional when choosing them.

As children's authors, our main goal is to connect with and be found by more readers. Everyone uses hashtags like *#childrensbook* or *#picturebook*. But beyond these more common, author-related hashtags, we will want to get a bit more creative when looking for additional, more unique hashtags.

To do so, we can use our book's characters and topics to our advantage.

Over the years, I have identified five hashtag categories we can explore and really dig into to help us stand out from the masses and increase our chances of being seen by just the right people.

CATEGORY 1: *People and Communities*

Here, we'll want to remember that besides the little ones who read our books, there are always grown-ups who have to purchase our picture book first.

We'll want to ask ourselves: *Who are those people? And how might they be connected to our book?*

For example, oftentimes it's moms who purchase children's books. So what are some hashtags moms are using to identify themselves on social media?

To find out, all we need to do is start typing in "mom" in the search bar on a social media platform and see what the auto-fill dropdown suggests. There are so many different hashtags, such as *#momsofinstagram, #momsover40,* or *#momsoftoddlers.*

What hashtags are teachers using?
What hashtags are librarians using?

CATEGORY 2: *The Topic of Our Book*

This category can be either very broad or very specific. For example, if our story teaches about kindness, we can start typing in "kindness" and see what comes up. Other great examples might be "bullying" or "patience."

Or maybe our book is about kids playing soccer. In that case, we could look for kid- or youth-soccer-related hashtags. If our story is about adoption, what hashtags are adopting families using?

By aligning our hashtags with the actual topic of our book, we increase the likelihood of being discovered by people who already care deeply about that subject.

CATEGORY 3: *Characters of Our Book*

Again, this can be super broad or very specific. If our book is about dogs, what are some dog-related hashtags we could find?

More specific hashtags would dial in on particular breeds. For example, if our book features a dachshund, what breed-specific hashtags could we use?

If our book is about unicorns, sheep, firefighters, or mail carriers, we can search for hashtags that relate directly to those characters or professions.

These types of hashtags help place our book into interest-based communities that already exist.

CATEGORY 4: *Relevant Locations & Places*

Location-based hashtags are often overlooked, but they can be incredibly powerful.

If our story is about firefighters, for example, it might make sense to use hashtags related to places associated with them, such as *#firestation* or *#firetruckenthusiast*. If our story takes place in a specific region, like the Midwest, are there regional hashtags we could use?

Do our local libraries or school systems use specific hashtags? To find out, we can visit their Instagram or X accounts and look at some of their previous posts to see which hashtags they're using.

These types of hashtags are often used less frequently, which means that even weeks or months later, our post may still appear when someone clicks on or searches that hashtag. So even if our post isn't seen right away, it might still be discovered later.

NINJA TIP:

If they exist, consider using your city's or county's hashtags. Or if your city has a local news channel or radio station with its own hashtag, include it.

And here's why:
This is how local media outlets often look for and discover newsworthy stories.

Local media is always on the lookout for interesting stories to share with their readers and viewers. Using location-specific hashtags doesn't cost us a dime, so it's absolutely worth trying.

CATEGORY 5: *Time & Seasons*

These hashtags can also be broad or very specific. They can relate to the four seasons or to specific holidays, such as Christmas or Halloween. They can also relate to school breaks or reading seasons.

Hashtags like *#summerread* or *#winterbreak* are great examples.

NINJA TIP:

Many content creators use season-related hashtags to find fresh, timely content for their blog posts, podcasts, or social media shares.

So even if our post doesn't get hundreds or thousands of views, it only takes **one** person to help our book be discovered by the right audience. Using relevant, timely hashtags can help us get there.

Using these unique, off-the-beaten-path hashtags helps our book appear outside of heavily saturated, book-only spaces. These are hashtags not every other author will think to use. And perhaps more importantly, they are highly specific to the topic of our book.

The main thing to remember here is to stay open and willing to experiment. There is no one-size-fits-all hashtag strategy.

And once we find hashtags that work well for us and our book, we'll want to note them down so we can reuse them for future posts. That way, we're not starting from scratch each time, and our marketing becomes easier, more intentional, and far more sustainable.

------------- • ✦ • -------------

Social media is not about going viral or getting everything "right." It's about visibility, consistency, and connection over time. When used intentionally, it becomes one of the most accessible marketing tools we have as children's authors, one that allows us to share our book, our message, and our journey without a financial barrier.

By showing up regularly, engaging with others, and using thoughtful hashtags, we make it easier for the right people to discover our book. And that is what good marketing does: it quietly removes friction, builds familiarity, and creates opportunities for our story to be found again and again.

———————— • ✦ • ————————

YOUR TO DOs FOR THIS CHAPTER:

- ❏ Based on what you've learned, create or update your social media accounts
- ❏ Based on what you've learned, brainstorm some relevant hashtags
- ❏ Using the *Social Media Wizard*, put together your posting schedule

Find all your templates and swipe files using this link below. You may want to bookmark this page, so you can refer to it as quickly and easily as possible.

⬆ *https://www.eevijones.com/marketing-downloads*

LINKS SHARED:

- *https://www.eevijones.com/social-media-prompt-generator*
- *best-hashtags.com*

CHAPTER 18
A Thoughtful Approach To Outreach

At this stage of our marketing journey, our book already exists in the world. It has a message, reviews, and a reason to be shared. What it needs now is reach.

This is where outreach comes in.

Outreach is the bridge between the work we have done behind the scenes and the people who have never heard of us yet. It is how our book leaves our immediate circle and begins to travel outward - into conversations, platforms, publications, and communities that already have attention, trust, and influence.

Many authors assume that marketing only happens on social media or through paid ads. But some of the most effective and long-lasting marketing does not happen on our own platforms at all. It happens when we intentionally place our voice, our story, and our expertise in spaces that already have an audience.

This chapter is about exactly that.

Guest articles, interviews, and thoughtful influencer outreach are strategic visibility tools. When done with care, they build credibility, expand awareness, and create discovery paths that continue working for us long after a post disappears or a launch ends.

Outreach marketing is not about asking for favors or pushing our book. It is about offering value, showing up prepared, and forming meaningful connections that benefit everyone involved.

In this chapter, we are going to look at how to approach outreach intentionally, ethically, and sustainably - in ways that feel aligned, respectful, and effective for us as children's authors.

Marketing is not just about being visible. It is about being invited into the right rooms.

———— • ♦ • ————

GUEST POSTING & MAGAZINE ARTICLES

Many websites and online magazines rely heavily on guest contributors. Unlike traditional print magazines (which typically hire journalists), online publications often welcome outside voices, especially from parents, educators, and therapists.

What if I were to tell you that all it takes to get on big-name websites and magazines is preparation and asking? All we need is a compelling story, an intriguing angle, a polished pitch, and a healthy serving of patience and persistence.

With these ingredients, I was able to write articles for places such as:

Forbes TEDˣ Scary Mommy E◉FIRE THE HUFFINGTON POST Kindlepreneur circle of moms POPSUGAR. Military.com

And so can you.

In the pages that follow, we're going to talk about how guest posting works specifically for us as children's book authors. Guest posting means writing an article or blog post for someone else's website or publication. It is one of the most powerful long-term marketing techniques available to us, because each article introduces us to brand-new readers, parents, educators, and professionals who may never have discovered our work on their own.

And best of all: besides our time, it's absolutely free.

When our article lives on a well-known site, it becomes a long-lasting discovery point that can continue sending readers our way for years to come. That tiny byline under our article acts like a quiet, ongoing ambassador for our book and our author brand.

! **Byline** = the line of text, usually below the headline, that names the author and gives them credit, often including their title, affiliation, or a link to their bio to establish credibility and allow readers to connect with them.

It's also beneficial for the website hosting our article, because they receive useful, high-quality content from someone with lived experience or expertise on a topic their readers care about. It's a win for everyone.

Yet, the majority of children's authors don't know about this marketing technique, or have never considered it.

Now, the truth is that while the idea of having our writing published on a site like *Scary Mommy*, *Motherly*, *HuffPost Parents*, or a well-known kidlit blog is exciting, the process of actually writing the article can feel a bit intimidating.

But getting our name into well-known publications doesn't have to take a lot of time or energy. Nor does our written piece have to be lengthy or research-heavy. In fact, we mostly want to use this technique to boost our credibility, which can help open far bigger doors along our author journey, if we know how to leverage it.

AIM FOR MEANINGFUL OVER MORE

When I first started out, I only wrote a small handful of guest posts, and I still use the credibility markers I gained from them to this day. So we really only have to use this technique a few times to reap its long-term benefits.

Just like you, I'm a busy children's author. I don't have endless hours to write. And the good news is, we don't need to.

High-impact guest posting is not about quantity. It's about intention and alignment.

I would rather invest time crafting one thoughtful, relevant article that reaches tens of thousands of readers and continues circulating year after year, than quickly push out several pieces that don't make an impact.

A single great article can:

- *access a large audience who relates to our book's topic*
- *bring traffic to our author website*
- *gently introduce our book in a natural, non-salesy way*
- *become a powerful credibility marker*
- *help create opportunities for interviews, collaborations, or school visits*

All we need is one clear idea that speaks directly to the audience of the site we are pitching.

NINJA TIP:

Guest posts keep working long after you stop writing them.

An article you write today could still be read, shared, or ranked in search results five years from now, quietly bringing readers back to you long after your book launch has passed.

This kind of long-term discoverability is what makes guest posting such a powerful marketing tool for us as authors.

WHOM TO PITCH TO

Guest posting works so well because we are approaching platforms that already have an audience. As long as we choose outlets that speak to people who would naturally be interested in our book's topic, writing a short article for these platforms can provide meaningful exposure.

To figure out which outlets to approach, we'll want to reflect on our goals:

- *Do we want more parents to discover our work?*
- *Do we want to establish credibility in our book's subject matter?*
- *Do we want steady, ongoing traffic to our website?*
- *Do we want to build new relationships and connections?*

Guest posting supports all of these goals.

Get very clear on your reason for guest posting. This clarity will guide you toward the right websites to pitch, and it will help you stay motivated when the writing feels intimidating. The short-term effort is small compared to the long-term ripple effect.

We can go about our outreach in two ways:

APPROACH 1: *Targeted Approach*

The targeted approach means reaching out to blogs that already cater to people who love the topic of our children's book.

For example, if our book is about monster trucks, we could approach a blog that already writes about monster trucks.

Ask yourself:

"Would this audience be interested in what I have to say? Does my article naturally align with what they already care about?"

If the answer is yes, the blogger is far more likely to say yes.

APPROACH 2: *General Approach*

The general approach means reaching out to broader parenting blogs that serve families with children in your target age range.

For example, if your book is for ages 2–5, it would make sense to approach sites like *Scary Mommy*, which has entire sections dedicated to parents of young children.

NINJA TIP:

Don't forget the blogs and publications you already know.

- *What family sites do you read regularly?*
- *What parenting blogs do you already enjoy?*
- *What newsletters are you subscribed to?*

See whether these platforms accept guest contributors, and if they do, reach out.

NINJA TIP:

Make use of existing lists online. Search phrases like:

- "Best 100 Family Blogs"
- "Top 100 Dog Blogs"

If you're new to pitching, start with blogs further down the list. Smaller or growing blogs are often more open to first-time contributors.

WHAT TO WRITE ABOUT IN OUR GUEST POSTS / ARTICLES

When writing for already established outlets, we will want to shift our mindset and focus from "my book" to "my value."

Your instinct will be to write about your book. That's completely natural. But here's the truth that changes everything:

Pitches that read like ads are almost always declined.

No publication wants to run a free commercial, especially after they've worked hard to earn their audience's trust.

Your guest post is not about your book. Instead, your book is something you can gently weave in later.

Think about social media. What works better?

- *A sponsored post clearly selling a product*

- *A genuinely helpful or heartfelt post where the product is mentioned naturally*

The second one. Every time.

The same applies to guest posting. Articles are accepted and shared when they offer genuine value first. When we approach this from a place of generosity, service, and authenticity, everything becomes easier and far more effective.

ARTICLE CATEGORIES

When coming up with guest post ideas, it helps to categorize the topics into article categories:

CATEGORY 1: *"How To" Articles*

"How To" articles allow us to showcase our expertise or experience, and provide value to readers by helping them learn or accomplish something.

For example, if our book is a story about preparing for a new puppy, then some great article titles could be:

- *How to Prepare Your Kids for a New Puppy*
- *How to Know If Your Kids Are Ready for a Puppy*

While we don't want to make our book the main focal point of these articles, we can mention and reference our book as one of the ways available to us to help prepare our kids.

CATEGORY 2: *"Why" Articles*

"Why" articles are meant to influence the reader's opinion and explain why they should stop or start doing something.

For our puppy book, our articles could be about:

- *Why Having a Puppy Will Support Your Kids' Development*
- *Why Preparing Children Early Makes Puppy Adoption More Successful*

CATEGORY 3: *"List" Articles*

"List" articles streamline content and make it easy for the reader to digest the information we are providing.

- *7 Science-Backed Reasons Why Growing Up With a Puppy Is Important*
- *The 3 Most Important Things to Decide Before Agreeing to a Puppy*

CATEGORY 4: *"Round-Up" Articles*

"Round-up" articles bring together a group of experts, books, or tools to show multiple perspectives on a topic. This is one of my favorite categories, and it has helped me get my articles into national online publications like Scary Mommy.

- *The 5 Best Books to Prepare Your Kids for a New Puppy*
- *6 Simple Activities That Teach Kids How to Care for a New Puppy*

CATEGORY 5: *"Most Important / Number One" Articles*

"Most Important / Number One" articles focus a reader's attention on a single tip or strategy.

- *The Number 1 Thing You Should Know About Owning a Puppy*
- *The #1 Rule When Preparing Your Kids for a Puppy*

CATEGORY 6: *"Piggyback" Articles*

"Piggyback" posts mention celebrity names, notable individuals, or categories of experts in their headlines to entice people to click and read.

- *Prepare for Your New Puppy, Oprah Style: 5 Ways That Ensure an Easy Adoption*
- *What Dog Experts Say About Successfully Preparing for a Puppy*

CATEGORY 7: *"Confession" Articles*

Writing a "confessional" first-person article is a powerful way to share our story, who we are, and what we believe in.

- *Confession of a Mom of Two, Adopting a Brand New Puppy*
- *When a Puppy Accomplished the Healing of Our Family*

If we can't weave in our book naturally into the article or post itself, we can mention it in our byline by writing something like:

"[NAME] is the author of the award-winning children's book [TITLE], created for families who believe that the bond between children and puppies is something truly special. To learn more, visit [WEBSITE]."

HOW TO PITCH OUR GUEST ARTICLE:

When pitching large media outlets, it's important that we follow their submission guidelines. We'll want to make sure to follow the instructions exactly, because doing so will increase our chances of getting in.

To find a website's submission guidelines, we can enter the following into our search engine:

[NAME OF PUBLICATION]	+	*Submission Guidelines*
	+	*Guest Posting*
	+	*Contributor*
	+	*How to Pitch*

Some websites will want us to submit our fully written guest article. Other places, however, will just want to see our pitches first.

There are 5 things we should include in every pitch we send:

1. Our subject line should indicate that it's a pitch
2. Create a connection (for example, citing a specific article that's had an impact on us)
3. Introduce a few of your credibility markers
4. Share 1 to 3 story ideas, followed by a short description of each
5. Offer to send more information (for example, a detailed outline or more story ideas)

Here is a template we can use as a guide:

Subject: [Insert headline of one of your pitches]

Hi [Media Contact Name],

[Create a connection; for example, "I loved your recent article about XYZ..." - make sure to be specific]

[Introduce yourself with a few of your credibility markers that are relevant to your pitch topic; for example, "I'm a certified puppy trainer and I've been featured in XYZ"]

[Provide 1 to 3 story ideas, with a short description for each idea]

[Offer to send more ideas if they want]

[Signoff]

[Insert your media bio (optional)]

Let's see what this pitch email might look like for our puppy book example.

Subject: Contributor article: Why kids should be part of the puppy adoption process

Hi Carl,

I recently read your article about helping families choose the right breed for their home, and I loved how thoughtfully you addressed the reality of preparing children for pet ownership. As a mom of three who adopted a puppy last year, that article brought me right back to our own whirlwind of excitement, questions, and adjustments.

During that experience, I realized just how important it is to intentionally involve kids throughout the adoption process - something many families don't think about until the puppy is already home. Including my children early made the transition smoother, strengthened their sense of responsibility, and helped our new puppy feel welcomed and understood from day one.

I would love to contribute an article to *Pet Parent Monthly* that supports your mission of helping families make thoughtful, informed decisions. Here are a few story ideas that I believe would resonate deeply with your readers:

1. Why Kids Should Be Part of the Puppy Adoption Process

A heartfelt but practical look at the benefits of involving children early, from emotional readiness to easing common first-week challenges.

2. The 5 Most Overlooked Ways to Prepare Young Kids for a New Puppy

Family-tested strategies that help parents get toddlers and young children ready for a new four-legged family member.

3. The #1 Thing Parents Forget When Bringing Home a Puppy

A single, powerful mindset shift that can make a dramatic difference in how smoothly the first weeks unfold.

I'd be happy to send full outlines or share additional story ideas if you'd like to explore further.

Warmly,

[Your Name]
Optional media bio: [Insert your brief media bio here if desired]

Pay attention to three key elements in this example pitch:

1. **The thoughtful use of credibility markers:** In this case, the author's lived experience of going through the puppy adoption process. This builds trust quickly and naturally, without needing formal credentials.

2. **The compelling, audience-centered headlines and story ideas:** Each one is designed to serve the publication's readers, not to promote a book.

3. **The intentional omission of the author's book:** Notice that the puppy book was not mentioned at all. The email's purpose is simply to spark interest and show the editor why your perspective matters.

Our goal here is not to "give it all away," but to tease just enough value and curiosity that the editor wants to hear more. Once our article is accepted, that is where we can naturally weave in a brief mention of our children's book.

Guest posting is one of the most powerful long-term marketing techniques we have as children's authors. A single published article can continue to build visibility, credibility, and discoverability for months or even years after it goes live.

So pitch your wonderful ideas, share your stories, and put yourself out there. I'm cheering for you every step of the way.

INTERVIEWS & PODCASTS

Podcast interviews (and interviews in general) are one of the most effective and overlooked long-term marketing strategies available to us as children's authors. The majority are absolutely free to appear on, accessible from anywhere, and remarkably evergreen. A single episode can introduce us to new readers for years to come.

Unlike social media, where attention spans last only seconds, podcast listeners willingly spend 30 to 60 minutes hearing our story, our mission, and the heart behind our book. That level of attention and connection is almost unheard of in today's digital world and makes podcasts a powerful place to share our message.

So let's identify the right podcasts, how to approach them thoughtfully, prepare for our interview intentionally, and make the absolute most of this beautiful opportunity.

WHY PODCAST INTERVIEWS WORK SO WELL

Podcasts combine all the best parts of modern marketing: low cost, deep connection, niche audiences, and long-term discoverability. While social media posts fade quickly, podcast episodes remain accessible indefinitely. Many listeners even go back through an entire catalog when they discover a host they love.

In addition to being evergreen, podcasts offer several additional meaningful advantages:

- They are free to appear on and require no travel.
- There are millions of shows, many of them actively seeking guests.
- They reach highly specific audiences, making it much easier to match our book to listeners who already care about the topic.
- They build trust quickly, because listeners already trust the host.
- They nurture deep connection, allowing strangers to hear our voice and story for an extended period.

For us children's authors, this is priceless. We aren't fighting for attention. We're being invited into someone's home, commute, or morning routine.

CHOOSING THE RIGHT PODCAST

A common mistake new authors make is pitching to author-only podcasts. While these can be enjoyable, their listeners are usually other writers, not the parents, grandparents, teachers, therapists, and caregivers who actually buy children's books.

Instead, think about your potential audiences in two layers:

1. General Audience Matches

These are groups who regularly purchase or recommend children's books, like:

- Parents and grandparents
- Teachers and librarians
- Counselors and therapists
- Homeschooling communities
- Caregivers and early childhood educators

Here, we want to ask ourselves:

What podcasts are these groups already listening to?

2. Topic-Specific Matches

This audience aligns directly with the theme of our book. For example:

- **A story about therapy dogs:** *podcasts for therapy dog handlers or child therapists*
- **A book about breastfeeding:** *lactation podcasts, midwife podcasts, postpartum support shows*
- **A book about friendship or kindness:** *parenting and SEL (social-emotional learning) podcasts*
- **A story about adoption:** *adoption preparation or foster family podcasts*

If a niche exists, there is almost always a podcast supporting it. Looking at our book topic through this lens opens doors to incredible opportunities.

WHERE TO FIND THESE PODCASTS

There are several simple ways to locate podcasts that align beautifully with our message and audience.

GOOGLE SEARCH:

Here, we can use phrases such as:

- "Top podcasts for parents of toddlers"
- "Family podcasts"
- "Podcasts for teachers"
- "Podcasts for anxious kids / mindful parenting / child behavior support"

These search results help us identify broad but relevant parenting and family-oriented shows.

FEEDSPOT SEARCH:

Feedspot.com (⬆) is one of the most helpful directories for podcasts, magazines, blogs, and so much more for authors. It allows us to:

- Search by our book's theme
- See a podcast's episode frequency
- See each show's website

The premium version provides more details, such as the host's email address, but the free version works perfectly well for finding niche-specific podcasts.

FeedSpot Reader

Read your favorite Blogs, Podcasts, News Websites, Youtube
Channels and RSS feeds from one place on Feedspot ○

Email Id

Password

☐ I'm not a robot

reCAPTCHA is changing its terms of service.
Take action.

reCAPTCHA
Privacy - Terms

By continuing you indicate that you have read and agree to Feedspot's Terms
of Service and Privacy Policy.

Sign Up   Cancel

 **NINJA TIP:**

Follow the breadcrumbs. Search for fellow authors with similar themes and see
where they have been interviewed. Look up their name in Apple Podcasts or
Spotify and use that list as inspiration.

HOW TO PITCH OURSELVES SUCCESSFULLY

Before pitching, we will want to clarify whether the podcast is free or paid, how large the audience
is, and what the show's main theme is, because these details determine how we shape our
outreach message.

Just like with guest posting, the most transformative mindset shift is this:

*Our pitch is never about our book. It is about the value we bring to the podcast's
audience.*

When pitching, we will want to:

- Keep our message short.
- Break our paragraphs into small, inviting sections.
- Personalize our outreach by referencing something specific we learned from the show.
- Speak from a place of service rather than promotion.
- Expect no's and keep going, because pitching is truly a numbers game.

! *Hosts say yes when they feel confident that we will bring value to their audience, not because we have a book to promote.*

Most hosts don't want us to promote our books on their show. Instead, they are looking for interesting stories that are relevant to their audience. So rather than introducing our book directly, we want to ask ourselves how we can tie in our book's topic.

If we're on a parenting podcast, we might talk about how we made time in a busy family schedule to write and publish our book. Or we could share how we came up with the book's topic.

The possibilities are endless. And when we think outside the box and make it relevant to the podcaster and their audience, we are far more likely to receive an enthusiastic yes.

PREPARING FOR OUR INTERVIEW

Once we've been invited on, this preparation phase is where exceptional interviews are made. A prepared guest stands out immediately, both to the host and to the audience.

Here, we will want to make sure we complete these five important steps:

PREP 1: *Listen to Multiple Episodes*

This helps us learn the host's style, pacing, and the types of questions they like to ask. It also reveals whether we should prepare structured answers or expect a more conversational flow.

PREP 2: *Draft Our Guest Bio*

Instead of letting the host pull a bio from our website, we can prepare a version tailored specifically to their audience. For a parenting podcast, we might highlight our parenting experience. For a writing podcast, we could emphasize our writing credentials. For a professional niche, we may want to mention relevant expertise.

PREP 3: *Prepare Your CTA (Call-To-Action)*

A CTA is a clear next step for listeners, such as:

- *Visiting our website*
- *Downloading a free printable or activity*
- *Joining our email list*
- *Learning more about our book*

214

We may even create a CTA specifically for that podcast's audience.

PREP 4: *Prepare Your Answers*

Especially if we've never been on a podcast before, we will want to practice sharing our story from the perspective of the host's audience. If we're speaking to moms or dads, we answer as a mom or dad. If we're speaking to entrepreneurs, we emphasize the entrepreneurial side of our journey.

The story stays the same. We are simply adjusting the angle so it resonates.

PREP 5: *Practice Out Loud*

Speaking our responses aloud helps eliminate filler words, shorten long explanations, and increase our confidence. Over time, we will develop a set of polished responses we can easily adapt for future interviews.

AFTER THE INTERVIEW: MAKING THE MOST OF OUR MOMENTUM

Many authors feel relieved once the interview is recorded, but this is actually where our opportunities expand.

AFTER-ACTION 1: *Immediately After Recording*

Immediately after the recording, we will want to thank the host warmly. A sincere note of appreciation stands out in a world where very few guests take the time to do so. We can also ask if there is anything we can do to support them, such as recommending other authors, sharing their show, or helping them connect with future guests.

AFTER-ACTION 2: *When the Episode Goes Live*

We will want to share our interview proudly and widely. This is a meaningful milestone worth celebrating. We can share the episode on:

- *Instagram (including Stories)*
- *Facebook*
- *Our author website*
- *Our email list*

NINJA TIP:

When sharing your interview, explain why it matters to you. Your audience will feel that excitement and be more likely to listen.

NINJA TIP:

Tagging the podcast host and expressing gratitude strengthens the relationship and increases the chances that the host will share your post as well.

AFTER-ACTION 3 : *Add the Interview to Your Media Page*

If we have a website, we will want to list the interview on our media page and include recognizable podcast logos. These markers build instant credibility.

AFTER-ACTION 4: *Use It to Strengthen Future Pitches*

When pitching additional podcasts, we can now mention the shows we've already appeared on. This helps establish trust and signals that we are an experienced, reliable guest.

AFTER-ACTION 5: *Listen to Your Episode*

Take time to reflect on what we loved, what we'd like to refine, and which unexpected questions we can now better prepare for. This reflection accelerates our growth for future interviews.

NINJA TIP:

Once we start sharing interviews, it can be tricky to get people to check them out.

Instead of simply posting a static image, try sharing a 10-second audio or video snippet of a particularly juicy moment from the interview. This sparks curiosity and invites listeners to check out the full episode.

EXTRA NINJA TIP:

Include subtitles so sound is not required to understand the message.

Podcast interviews offer a beautifully warm, human way to share the heart of our children's book.

They help readers discover our work organically, allow us to speak deeply about our message, and continue supporting our marketing long after the episode first airs.

Whether we are pre-launch, mid-launch, or years past publication, our story is still relevant and our voice is needed.

REMEMBER:

Start small.
Start intentionally.
And start from a place of giving, not asking.

You are building connection, community, and visibility for your beautiful book, and I'm cheering you on every step of the way.

——————————— • ✦ • ———————————

EDITORIAL REVIEWS - Part 02 (<u>AFTER</u> the Launch)

INFLUENCER EDITORIAL REVIEWS

In the pre-launch section of this book, we talked about editorial reviews from professionals whose expertise directly connects to the topic or message of our children's book. Those reviews are powerful because they offer something called *contextual authority* - credibility rooted in someone's real-world experience with our book's subject matter.

But editorial reviews don't end once our book is published.

In fact, one of the strongest post-launch strategies we can use is to expand our editorial review circle even further by reaching out to influencers.

Influencers are a unique category in the world of editorial reviews because they bring something traditional reviewers cannot:

Built-in reach.

Influencer reviews carry both *authority* and *reach*.

- Where a librarian offers expertise, an influencer offers exposure.
- Where a fire chief offers contextual authority, an influencer offers amplification.

While experts speak with authority, influencers amplify that authority to thousands, sometimes even tens of thousands, of people who already trust their recommendations. This blend of credibility and visibility is what makes influencers such an extraordinary asset in the post-launch phase.

At its core, influencer marketing simply means partnering with someone who already has the attention of the audience we hope to reach. And for children's authors, this can be a treasure trove of opportunity.

Their support can spark new sales spikes long after launch day, create fresh waves of awareness, and open doors to features, interviews, podcast appearances, newsletter mentions, and more. It's a strategy we can revisit again and again throughout the life of our book.

Examples of influencers who serve our target audience could be:

- *Parenting influencers*
- *Homeschooling influencers*
- *Bookstagrammers and BookTok creators who review children's books*
- *Kidlit bloggers*
- *Family-focused YouTubers*

HOW TO CHOOSE THE RIGHT INFLUENCERS

The first and most important step in choosing whom to reach out to is *alignment.* We never want to reach out simply because someone is "big." Instead, we want to ask ourselves:

Would their audience benefit from learning about my book?

If the answer is yes, we've found a match.

This ensures that our outreach feels thoughtful, respectful, and mutually beneficial. When our book naturally supports the work the influencer is already doing, or speaks to the audience they are already serving, the request no longer feels like a pitch. It feels like a partnership.

For example, when I reached out to Teri Crane, known nationally as the "Potty Pro," my request for my book *Teeny Totty Uses Mama's Big Potty* was a beautifully natural fit. Her audience was made up of parents navigating potty training, and my book directly served that need.

This kind of alignment dramatically increases the likelihood of receiving a yes, and it ensures the influencer can share our book with enthusiasm and authenticity.

INFLUENCER MARKETING THAT COSTS NOTHING BUT A BOOK

Now, you may be thinking, *"But Eevi… I can't afford to commission an influencer."*

What if I told you that my most successful influencer "partnerships" have all been unpaid?

Not because I negotiated masterfully.
Not because I asked for a favor.
But because the alignment was perfect.

In every case, all it took was thoughtful research, a copy of my book, and a heartfelt message explaining why I believed the book might matter to them personally.

STORY 1: *Bethany - A Mom of Four*

When I first published my illustrated gift book *Precious: For New Moms and Moms-To-Be*, there was one person I immediately thought of: Bethany, a mother of four sweet little boys whom I had quietly followed on Instagram for years.

I adored her kindness, the way she interacted with her children, and her gentle presence in the world. So when her family welcomed their fourth baby boy, I mailed her a copy of my book along with a simple, sincere note.

No ask.
No expectation.
Just alignment.

And without me prompting her in any way, Bethany shared my book with her audience of more than one million people. That single moment created an unbelievable wave of visibility. And besides a copy of my book, it cost absolutely nothing.

STORY 2: *Actress Jamie Lee Curtis - A Conversation About Menopause*

When I saw actress Jamie Lee Curtis speak publicly about her own struggles with menopause, I felt called to send her a copy of my then newly published book *Menopause: Let's Normalize It Already.*

Again, I didn't ask her to read it. I didn't ask her to post it. I simply wrote a heartfelt note explaining why I felt my book might resonate with her.

And once again, without me ever asking, she shared my book on Instagram with her more than six million followers.

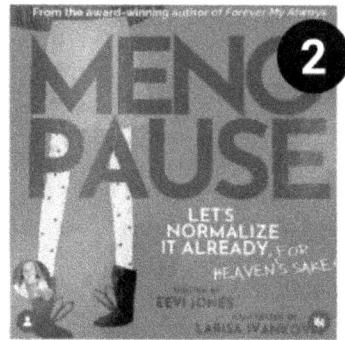

jamieleecurtis Thanks @eevi_jones the WORLD needs this BOOK!

jamieleecurtis ⊙

THE SECRET INGREDIENT = *Alignment + Awareness*

This is where influencer outreach becomes truly powerful.

If an influencer is:

- Getting a new puppy… could your book help prepare children for a new family member?
- Sharing that their child is a picky eater… could your book gently guide families through mealtime challenges?
- Talking about big emotions, anxieties, bedtime routines, or school transitions… could your story provide comfort or support?

If we approach social media through the lens of *awareness*, our marketing brain will begin to see opportunities everywhere.

That's when we start noticing dozens of moments where our book could genuinely add value to someone's life. And when the connection is perfect, influencers will often share our work voluntarily, because it is meaningful to them.

NINJA TIP:

A small but mighty truth: not everyone will respond. Influencer outreach is, in many ways, a numbers game.

- Not everyone will reply.
- Many will never open your message.
- Some will simply be too busy.

But the more aligned our book is with the influencer - their story, their values, their current life moment - the more likely they'll respond with genuine enthusiasm.

NINJA TIP:

Don't ask for anything.

Just send the perfect book to the perfect person at the perfect time.

When the alignment is right, the share often happens naturally.

NINJA TIP:

Once a review or share is received, a heartfelt thank-you matters more than we realize.

Whether that's a handwritten note, a small thoughtful gesture, or something memorable like a bouquet of flowers, expressing gratitude not only honors the moment but also opens the door to a lasting relationship.

Many wonderful, ongoing opportunities have grown from these small, intentional moments of connection.

Every outreach method we covered in this chapter has one thing in common: it puts our book in front of people who are already paying attention.

Whether it's a guest article, a podcast interview, or an influencer share, each of these strategies helps us borrow trust, visibility, and reach from platforms and people who have already done the work of building an audience. That is smart marketing.

This kind of outreach doesn't rely on algorithms, trends, or paid ads. It relies on alignment, preparation, and the willingness to show up with something meaningful to offer. And when done thoughtfully, it creates credibility markers, long-term discoverability, and opportunities that continue to support our book long after launch day.

Marketing is not about shouting louder. It's about being seen in the right places, by the right people, at the right time.

And with these outreach tools in hand, we're no longer waiting to be discovered. We're intentionally placing our book into conversations where it belongs.

YOUR TO DOs FOR THIS CHAPTER:

- ❏ Pay attention to where your book could add value, and you'll begin to see opportunities everywhere

Find all your templates and swipe files using this link below. You may want to bookmark this page, so you can refer to it as quickly and easily as possible.

⬆ *https://www.eevijones.com/marketing-downloads*

LINKS SHARED:

- *https://www.feedspot.com*

CHAPTER 19
Leveraging The Momentum You've Built

I decided to add this chapter to our marketing book because what you will learn in these next few pages will help you amplify the results you receive from all your hard marketing and promotional efforts, so you can get the absolute most out of these opportunities.

We will look at how we can share our beautiful wins, whether that's a newly received review, a fulfilling interview that went really well, or the awarding of a well-deserved award.

Whenever we receive reviews for our beautiful children's books, win an award, or are interviewed for a podcast, blog, or magazine, we get incredibly excited. And we absolutely should, because we've worked so very hard to write our book, gather reviews, and secure these interviews.

But beyond sharing these wonderful and well-deserved accolades with our friends and family via a post on places like Facebook or Instagram, we often don't take as much advantage of these beautiful opportunities as we should, could, and ought to.

So in this section, we will look at:

- *things that help increase our visibility*
- *things that encourage people to continue sharing our work*
- *things that help build and strengthen connections with fellow authors*
- *things that boost our credibility*

The biggest mistake most of us make when it comes to sharing anything related to our children's book is this:

Once we have shared our children's book, or any type of book-related media win such as an interview, with a single social media post, most of us stop. For whatever reason, we think that sharing this media coverage once is enough.

But from here on out, I want you to remember this:

Now, to show you what I mean by "leverage," I'm going to share a few examples of how I've been leveraging some of my media coverage over the past couple of years. Hopefully, this will get your creative juices flowing as well, so that the next time you receive an amazing review or land a wonderful and highly anticipated interview, you know exactly what you can do on your end to get the most out of this type of publicity.

No matter what type of media coverage you receive, always ask yourself this one question:

How can I make the absolute most of this opportunity?

Media coverage and opportunities can include:

- *Reviews*
- *Interviews for articles*
- *Podcast interviews*
- *Someone sharing our book on social media*
- *Book awards we've won*
- *Bestseller status*
- *And so much more*

Let's look at how we can leverage something we may have written for or about our children's book.

———— • ✦ • ————

LEVERAGE: *Guest Posts*

Over the past few years, I've written quite a few guest posts for places like *Scary Mommy, Business Insider*, and *Kindlepreneur*.

Kindlepreneur is one of my favorite blogs and one I had been reading for years. So once my article appeared on this blog, I got to work making the absolute most of this opportunity.

Instead of sharing my guest post just once with friends and family, I began sharing it everywhere:

- *I shared it via email with my readers.*
- *I shared it on my website.*
- *And I still send people to this article to this day.*

I really went out of my way to get lots and lots of eyeballs on it. Now, I could have just said:

> **"Great job, Eevi! You wanted to write a blog post for this site, and you did it! Congratulations. My job here is done."**

That's what most people do. And because that's what most people do, this is exactly where *you* can step in and set yourself apart.

Sharing this blog post so intentionally is what set me apart from many others who had also written articles for the same site. And it resulted in three main outcomes:

ONE: *Lots of Shares*

Sharing this article within my own circle helped get the ball rolling, especially right after it was published. Over the years, this article has been read tens of thousands of times and shared more than 2,000 times, making it one of the most read and shared articles on this entire website.

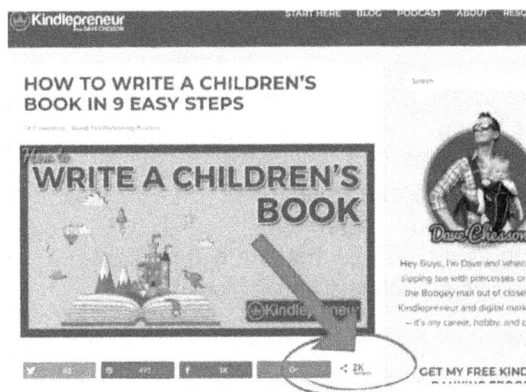

TWO: *Lots of Comments*

Something many guest posters forget to do is check the comments section of their article. This is such a missed opportunity to connect with readers and the blog owner.

After my article was published, I didn't disappear. I continued checking the comments section and responding to readers' questions. That's why this article now has over 180 comments.

This doesn't happen often on blog posts, is incredibly helpful to readers, and does not go unnoticed by the blog owner.

 By **Eevi Jones** 182 💬

THREE: *Podcast Interviews*

Because I stayed engaged and responded to comments, Dave (the blog owner) invited me to appear on his podcast.

That invitation led to many more guest posting opportunities and podcast interviews, because he continued recommending me to other influential bloggers, all without me ever having to ask.

 **NINJA TIP:**

Once an interview or blog post goes live, instead of sitting back and thinking your work is done, that's when you want to step up your game.

To truly leverage this opportunity:

- Share what you've written more than once.
- Make your shares intriguing so people actually want to click.
- Thank the blog owner publicly.
- Respond to comments and questions.
- Add the article to your media page.
- Add the blog's logo as a credibility marker, if appropriate.
- Mention this feature when pitching future blogs.

When leveraging an opportunity such as this one, remember this:

A podcast host or blog owner is far more likely to bring you back or recommend you to others if they know you will share and send eyeballs their way. They gave you a platform, so make sure you pay it forward.

———— ◆ ————

LEVERAGE: *Interviews*

A few years ago, I was interviewed for a *Forbes* article. At last check, that article had been viewed **32,711** times.

The average view count for that contributor's last 20 articles was around 11,515, many well below 10,000. So why was mine three times higher?

Because I shared it everywhere.

- *on Instagram*
- *in my Instagram Story*
- *on Facebook amongst my family and friends*
- *on my website's media page*
- *in my emails*

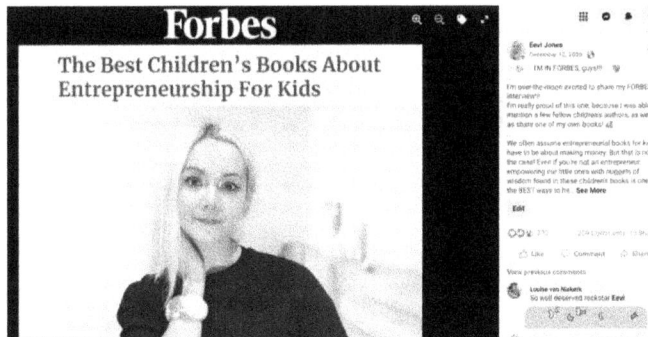

I shared it for four reasons:

- **REASON 1:** I was proud of being interviewed by *Forbes* again.
- **REASON 2:** I wanted as many people as possible to read it.
- **REASON 3:** I wanted *Forbes* to feature it more prominently (which would generate even more views)

- **REASON 4:** I wanted the contributor to happily interview me again.

Beyond sharing, I also leveraged it in other ways:

MY MEDIA BIO:

First, I updated my media bio, which I share in places like my website and my Amazon author profile.

> She has appeared in numerous publications and top podcasts including *Forbes, Business Insider, EOFire, Scary Mommy, Huffington Post, EP Magazine, SCBWI,* and more.
>
> Eevi lives near D.C. with her husband and two children. She can be found online at

MY WEBSITE:

Second, I added the feature to the media banner displayed on my website. Doing so instantly boosts our credibility with visitors, because they can see right away where else we've been featured or where else we've appeared. That way, people can quickly confirm that we are real and that we truly are who we claim to be.

TEDˣ Scary Mommy Forbes EOFIRE CREATIVE CREATIVINDIE reedsy Kindlepreneur BUSINESS INSIDER THE HUFFINGTON POST

MY EMAIL SIGNATURE:

And third, I added it to my email signature block. This is such a wonderful opportunity to pique a recipient's interest, no matter the subject of the email. This is how I've received a number of author-visit invitations, without ever having introduced myself as a children's book author. My email signature did all the work for me. We will talk much more about your email signature in chapter 23.

Eevi Jones
USA Today & WSJ Bestselling Writer &
Award-Winning Children's Book Author

Founder | Children's Book University®
As seen in *Forbes, HUFFPO, Kindlepreneur*
WEB: www.EeviJones.com
BOOKS: www.BravingTheWorldBooks.com

To truly leverage this type of opportunity, do this:

- Once you've shared your interview, share it again.
- Thank the people who helped make this article or interview possible. When sharing about it, be sure to tag them.
- Thank the contributor or interviewer, and again, be sure to tag them.
- Thank the photographer or anyone else involved, and tag them when sharing.
- Add your interview or feature to your media page on your website, if you have one.
- Add the logo to your website banner.
- Add the feature to your media bio and your email signature.
- When reaching out for future features and interviews, mention those you've already appeared in.

When leveraging an opportunity such as this one, remember this:

NINJA TIP:

Believe it or not, journalists, interviewers, editors, and contributors often don't receive thank-you messages from the people they feature. So be the one who stands out, in the best possible way, and reach out to express your appreciation. They will remember you for it. Plus, it's the right thing to do.

⸻ • ✦ • ⸻

LEVERAGE: *Awards & Bestseller Banners*

Once I started winning awards with my children's books, I added "award-winning" to my author bio. And when I became a *USA Today* and *Wall Street Journal* bestselling author, I added that to my author bio and email signature as well.

Just like before, I started sharing these accomplishments everywhere.

- *I shared them in my email signature.*
- *I shared them in my author bio on my website.*
- *And I shared them on my Amazon sales pages.*

To truly leverage this type of opportunity, do this:

- Once you've shared your incredible win, share it again.

- Thank the people who helped you along the way in publishing your beautiful children's book, and tag them in your shares.
- Thank any contributing parties, such as your illustrator and editor, and tag them when sharing.
- Add your win to your website.
- Showcase your win in your media bio and email signature.
- When reaching out for interviews, weave your wins into your outreach message.

When leveraging an opportunity such as this one, remember this:

NINJA TIP:

Despite what others may say, people do often judge a book by its cover. This also applies to titles and distinctions. Be sure to showcase everything you've accomplished with your children's book. Winning an award is a big deal, so be proud of it and share it.

——————— • ◆ • ———————

LEVERAGE: *Reviews*

Reviews can come in all sorts of shapes and sizes:

- Professional reviews from institutions like Kirkus
- Reviews from friends and family
- Reviews from readers we don't know
- Opinions about our children's book shared in interviews and podcasts

Reviews are extremely important, especially in the early stages of a newly published children's book. Every single review is treasured and celebrated by the author, so why not share it?

Sharing an especially beautiful review can do wonders:

- *It shows your excitement.*
- *It lets others know how important reviews are to authors.*
- *It may inspire or remind others in your circle to leave a review.*
- *It may encourage others to purchase your book and even share it.*

Often, our book is praised in places beyond Amazon reviews. These mentions don't need to remain hidden. If a review or quote can't be added as a regular Amazon review, we can add it ourselves using Amazon's *Editorial Review* section (see chapter 7).

Editorial Reviews

Review

PUBLISHERS WEEKLY - EDITOR'S PICK

Jones's sweet children's book encourages young people to explore the world and take chances to become the "truest version" of themselves. Reminiscent at times of the Dr. Seuss classic *Oh, the Places You'll Go!*, Jones uses simple rhyming verse to offer kids of all ages essential advice about overcoming challenges, choosing the right friends, and how to "trust in their own magic." One of the most welcome, important-and hardest to grasp- components of Jones's message is its warning against the pitfalls of privilege: "Gain confidence through your success, not entitlement and birth. For through the daily and smallest of wins your true self-it will emerge."

For parents who feel emotional when envisioning their babies venturing out into the world, this touching story will likely trigger a tear or two. However, it will also give adults important opportunities to talk to youngsters about crucial life skills, like growing confidence and overcoming fear. With distinctive illustrations and mostly smooth, easy-to-follow rhymes, Jones's uplifting tale will inspire curiosity in young people-and leave parents wishing they could go back in time to impart knowledge to younger versions of themselves.

TAKEAWAY: This delightful story encourages children of all ages to explore the world and take chances to become the "truest version" of themselves.

GREAT FOR FANS OF: Emily Winfield Martin's *The Wonderful Things You Will Be*, Mark Pett and Gary Rubinstein's *The Girl Who Never Made Mistakes*.

To truly leverage this type of opportunity, do this:

- Share beautiful reviews on social media, and consider creating a simple visual in *Canva*.
- Thank any contributing parties, such as your illustrator and editor, and tag them.
- If reviews can't be submitted as standard Amazon reviews, add them to the *Editorial Review* section.

When leveraging an opportunity such as this one, remember this:

NINJA TIP:

Unless someone has written and published a book themselves, most people don't realize how important reviews are. Sharing your excitement openly helps them understand how they can support you.

———— ♦ ————

LEVERAGE: *Shout-Outs*

Shout-outs are near and dear to my heart, because they come purely from the generosity of others.

Not too long ago, one of my biggest article interviews went live with a major publication. In that article, I shared the work of fellow children's authors. I still remember how, many years ago, one of my first books received a major shout-out. I wanted to shout it from the rooftops and share it with everyone. That's how proud and excited I was.

But do you know how many of the authors I featured in that major publication shared it with their communities? One!

What a missed opportunity to:

- *Share it on their own social media*
- *Share it with their friends and family*
- *Share it on their website, stating that they had been featured in a major publication*
- *Connect with the people who provided them with this opportunity of having their book mentioned and featured*

To truly leverage this type of opportunity, do this:

- If you receive a shout-out, no matter how big or small, thank the person who took the time to do so. If you don't, they will likely never do it again.
- Re-share the shout-out on your own channels.
- Depending on the shout-out, evaluate whether it should be showcased on your website.

When leveraging an opportunity such as this one, remember this:

NINJA TIP:

Any time your children's book is mentioned or shared, someone took time out of their day to do that. These gestures are generous and should never be taken for granted. Show your appreciation and pay it forward.

When it comes to social media and human psychology, here's something important to remember:

People love and appreciate nothing more than having the work they created

1. liked
2. shared

It's great for business, great for self-esteem, and, in our case, great for our children's books. This holds true whether that person is an author, a business owner, an entrepreneur, or even a celebrity.

"Sharing is caring."

I'm sure you've heard that phrase before. But many people see it as a one-sided action. A one-sided kind of sharing. My hope is that after reading these last few pages, you now realize that we, as authors, can take sharing to the next level by sharing that share.

That's when it becomes a true win-win.

A win for the person whose book has been shared - you. And a win for the person who so generously provided you with an opportunity or platform to talk about your book.

If we elevate those who elevate us, we will go so much farther.

I truly hope these examples helped get your creative juices flowing and gave you concrete ideas for what to do with all the wonderful shout-outs, interviews, reviews, and features you have received, are receiving, or will receive.

Momentum matters. So be sure to make the most of every opportunity that comes your way.

And next time you see a fellow children's author share one of their wins, show your support. Give their post a like. Leave a comment. And maybe even share it.

When it comes to being a children's book author - or any kind of author - connection matters. Community matters. Supporting one another matters.

We are not each other's competition. We are each other's allies. And we are stronger because of it.

————————— • ✦ • —————————

In this post-launch phase, we saw our marketing begin to mature.

What we do during this stage determines whether our book's initial momentum fades quickly or turns into something steady, strategic, and sustainable.

Everything we focused on in this part of the book was intentional.

- We built assets that help others take us seriously and say yes more easily.

- We strengthened our online presence so our book can be discovered outside of launch week.
- We learned how to reach out thoughtfully, share our story in meaningful places, and position our work in front of the right audiences.
- And most importantly, we learned how to *leverage* every win, review, interview, and opportunity instead of letting it live only once and then disappear.

This post-launch phase is about building infrastructure, so when opportunities arise, our book is ready. And when momentum appears, we know how to extend it.

Now that these foundations are in place, we are no longer marketing reactively! We are marketing *intentionally*.

And that brings us to the next phase.

———— • ◆ • ————

YOUR TO DOs FOR THIS CHAPTER:

❏ Ask yourself: how can you leverage your already achieved accomplishments?

Find all your templates and swipe files using this link below. You may want to bookmark this page, so you can refer to it as quickly and easily as possible.

↑ *https://www.eevijones.com/marketing-downloads*

PART VI
MARKETING FOR
LONG-TERM VISIBILITY

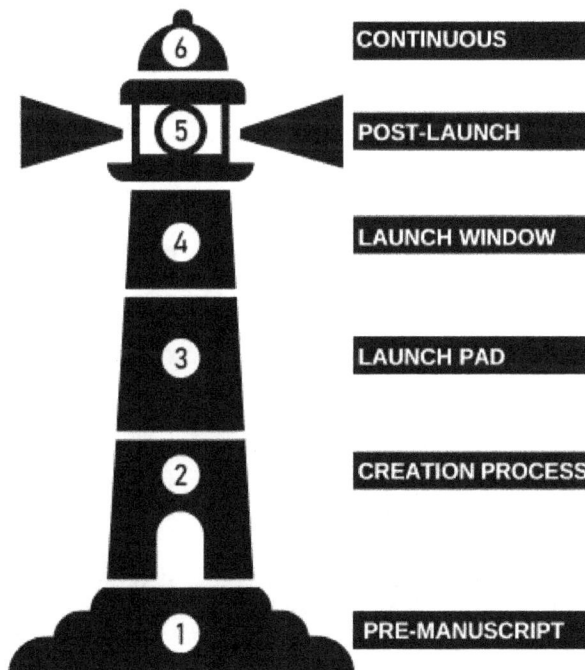

6 — CONTINUOUS

5 — POST-LAUNCH

4 — LAUNCH WINDOW

3 — LAUNCH PAD

2 — CREATION PROCESS

1 — PRE-MANUSCRIPT

CHAPTER 20
Talking About Your Book With Ease

In this part of the book, we will shift our focus from short windows of activity to long-term systems. Systems that keep our book relevant, discoverable, and supported not just for weeks or months, but for years to come.

- *This is where marketing becomes sustainable.*
- *This is where our book continues to work for us.*

And one of the most important long-term skills we can develop as authors is learning how to confidently and naturally talk about our book.

————————— • ◆ • —————————

I'm so excited to share this next part with you, because it has the potential to really help you in everyday scenarios and situations when it comes to the marketing of your precious children's book.

One of the biggest stumbling blocks for so many of us authors is how to talk about our beautiful children's book.

- We don't know what to say.
- We worry about coming across as too salesy.
- Or we don't really know how to bring up our children's book in a conversation in the first place.

Whether that's during in-person events like office parties or get-togethers, or during more targeted events like vendor events, markets, or fairs where we are trying to sell our book, so many of us don't really know what to say.

So before diving into more marketing strategies that are meant to help you with your visibility, I thought it would be helpful to prepare how we can best talk about our precious children's book.

Because even when it comes to something as basic as talking about our book, **preparation and practice are everything.**

Oftentimes, during an event or get-together, we may feel it's quite challenging to transition from talking about the weather to talking about ourselves and our children's books.

And if it's during vendor events, we may worry that we sound too salesy.

And so that's what these next few pages are all about.

1. We will look at what exactly we can say to capture people's attention right away, so they will want to learn more about our book.
2. We will look at creating smooth transitions, so we can easily segue into talking about our beautiful book during any given conversation, so that it no longer feels awkward or salesy to talk about our beautiful children's book.
3. And we will also look at a number of really confidence-infusing responses to the one question that is dreaded by so many of us: *Did you self-publish?*

Preparing for vendor events, holiday markets, and book fairs (which we will learn more about in chapter 25) is one thing. But approaching others and actually talking about our book is a whole different story.

Many of us get nervous or feel awkward talking about ourselves, myself included. Or we are simply unsure what exactly to say to truly capture people's attention right away.

And so, having been an author for many years, something that I've found helps so, so much with overcoming this is to prepare.

- Prepare *what* we are going to say.
- And prepare *how* we are going to say it.

Because if we prepare what we are going to say beforehand, we can practice, so we feel less pressure and, perhaps more importantly, less salesy.

So let's first look at how we can prepare our own introduction and what we can say to capture people's attention right away, so that they will want to learn more about us and our book.

We'll look at two different scenarios:

SCENARIO ONE is an introduction we can use in regular, everyday settings, when we're meeting new connections and are being asked what we do for a living.

SCENARIO TWO is an introduction we can use during vendor events, where people can see that we are selling our children's book.

For both scenarios, we want our introduction to be:

1. *Interesting and intriguing, engaging our listeners emotionally*
2. *Extremely short*
3. *As clear as possible, very much like an elevator pitch*

It's important to note that this elevator pitch is neither our author bio nor our book description. Both our author bio and our book description are much more detailed and much longer.

Instead, an elevator pitch is much more succinct, where we share our **who**, our **what**, and our **why**, all in ideally less than 10 to 12 seconds.

I personally don't really like the term elevator pitch, because the word "pitching" alone already sounds a bit salesy. So I like to call it our **Hello-Line** instead.

———————— ◆ ————————

SCENARIO ONE: *Meeting New Connections*

When meeting new connections, what could our *Hello-Line* be when we are being asked what we do for a living?

Let's say we are an engineer, but would much rather talk about our beautiful book that is all about self-love and self-compassion. When asked what we do, we could say something like this:

> *"Hi! I'm Eevi. I'm an engineer by day, tinkering with gears and gadgets, but my true passion lies in the enchanting world of children's literature. I'm a children's author dedicated to crafting stories that celebrate the extraordinary qualities within each child."*

Here, our *Hello-Line* consists of three main parts:

WHAT WE DO FOR A LIVING **+** **TRANSITION** **+** **DESCRIPTION OF MAIN ISSUE / CONCEPT OUR BOOK IS TACKLING**

The part following our transition should be a short description of the main issue or concept our book is tackling, or the main thing we want people to know about our book - whether that's self-love, kindness, confidence, or simply a story meant to entertain.

Here, we're very much making use of the value we identified for our book in Part 1 under the *Lead With the Heart Method.*

NINJA TIP:

Notice here that we are **not** mentioning the title of our book in our initial *Hello-Line*. We should put our *Hello-Line* together in such a way that it naturally sets up the follow-up question the other person is now very likely going to ask - which is to share more about our book.

What I have found over the years is that most people are quite intrigued when they hear we are writing children's books. So more often than not, they will want to hear more. Piquing people's interest like this is usually quite easy to do.

Let's look at another example. Let's say we are an accountant, but have just published a children's book about kindness. When asked what we do for a living, we could say:

> *"Hi! I'm Eevi. While my weekdays are filled with numbers and spreadsheets as an accountant, my heart beats to a different rhythm on the weekends. I'm a children's author on a mission to write books that celebrate kindness, teaching young minds the magic that unfolds when compassion and empathy come together."*

Here again, our Hello-Line consists of

1. what we do for a living,
2. a transition, and
3. the main concept of our book.

Here are just a few more scenario examples:

1. Spouse's Business Holiday Event

PERSON: *"So, what do you do for a living?"*

YOU: *"I work in marketing, but I'm also a children's author. It's been such a joy combining my love for storytelling with my professional life."*

2. Networking Event

COLLEAGUE: *"So, what do you do outside of work?"*

YOU: *"Aside from my work in marketing, I'm also a children's author. I recently published a* *book aimed at fostering creativity and wonder in young minds."*

3. Team Meeting Icebreaker

COLLEAGUE: *"Let's go around and share something interesting about ourselves."*

YOU: *"Sure! Apart from my role here, I'm also a children's author. I recently published a book that promotes creativity and resilience in kids. It's been a fulfilling side project."*

4. Team Meeting

TEAM MEMBER: *"Any updates or accomplishments to share?"*

YOU: *"Absolutely! Aside from our team projects, I've been wearing my author hat lately. I just published a children's book, spreading positive messages through storytelling."*

Now, while these are mostly responses to someone asking us what we do for a living, we don't have to wait for others to ask us these questions. Instead, we can be the ones asking those questions first and then reply with our *Hello-Line* once it's our turn.

SCENARIO TWO: *At Vendor Events / Markets / Fairs*

Now let's look at what we could say during a vendor event to get others interested in our book. This scenario is a bit different, because people won't ask us what we do for a living. Instead, we are the ones approaching others first.

The other difference is that we are there to sell our book. We're standing in front of our table or stand, probably holding our book in our hands. So the setting and people's mindset are very different, because everyone is there to browse across the market and purchase from vendors. So we can be a bit more direct with our book here.

Let's say our book is about confidence. Here's what our *Hello-Line* could sound like:

> *"Hi guys! I'm Eevi, a local children's author. If you believe in nurturing confidence in little ones in the most magical way, feel free to check out my book The Magic of Choice. The story explores the power of choices and the incredible confidence that blooms when kids trust their decisions."*

Here, our *Hello-Line* again consists of three main parts.

WHO WE ARE	+	CONCEPT OF OUR BOOK & HOW THE OTHER PERSON MAY RELATE TO IT	+	INVITATION

NINJA TIP:

If this is a local event, make sure to weave into your *Hello-Line* that you are a local author. Oftentimes, that makes you even more interesting and relevant to the people visiting that event.

When talking about our book's main concept or theme, we'll want to show how it may be relevant to the person we're talking to. Most everyone believes in nurturing confidence in little ones. So if that's a theme in our story, that's what we could mention here in order to tie it to our book.

But what if our book doesn't have a teaching point and is simply meant to be a fun read?

Let's say I'm the author of *Dragon's Love Tacos* by Adam Rubin. My *Hello-Line* could be:

> *"Hi guys! I'm Eevi. I'm a local children's author. Did you know that while dragons love tacos, they really, really hate spicy salsa?"*

Here, our Hello-Line again shares (1) who we are, and (2) something that might pique the interest or tickle the funny bone of the person we are speaking to. And while this particular example does not include a direct invitation to learn more about our book, people are bound to ask why dragons hate spicy salsa - which then gives us a natural opportunity to invite them to check out our book.

Here are just a few more examples:

YOU: *"Hi guys! I'm Eevi, a local children's author. If you believe in nurturing confidence in little ones in the most magical way, feel free to check out my book "The Magic of Choice." The story explores the power of choices and the incredible confidence that blooms when kids trust in their decisions."*

YOU: *"Hi guys! I'm Eevi. I'm a local children's author. If you believe in the importance of embracing a humble heart and encouraging little ones to discover the magic of being less of a bragger and more of a team player, come say hi, and let's chat about 'Ego, Sheep, and Knittery.'"*

YOU: *"Hi guys! I'm Eevi. I'm a local children's author. Did you know that we can teach our kids that they have a choice in how they react to life's ups and downs. That's what my book*

241

'Sometimes It Rains' helps little ones with, so they can learn about the power of choice and resilience in a fun and engaging way."

YOU: *"Hi guys! I'm Eevi. I'm a local children's author. How do you think a toddler would react if they really wanted grapes, but all we have is an apple?"*

A SAMPLE VENDOR CONVERSATION: *From Start to Finish*

Below is an example of how we can engage someone in a conversation about our beautiful children's book without being pushy or overly salesy. We can introduce ourselves and our book, make the conversation personal and engaging, and then gently guide the conversation toward a purchase in a natural, non-pushy way.

ME: *"Hi! I'm Eevi, the author of the book "Sometimes It Rains," which helps little ones understand that it's okay to want something, but not get it sometimes. Or that it's okay wanting to be happy, but feeling a bit sad sometimes instead."*

SHOPPER: *"Hi Eevi! That sounds like a wonderful book. I have a little one who sometimes struggles with those very feelings. Can you tell me more about how the book addresses these emotions?"*

Now we can provide a bit more depth about our book and how it can help children. Here, we will want to keep the tone light and engaging to encourage further interest.

ME: *"Absolutely! The book is written in rhyme, in which little readers are introduced to everyday-situations they may encounter, that illustrate how we could respond when things don't go as planned. Sometimes, we may get the red cup instead of the green. Or we may have to wait for our turn."*

SHOPPER: *"That sounds like a book my child would benefit from. I love that it uses everyday situations to teach important life lessons. How can I get a copy?"*

ME: *"I have a copy for you right here. The book is $15. And if you'd like, I'd be so happy to sign it and add a personalized dedication for whomever you'd like to gift it to."*

This response will help make the process of buying the book straightforward and also adds a personal touch by offering to sign it and add a dedication.

SHOPPER: *"That's wonderful! I'd love a signed copy with a dedication to my son, Sam. Thank you, Eevi. It was so nice to meet you and learn about your book."*

TRANSITIONS

Now that we have two frameworks we can use to introduce ourselves, let's look at what we can say during conversations with people we may already know, so we can easily transition into talking about our beautiful book during any given conversation - without it feeling awkward or salesy.

There are three distinguishable segue opportunities.

SEGUE OPPORTUNITY 01:

The first opportunity presents itself anytime people talk about (1) their kids, (2) their grandchildren, or (3) book-related topics like the library or a new book the other person has been reading. These moments are often a natural and easy way in.

Let's say someone we've been talking to just mentioned their grandchildren. We could then transition with something like this:

> *"Speaking of grandchildren, I recently wrote a children's book for little ones that's all about inspiring young minds to embrace their uniqueness and embark on imaginative journeys that foster creativity and self-discovery."*

NINJA TIP:

The key here is to prepare something that combines

- *something from our book with*
- *something most parents and grandparents would want to foster in their children - something we have already uncovered in Part 1 under the Lead With the Heart Method.*

SEGUE OPPORTUNITY 02:

The second opportunity presents itself anytime someone talks about something that relates to the topic of our book.

Let's say someone just mentioned that their little one has become quite the bragger. This would be the perfect moment for me to bring up my book *Ego, Sheep, and Knittery - Being Humble and Other Great Stuff*. I could transition with something like this:

> *"Speaking of bragging, I recently wrote a children's book that gently encourages little ones to discover the magic of being less of a bragger and more of a team player. It's meant to inspire kindness and humility."*

Finding these topic-related segue opportunities makes weaving in our book feel really natural and smooth.

SEGUE OPPORTUNITY 03:

The third opportunity presents itself anytime someone asks us what is new with us, which is a question that comes up quite often when we're around people we already know.

Let's say a friend we haven't seen in a while asks us what's new with us these days. We could say something like this:

> *"I've been working on some projects at the office, but I've also just published a children's book. It's all about encouraging little ones to dream big. It's been such a fun and heartwarming journey."*

Again, there really isn't anything else we need to say here, because the person we're talking to is now very likely going to ask us to share a bit more about this new endeavor.

Here are just a few more transition examples:

1. Casual Gathering

FRIEND: *"How's work going these days?"*

YOU: *"Work's good! I've been keeping busy with my day job in finance, but did I tell you about the children's book I recently published? It's been an exciting creative outlet outside the numbers."*

2. Family Get-Together

RELATIVE: *"How's everything with your job?"*

YOU: *"Work's going well, and you know, I've been exploring a new passion too. I wrote a children's book! It's amazing how different worlds can coexist, isn't it?"*

3. Coffee Shop Chat

ACQUAINTANCE: *"What's new with you these days?"*

YOU: *"I've been working on some projects at the office, but I've also just published a children's book. It's all about encouraging little ones to dream big. It's been a heartwarming journey."*

4. Meeting Friends

FRIEND: *"Hey, how have you been?"*

YOU: *"Great, thanks! I've actually been working on something exciting lately. I recently wrote and published a children's book. It's been such a joy to share stories that inspire little ones."*

5. Family Gathering

COUSIN: *"What's new with you?"*

YOU: *"Well, I've been channeling my creative side. I wrote a children's book. It's been a delightful journey watching kids dive into its magical world."*

6. Book Club Gathering

CLUB MEMBER: *"What's everyone been reading lately?"*

YOU: *"Well, aside from our book club picks, I recently authored a children's book. It's been fascinating to see how kids interpret the magical adventures within its pages."*

FOLLOW-UP QUESTIONS

Others will often be intrigued to learn that we wrote a children's book. So more often than not, there will be follow-up questions.

Just like we prepared our initial *Hello-Line* and our transitions, I encourage you to also prepare for the follow-up questions people may ask.

Very common follow-up questions are:

1. *Can you tell me more about the theme or message of your book?*
2. *What age group is your book intended for?*
3. *Where can I get your book?*

Having answers ready for the questions that come up most often is what will really help set us apart and help our book shine.

And to help you brainstorm what questions may come up, I've put together a list of the most common follow-up questions, along with a sample response for each, so you can begin to think about your own replies.

1. What inspired you to write a children's book?

"I've always been fascinated by the power of storytelling. The inspiration for my children's book came from a desire to share positive messages and encourage creativity among young readers."

2. How did you get started?

"I found a really helpful book on Amazon called "How To Self-Publish a Children's Book" by Eevi Jones. She also has a wonderful YouTube channel where she shares lots of valuable information. I can send you the information if you're interested."

3. Did you face any challenges while writing or publishing the book?

"Absolutely. The journey had its challenges, but it was incredibly rewarding. Overcoming obstacles during the writing and publishing process only strengthened my commitment to bringing this story to life."

4. Can you tell me more about the theme or message of your book?

"Certainly! My book is called "Finding My Awesome" and revolves around the theme of resilience and the importance of embracing uniqueness. It encourages children to face challenges with courage and kindness."

5. Have you always wanted to be an author?

"Becoming an author was a bit spontaneous for me. I had this story itching to be told, and the journey into the world of children's literature unfolded from there."

6. What age group is your book intended for?

"I wrote the book with early readers in mind, typically targeting the age group of five to eight years old. It's a stage where kids are developing important values and concepts."

7. Are there any specific lessons or values you hope children take away from your book?

"Absolutely. I hope children take away the importance of kindness, resilience, and the understanding that each of them has something unique and valuable to offer."

8. How did you illustrate your book?

"I collaborated with a talented illustrator. I really wanted each page to be vibrant and engaging, enhancing the overall storytelling experience for young readers."

9. Do you have plans for more children's books in the future?

"Yes, definitely! I'm currently working on a few ideas for future children's books. It's an exciting journey, and I can't wait to share more stories with young readers."

SELF-PUBLISHING RELATED QUESTIONS

Two questions we are bound to get asked are these:

- *How did you go about publishing your book?*
- *Did you self-publish your book?*

Let's look at a number of really great, confidence-infusing responses to these questions - questions that are dreaded by so many of us.

- *"I chose to self-publish because it gave me creative control and allowed me to bring my vision to life exactly as I imagined. It's been a fulfilling journey, and I'm proud of the result."*

- *"I decided to self-publish, and I'm grateful for the independence it offered. It allowed me to take charge of every aspect, from the storyline to the cover design. It's been a learning experience, and I value the freedom it provides."*

- *"I opted for self-publishing because it offered a valuable learning experience. It allowed me to understand the intricacies of the publishing world and connect directly with my readers. I've grown so much throughout this process."*

- *"I self-published my book, and it was a labor of love. Having complete control over my project allowed me to pour my heart and soul into every page. It may not be the traditional route, but it's been deeply rewarding."*

- *"I decided to self-publish because it allowed me to build a direct connection with my readers. Their feedback has been invaluable, and it's heartening to see the impact my work has on them. That connection is what matters most to me."*

If you've ever felt apprehensive about answering these questions or weren't quite sure how to respond, I hope this list of responses leaves you feeling more confident than ever when talking about your beautiful book.

By sharing our book in a way that relates to the person we're speaking to, we are no longer trying to just sell something. Instead, we are trying to help the people who need our book the most discover it.

Once we shift our mindset to thinking about how our book can help others, we naturally feel much more comfortable talking about it.

When using your *Hello-Lines*, remember these two things:

NINJA TIP:

Once you have prepared your responses, make sure you practice them until you feel comfortable saying them.

NINJA TIP:

The more excited we are when we speak about our book, the more excited our listeners will become. They will match our energy.

Not every situation will lend itself to sharing about our book. But being on the lookout for opportunities to do so helps immensely.

Just like we seem to see a car brand everywhere once we've decided to buy it, we will also start seeing more and more opportunities to share our book. Thinking about these opportunities sharpens our awareness.

———·◆·———

YOUR TO DOs FOR THIS CHAPTER:

- ❏ Prepare your *hello-line*
- ❏ Prepare possible follow up questions and your answers to them

Find all your templates and swipe files using this link below. You may want to bookmark this page, so you can refer to it as quickly and easily as possible.

⬆ *https://www.eevijones.com/marketing-downloads*

CHAPTER 21
The Power Of A Signature

Learning how to talk about our book goes hand in hand with learning how to sign or autograph it, because that, too, is a very important part of our branding as an author.

If you've ever sent out your beautiful children's book without signing it, then I encourage you to never do so again.

In this chapter, we will look at:

1. **WHY** we should always sign our children's book
2. **WHY** we should always write a personal message whenever we give or send our book to someone
3. Lots and lots of fun and creative personal message examples and ideas to inspire us to come up with our own list of go-to staples we can use whenever we're sending out our book

Most books have what is called a *dedication*, like Aaron Blabey's book *Pig the Pug* right here.

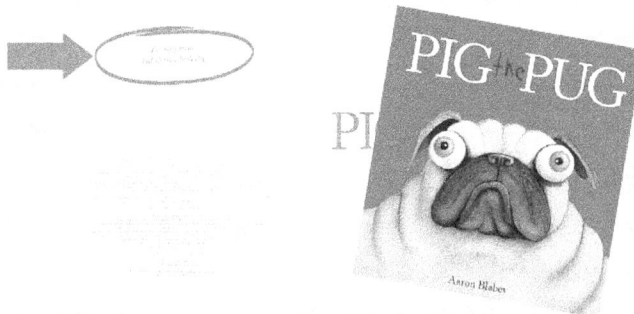

It's part of the interior of the book, so it's the same in every printed copy.

A personalized note and signature, however, is something authors usually write into their book when they are at book signings, when they are gifting their book, or when they are sending it to someone.

If you're like me, you may have wondered whether or not you should be signing your book before giving or sending it to someone. After all, who are we to assume others want us to scribble in their copy of our book, right?

Especially in the beginning, I felt quite pretentious whenever I signed my book, because I always thought only famous authors should get to do so.

And I know so many fellow authors feel this way, because I receive so many beautiful children's books from my *Children's Book University®* students, my clients, and my readers. And so many of them - in fact, the majority of them - are not signed.

Seeing this always makes me so sad, because I know that the author who was so sweet and kind to send their beautiful book my way likely had an inner dialogue about whether or not they should sign it, and decided against it because they didn't feel worthy.

So let me tell you this right now:

YOU are worthy to sign your beautiful book. You absolutely are.

From this day forward, whenever we are sharing a copy of our book, we are going to sign it. Without exception.

Because believe me - receiving a book directly from its author will always be special. And adding our personal, handwritten touch only enhances this beautiful gesture.

I love seeing special notes in the books that are sent my way. And so does everyone else who receives your book. I promise.

----------- • ✦ • -----------

Now that we've established that we will *always* personalize our books with a signature and a special note, let's look at some fun examples so we can begin putting together our own list of just two to three short, go-to messages we can handwrite whenever we're signing our book.

When choosing our message, it's always helpful to consider three things:

1. *WHO* is the recipient?
2. *WHAT* is our book about?
3. *WHAT* is the signing occasion?

Most recipients fall into one of four categories:

1. Kids the book is meant to be gifted to
2. Family members, friends, and others we already know
3. New buyers we just met during book signing events
4. Reviewers or influencers we are sending our book to

Knowing who our book is for can be really helpful for two main reasons.

REASON 1: If we know the recipient's actual name, we can make our note extra special by addressing them personally.

Here, for example, are two books that were signed by addressing me or my boys as the recipients:

REASON 2: If we know who the book is for, choosing the wording and tone of our note becomes much easier.

This signed note, for example, is by *New York Times* bestselling author Nick Sansbury Smith in one of the books he sent my way. Because he knew exactly who the book was for, he was able to truly personalize his message.

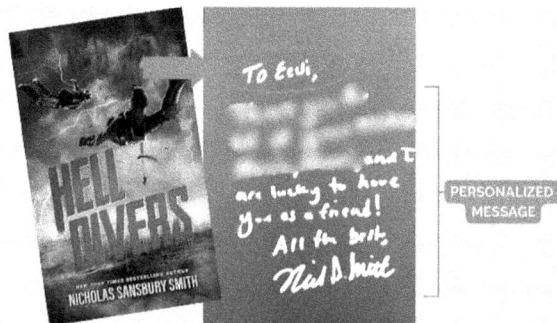

Knowing our recipient also helps us choose the tone of our note. If our book is for little ones, we might want to write in the voice of our main character. We could choose something silly, playful, or encouraging.

Lauren Eresman's beautiful book *The Treehouse Trio* is a wonderful example. She encouraged my boys with the words: "Try. Fail. Learn. Grow. Repeat. Just don't give up!"

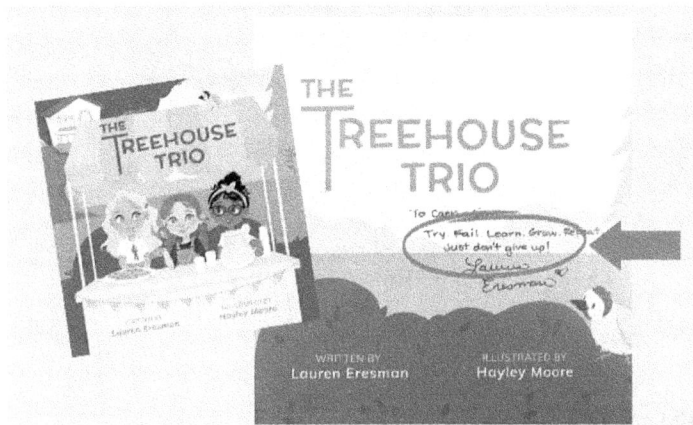

If our book is for a family member or friend, we may want to write a message that expresses gratitude and appreciation.

Ann-Margret Manley's signed note is a perfect example. In her precious book *Jeni's Bubble - A Sticky Tale About Not Giving Up*, she wrote such a sweet message thanking me for believing in her.

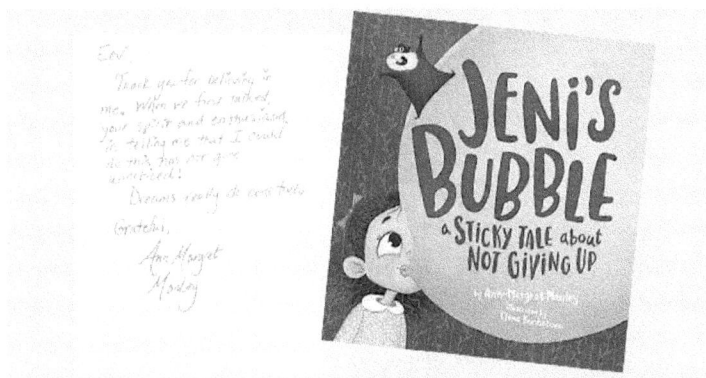

If our recipient is an influencer, reviewer, or someone we may not personally know, we may want to stay a bit more professional and on-brand.

Gretchen Rubin's signed message is a great example. She simply addresses the recipient and adds a short "Onward!" - a phrase she often uses in her emails and on social media, making it very much her signature phrase.

NINJA TIP:

When sending our book to influencers, we may not want to add their name directly into the book itself.

Oftentimes, depending on the influencer, a book may come back as undeliverable, especially if it was sent unsolicited. By not including their name in the book, we can reuse it and send it to someone else if needed.

That said, personalizing our outreach is still incredibly important. But instead of writing a personalized note directly into the book, we can include a personalized letter or card with the book, just like I did here:

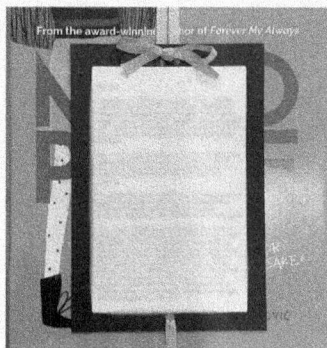

UNCOVERING OUR SIGNATURE PHRASE

Now that we understand why knowing *who* our book is for matters, let's look at *what* we could or should say in our note.

When drafting a message we can use again and again, I always find it helpful if it ties directly into the message or theme of our book.

Again, Lauren Eresman's *The Treehouse Trio* is a wonderful example. Her book inspires young readers to follow their dreams, support one another, and get back up after failure. Her phrase:

"Try. Fail. Learn. Grow. Repeat. Just don't give up!"

sums that up beautifully and makes for the perfect signing phrase.

Another great example is Nicole McDonald's book *Dash's Week*, which is all about helping others by simply being ourselves. Her note, ***"Just Be You,"*** ties in perfectly.

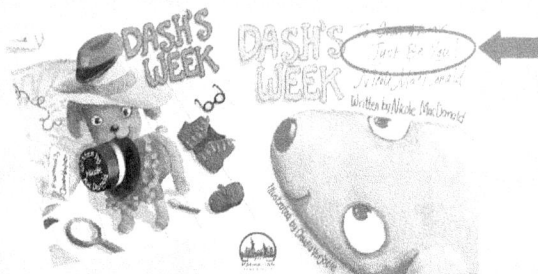

One of my absolute favorite examples is happiness researcher Shawn Achor's book *Ripple's Effect*. The book teaches little readers about the power of a smile and how each of us can make the world a better place. Signing it with ***"Happiness Is a Choice!"*** is absolutely perfect.

So how can we uncover our own signature phrase? It may help to ask ourselves questions like:

- *What is the one thing I want little ones to take away from my book?*
- *Is there a phrase that's repeated throughout the story?*
- *Is there something especially funny or catchy my characters say?*
- *Is there a message I want to emphasize and highlight?*

These are all questions that can guide us in discovering our *signature phrase*.

In my book *The Magic of Choice - My Power Within*, I love signing it with: ***"Remember - you always have the power to choose!"*** - because that's what this book is all about.

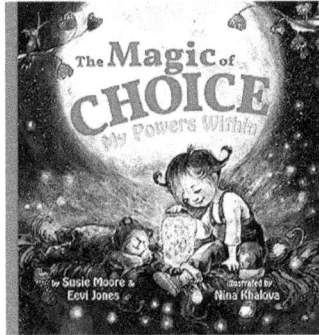

When I send out *Letting Go - For the Soon-to-Be Empty Nester*, I often sign it with: ***"What a magnificent human you have raised!"***

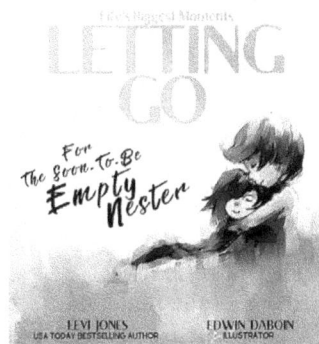

And when signing *The Girl That Makes Mistakes - Growing Confidence One Day at a Time*, I like to add: ***"May you always remember that you're the hero of your own life!"***

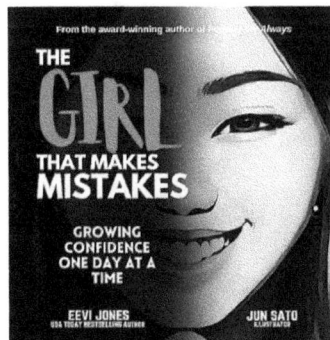

Wendy Van De Poll's note in *The Adventures of Ms. Addie Pants - The Rescue* is such a sweet example. She added her dog's name, Addie, along with a paw print.

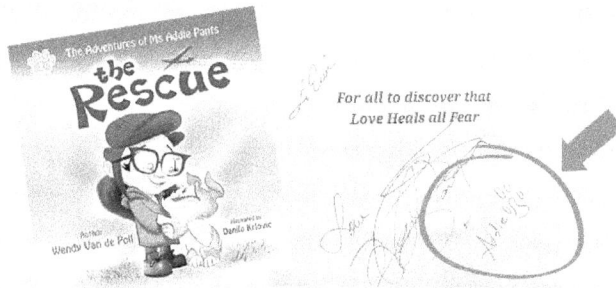

If your story is about a dinosaur at bedtime, you could add a simple doodle and the words *"Sweet dreams!"*

If your story is encouraging, you could draw a few stars and write *"Reach for the stars!"*

If your book is about food, cookies, or eating, you could add a tiny bite mark along the edge of the page with the words *"Happy munching."*

The sky really is the limit.

If your book has a playful title, you might even incorporate it into your note, just like Laura Belgray did with her memoir. While not a children's book, it's such a fun example of using the title as part of the signed message.

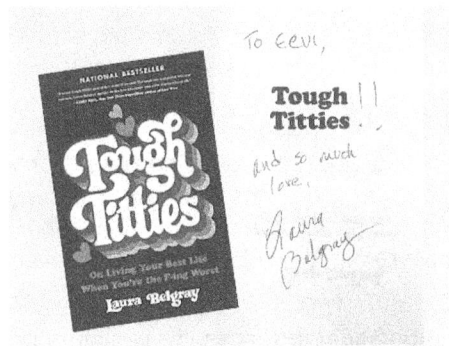

But how can considering the *signing occasion* help us draft the perfect note?

If we're gifting our book to friends or family, or using it to thank someone and express our gratitude, our message may be longer and much more personal - and therefore different from person to person.

If, on the other hand, we're drafting a message we plan to use during book signings, we'll likely want to keep it short so we can sign our books more quickly. That's when having just a few succinct, go-to options on hand becomes so helpful.

Again, Gretchen Rubin's *"Onward!"* is such a great example, because it's something she says all the time. It also has the added bonus of being very short, making it perfect for book signings where things usually move quickly.

NINJA TIP:

Simply ask the person who wants their book signed whether it's for a special occasion.

If it's a birthday, we can make our note birthday-specific:

- *The happiest of birthdays, [NAME].*
- *To [NAME] - the luckiest birthday kid!*
- *Happy 7th birthday, [NAME]!*
- *I hope you're having the BEST birthday!*

Here are a few simple, general fallback messages you can always use:

- *Happy reading!*
- *Enjoy the book!*
- *Enjoy [NAME OF BOOK'S CHARACTER]'s little adventure!*
- *I hope you love this book as much as I loved writing it!*
- *The journey of a lifetime starts with the turning of a page.*
- *May you always find joy and love in your life.*
- *Wishing you many nights of bedtime stories and sweet dreams.*
- *I hope this book will open up your heart to the world of magic and imagination.*
- *Grow your imagination and never stop dreaming, learning, and living.*
- *Be the hero of your own story, [NAME]! Remember - never give up!*

Signing our book and adding a personalized message is such a powerful opportunity to connect with our readers, make our book extra special, and let our personality shine through.

In a sea of authors and books, branding is a big - and often forgotten - part of our marketing strategy. These small, human touches are what make our book memorable long after it's been read and help create a deeper emotional connection between our story and its reader.

We have so many beautiful options when it comes to signing our books. So before sending out your next copy, make sure to sign it and add a note that represents you and your book thoughtfully and authentically.

Because you and your book are absolutely worth it.

One way we can ensure the other person continues to learn more about us and our book is by giving them something tangible that piques their interest even further - our author business card.

These can be surprisingly versatile, so let's look at those next.

———————————— • ◆ • ————————————

YOUR TO DOs FOR THIS CHAPTER:

- ❏ **Using what you have learned,** uncover our own signature phrase

Find all your templates and swipe files using this link below. You may want to bookmark this page, so you can refer to it as quickly and easily as possible.

⬆ *https://www.eevijones.com/marketing-downloads*

CHAPTER 22
A Small Card With Big Impact

There are moments when people feel genuinely excited about our book, ask thoughtful questions, and want to stay connected - and then the moment passes. An author business card exists for exactly that moment.

It gives us a simple, intentional way to continue the conversation, make our work easy to find, and keep our book discoverable beyond that one interaction.

When designed with care, an author business card becomes a small but powerful marketing tool that supports our visibility, our branding, and our long-term reach.

So in the next few pages, we'll take a closer look at:

1. **Why** and **when** creating a business card makes sense for us children's authors
2. **What** elements we want to make sure to include on our card
3. **What** elements we want to make sure **not** to include on our card
4. Fun and creative design ideas to help our card stand out
5. **How** to use our business card in a truly unique and effective way
6. **Where** to go to create and print our business card

WHY SHOULD WE HAVE A BUSINESS CARD?

Now..., you may be wondering:

> *Does it make sense to create a business card for myself as an author?*
> *Would the investment be worth it, especially if we're not a full-time author?*

I've been an author for over a decade, and there have been so many moments where I wished I had a card with me. So now, I always carry at least a couple of cards wherever I go.

So the short answer is: YES - creating our own author business cards is absolutely worth it.

And that's because a well-designed business card helps us in more than just one way.

- It helps us share our most relevant information quickly and easily.
- Having a designed card looks far more professional and put together than scribbling our information down on a piece of paper.
- Being able to share our information this way simply makes everything feel more official.

Investing in ourselves in this way signals that we believe in ourselves and that we take being an author seriously. And if we take ourselves seriously, so will others.

───────────── • ✦ • ─────────────

WHERE WOULD WE GET TO SHARE OUR WONDERFUL BUSINESS CARD

1. EVERYWHERE

As I already mentioned, I now always carry a few cards with me wherever I go. One of the first things people often ask me once they hear that I'm a children's author is whether I have a card, so they can look me up, learn more about me, and hopefully purchase one of my books.

If you feel awkward or salesy talking about your children's book, or if you're not quite sure how to bring it up in conversation, make sure to read chapter 20, where we learned how to talk about our book.

That way, we can introduce the topic much more naturally, which then gives us the perfect opportunity to share our business card.

2. SPECIFIC EVENTS

Another important use for our business card is during vendor events, book fairs, and other public events where we're showcasing our book, including school visits.

Having an author business card handy during these events looks professional and helps us stay on people's minds long after the event is over.

3. STANDING OUT & GOING THE EXTRA MILE

A third great use for our business card is to include it with our books - either tucked into the package when we're mailing them out, or placed directly inside the book.

Something I love doing is adding my card to the very front of my books using self-adhesive corners, like the ones often used for photos or scrapbooking. I like to use gold ones because they really elevate the look.

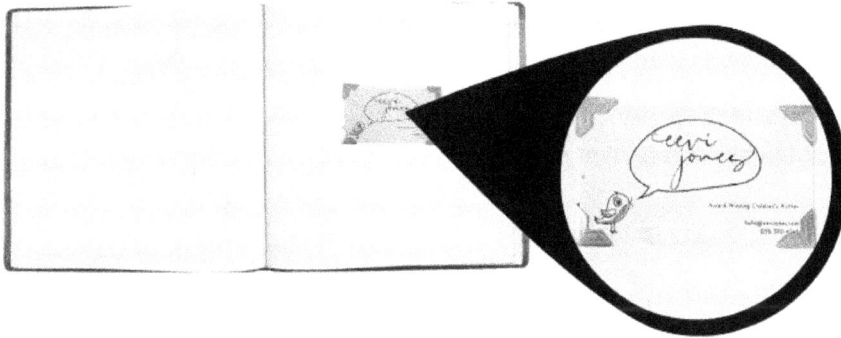

WHAT ELEMENTS SHOULD WE INCLUDE ON OUR CARD?

Now that we know when and where we might use our business card, let's look at the key elements we'll want to include.

This is where we want to be both methodical and practical, asking ourselves:

What is the main purpose of my business card?

- *Is it meant to help readers learn more about me and find my book?*
- *Is it meant to provide retailers or businesses with my official contact information?*
- *Am I aiming to be mostly practical, or do I want my personality to shine through the design?*
- *What is my budget?*

Thinking through these questions matters, because our answers will guide our design decisions and determine what we include.

For example, if I'm mostly sharing my card with readers, I wouldn't include my personal phone number. If I'm sharing it primarily with businesses or retailers, including a phone number might make sense.

So first, we want to be clear on the main purpose of our card.

Let's now take a closer look at the main elements we'll want to include on our card.

1. OUR NAME

If we write and publish our beautiful book under our real name, this is straightforward. If we use a pen name, we have a few options:

- *Use our legal name*
- *Use our pen name*
- *Include both*

If including both, we could write something like: *Daniel Handler, writing as Lemony Snicket.*

DANIEL HANDLER
WRITING AS LEMONY SNICKET ————

2. OUR TITLE

Next, we'll want to include our title.

If we're both the author and illustrator, we could use *Children's Author and Illustrator*. If our book has earned a bestseller badge, we could use *Bestselling Children's Author*. If we've won an award, *Award-Winning Children's Author* is a wonderful credibility marker.

One of my own cards, for example, lists: *USA Today & WSJ Bestselling Writer and Award-Winning Children's Author*.

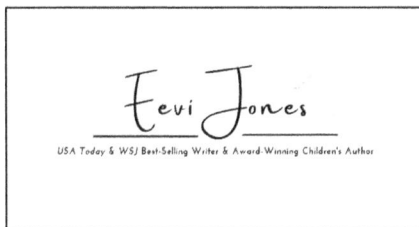

If we've earned these titles, we should absolutely be proud of them and share them.

3. OUR CONTACT INFORMATION

Next, we'll want to include our contact information - whatever details we feel most comfortable providing.

The three most common options are:

- *Our email address*
- *Our website*
- *Our social media handles*

NINJA TIP:

When including a website, it's best to stick to **one** URL.

I know it can be tempting to include more than one link. If you have multiple links you'd like to share, I encourage you to take advantage of the *One-Link* strategy we discussed in chapter 14. This allows us to share multiple links using just one.

For social media, focus on the platforms you're actually active on. For me, that's Instagram.

NINJA TIP:

REMEMBER: It's incredibly helpful to use the same handle across social platforms whenever possible.

This is one of my own cards. It shares my name, my title, my email, my website, and my Instagram handle.

Besides these main elements, there are a few optional elements we may want to add to our card.

4. AN AUTHOR IMAGE

While I don't personally include an image, this is absolutely an option. To make it look as professional as possible, there are a few things we'll want to keep in mind:

- We'll want to avoid using a selfie that clearly looks like a selfie.
- Even though it's just a small photo, it should still fit our genre. Something that really helps here is to look at the profile pictures of some of our favorite children's authors and notice the similarities. What are they wearing? How are they posing? What does their background look like?

These are some of my favorite children's authors. And just by looking at a few of them, I can already see clear trends and similarities when it comes to their poses and backgrounds.

Peter H. Reynolds   Anna Dewdney   Dan Santat   Nyong'o Lupita   Loren Long

5. A COVER IMAGE

A 3-D mockup image (instead of just a flat image of our cover) often looks a bit more professional, simply because it adds depth.

If we've written a series, we could even showcase all the books in that series, like we see in this example right here of my *Life's Biggest Moments* series.

6. THE LOGO OF OUR IMPRINT

We could include the logo of our imprint, if we have one, or the logo of our series.

This is absolutely optional. The top example here shows the logo of my imprint, LHC Publishing. The bottom example shows the logo of my award-winning children's book series *Braving the World*.

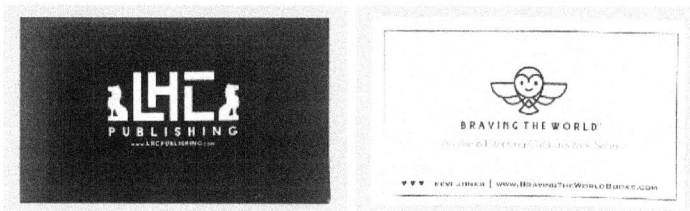

7. A QR CODE

QR codes provide an easy way to access websites more quickly than manually typing in a URL. This is especially helpful when our URL is long. So by adding a QR code to our card, we're making it as easy as possible for the person receiving it.

Whether we use it to lead someone directly to our website, to our book's sales page on Amazon, or to automatically open a new email with our address and subject line pre-filled, the possibilities are nearly endless.

And best of all, creating and using QR codes is absolutely free, with tools such as *qr-code-generator.com* (↑).

FRONT

BACK

NINJA TIP:

If we do include a QR code, we'll still want to include the written URL as well. That way, even those who aren't able to use a QR code can still access our information.

- ◆ -

WHAT ELEMENTS SHOULD WE AVOID ON OUR CARD?

Now let's look at a few things we may want to avoid including on our business card.

1. OUR ADDRESS & PHONE NUMBER

Information we may want to stay away from sharing includes our physical address and phone number.

This is often where functionality meets privacy. That said, this very much depends on the purpose of our business card.

2. TIME-SENSITIVE PROMOTIONS

We'll also want to avoid time-sensitive elements, such as references to upcoming book readings, author visits, or book fairs.

It's also best to steer clear of seasonal language, like "best read this summer."

3. PRICING

Because we can adjust our book pricing at any time, it's best not to include pricing or discount information on our business card.

This ensures our cards remain relevant and usable for a long time.

4. HARD-TO-READ FONTS

We'll want to avoid fonts that are difficult to read. While calligraphy or handwriting-style fonts can look beautiful, they aren't always the best choice if clarity suffers. Here, clarity should always come before aesthetics.

Daniel Handler
WRITING AS LEMONY SNICKET ————————

5. GENRE-INAPPROPRIATE FONTS

We also want to make sure our fonts match our genre. For example, western-style fonts or fonts associated with horror movies wouldn't be a great fit for children's books.

Daniel Handler
WRITING AS LEMONY SNICKET ————————

Daniel Handler
WRITING AS LEMONY SNICKET ————————

DANIEL HANDLER
WRITING AS LEMONY SNICKET ————————

6. HARD-ON-THE-EYES DESIGNS

Beyond fonts, we'll also want to ensure our text isn't too small and that it stands out clearly from the background. Color contrast matters, and busy backgrounds can make cards hard to read.

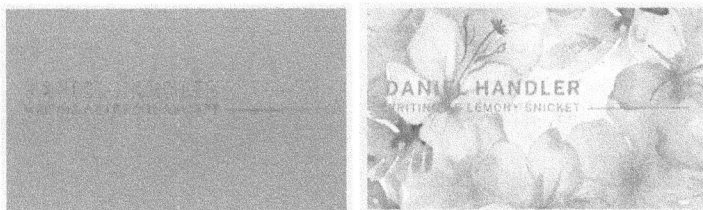

7. LOW IMAGE QUALITY

We always want to use high-quality images so they don't appear blurry or pixelated. A resolution of 300 DPI (dots per inch) is ideal.

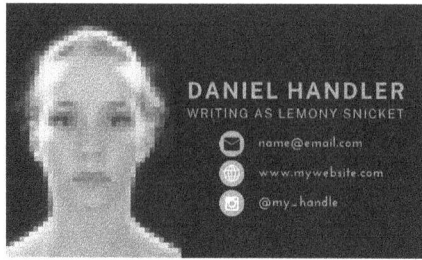

DANIEL HANDLER
WRITING AS LEMONY SNICKET

✉ name@email.com
🌐 www.mywebsite.com
📷 @my_handle

FUN & CREATIVE DESIGN IDEAS FOR OUR CARD

Now that we've covered the dos and don'ts, let's move on to the fun part - design. As children's authors, we have so much creative freedom here.

A helpful question to ask ourselves is:

Do we want our business card to feel more classic?
Or do we want it to be a direct extension of our book?

DESIGN IDEA #01: *Incorporating our book illustrations*

Because we already have illustrations created for our book, we might as well use them. A fun and unique option is to feature an illustration as the background or as a spot illustration. In the examples below, I even added a little tagline:

Freddy the Frog - Plenty of Adventures, One Hop at a Time.

DESIGN IDEA #02: *Coordinating background*

To take it a step further, we could coordinate the background on the back of our card with the front, creating a cohesive and colorful look.

DESIGN IDEA #03: *Horizontal vs. vertical*

We can also play with orientation. Instead of the traditional horizontal layout, we might try a vertical design.

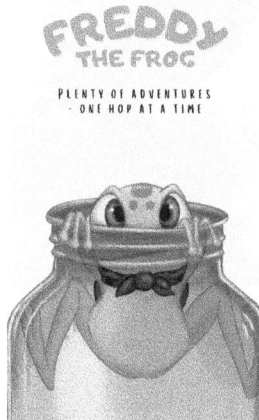

DESIGN IDEA #04: *Incorporating cut-out shapes*

One of my favorite ideas is using cut-out shapes that tie into our book's theme.

For example, if our book features a bunny eating a cookie, we could trim the corner of the card so it looks like a bite was taken out of it.

We could do the same with cheese by punching holes, or with a night sky by punching out stars or hearts.

There are so many inexpensive shape punch options available, making the possibilities endless.

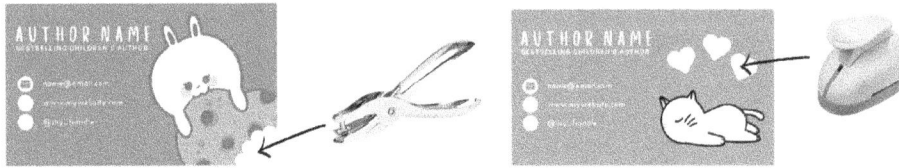

DESIGN IDEA #05: *Make it a bookmark*

Another creative idea is to design our business card as a bookmark. That way, it's not only informative, but also useful. To make it even more special, we could punch a hole at the top and add a tassel.

This is such an inexpensive way to stand out, since tassels can be purchased on Amazon in bulk for just a few dollars.

We could even add a fun activity to the back, like a picture search where children cross off items they find in the book.

HOW TO USE OUR BUSINESS CARDS IN UNIQUE WAYS

We've already talked about QR codes, but what if we took this idea one step further?

I call this my *Creating Micro-Moments of Discovery Method*, or my *Breadcrumb Method*.

This idea is one of my absolute favorites, because it's so simple and creative.

We're so used to thinking that people discover our books online. But what if they could also discover them out in the real world? All with the help of our small, yet mighty business card.

All we would have to do is design a fun little card that shows our book cover, a short and intriguing line about its message, and a QR code that leads directly to our website - or to a video trailer of us reading the first couple of pages of our book.

And here's where it gets fun:

Wherever we go, we take these little cards with us. We can leave them in local coffee shops, children's museums, art studios, or waiting rooms where families gather - whether that's at the doctor's office or the dentist.

If we've created bookmarks, we could leave them in libraries or place one inside every book we return. We could also add one to books in those little free libraries we see along the road, where people can pick up books to read.

We could even include one in local donation baskets, teacher gifts, or community giveaways.

Each one is like a tiny breadcrumb leading back to our world.

It's visibility that doesn't rely on social media or algorithms - just curiosity and creativity. Each time someone finds our card, we've created a micro-moment of discovery.

And the best part is that it's inexpensive, it's fun, and it keeps our story traveling even when we're not.

The more this little card tickles someone's curiosity, the better. Paired with a cut-out design, our cards can look fun, adorable, and eye-catching. We could even add a little ribbon and use it as a tag we can hang on things.

The examples below look even better in color, so I made sure to include them on your download page (↑).

NINJA TIP:

Don't just link your QR code to an Amazon page. Instead, consider linking it to your own website - or, even better, to a landing page with a short video of you saying hi, introducing yourself as a local author, and reading the first page of your book. Make it feel personal!

WHERE TO CREATE & PRINT OUR BUSINESS CARD

I create all my card designs directly in *Canva.com* (⬆), where we can either start from scratch or use Canva's templates and then add our illustrations and information.

One of the things I love about using Canva is that we can also order our printed business cards and bookmarks directly through the platform, which makes the entire process really simple.

If we're looking for additional paper stock options or design features like rounded corners or foil accents, a place like *Vistaprint.com* (⬆) is a wonderful option as well.

NINJA TIP:

I still recommend designing your card in *Canva* first, downloading the file, and then uploading it to *Vistaprint*. That way, we have far more design flexibility.

NINJA TIP:

Before ordering a large quantity, start by ordering just 50 cards - the smallest quantity available on *Vistaprint*. This allows us to see how we like them, make any tweaks, and then order more with confidence.

Over the years, I've created my fair share of business cards, and every single time it's been special and so much fun. As children's authors, our possibilities truly are endless.

We spent quite some time on author business cards - and that's intentional. This is something we'll share far and wide, often in small, everyday moments that quietly support our marketing. So we want to make a strong impression - one that sparks curiosity, invites connection, and makes people want to learn more about us and our beautiful book.

Designing our own uniquely branded business card is one of the easiest and most cost-effective ways to increase our visibility, reinforce our message, and keep our book discoverable long after a conversation has ended.

And remember - we're building our brand. Something that sets us apart in a world filled with millions of children's authors.

— • ◆ • —

YOUR TO DOs FOR THIS CHAPTER:

❏   Design your very own author business card

Find all your templates and swipe files using this link below. You may want to bookmark this page, so you can refer to it as quickly and easily as possible.

↑ *https://www.eevijones.com/marketing-downloads*

LINKS SHARED:

- *https://www.qr-code-generator.com*
- *https://www.canva.com*
- *https://www.vistaprint.com*

CHAPTER 23
Using Your Email Signature Strategically

We rarely think of email as a marketing tool - and that's exactly why it's so powerful. It's personal, it's practical, and it's already woven into our everyday lives.

Email is one of those things we use constantly when communicating with schools, parents, teachers, community members, businesses, and organizations. And so, every one of those emails carries an opportunity to reinforce who we are, what we do, and that our book exists.

When used intentionally, a personalized email signature can become a simple, evergreen marketing tool that works for us automatically - without feeling salesy, promotional, or forced.

In this chapter, we'll look at how to turn something we already use every day into a subtle but powerful way to increase visibility, strengthen our author brand, and help the right people discover our books naturally.

So let's take a look at:

1. The advantages of including an email signature block
2. What elements we'll want to make sure to include
3. How to create our very own signature block

———— • ◆ • ————

How fun would it be to make people aware of our books without having to directly tell them about them - all through the use of an email signature block?

This right here is one of my email signature blocks.

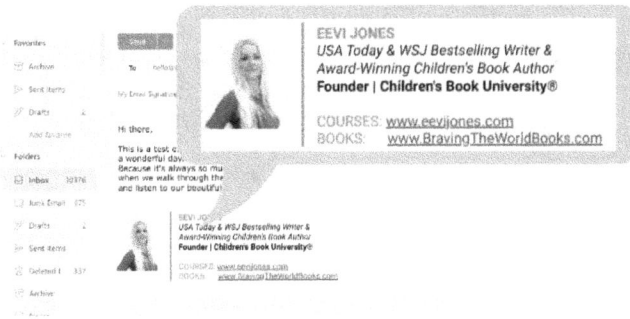

It shows my photo, my name, a short line about who I am, and two links - one to my courses and one to my books. And what makes an email signature block like this so useful is that all of these links are clickable.

So not only does a signature like this pique people's curiosity about what we do, it also gives them an easy way to click through and instantly learn more about us and our work.

This is how I've received a number of author-visit invitations without ever having introduced myself as a children's book author. My email signature did the work for me.

I actually discovered this completely by accident a couple of years ago. At the time, this wasn't intentional at all. While communicating with my oldest son's school office, my emails simply always included this signature. That's how the school learned that I was a local children's author, which eventually led to my very first author-visit invitation.

While this happened accidentally for me, I'm sharing it with you so you can implement it with intention.

An email signature block like this works because it taps into something very human: curiosity. When we see a name, a photo, and a short line that hints at something interesting, it's only natural to want to click and learn a little more.

———————— • ✦ • ————————

WHAT WE SHOULD INCLUDE

What we include in our email signature block entirely depends on our own preferences. Whether or not we include an image of ourselves is completely up to us. We could also choose to share the cover of our book instead.

It could look something like this example right here, where I'm featuring my book *Sometimes It Rains*.

EEVI JONES
USA Today & WSJ Bestselling Writer &
Award-Winning Children's Book Author
Founder | Children's Book University®

COURSES: www.eevijones.com
BOOKS: www.BravingTheWorldBooks.com

This immediately catches the reader's attention and helps them visually recognize our book.

While I would say the image itself is optional, there are three elements we *do* want to make sure to include:

1. OUR NAME: To visually set our name apart from the rest of the text, we could change its font color, make it bold, or even capitalize it.

2. A LINE THAT MAKES IT CLEAR WE ARE AN AUTHOR: This is where we can get a little creative.

Any credibility markers we've earned are wonderful additions here. For example:

- *Award-Winning Children's Author*
- *Best-Selling Children's Author*

My own line, for example, highlights my most important credibility markers and reads:

USA Today & WSJ Bestselling Writer and Award-Winning Children's Book Author

Another fun option is to simply incorporate our book title, such as:

Children's Author of *Sometimes It Rains*

The main goal of this line is to make it immediately clear that we write children's books.

3. A LINK TO OUR BOOK OR WEBSITE: We'll want to include at least one clickable link that allows readers to learn more about us and our work if they choose to. This could be a link directly to our Amazon page or to our own website.

Providing a direct link makes it as easy as possible for people to learn more, without requiring them to search for us on their own - which is an extra step many people simply won't take.

In my example above, I even included two links: one to my courses and one to my books.

OPTIONAL ELEMENTS: There are also a few optional elements we could add.

If we want people to connect with us on social media, we could include small clickable icons or buttons that link directly to our Instagram or Facebook accounts, or even to our LinkedIn profile.

HOW TO CREATE OUR EMAIL SIGNATURE

There are many ways to create an email signature. I personally like using an email signature generator tool, such as the one provided by *HubSpot.com* (↑), which is completely free. To find other options, you can simply Google the phrase *email signature generator*.

What I love about the HubSpot tool is that it allows us to fully customize our signature block, including layout, fonts, and colors. All we need to do is enter our information, upload an image, and choose a template.

This process is meant to be fun, so don't hesitate to play around with different layouts and styles.

Because our email signature is part of our author branding, here are a few DOs and DON'Ts to keep in mind.

DOs & DON'Ts:

1. **DON'T include too many images.** One image is plenty - whether it's your author photo or your book cover.
2. **DON'T include too many links.** Simplicity keeps things focused and easy to engage with.
3. **DON'T use hard-to-read fonts.** Our signature should be easy on the eyes and completely legible.
4. **DO test everything.** Send yourself a test email to make sure the links work and the layout looks the way you expect it to on the receiving end.

ADDING OUR SIGNATURE

The way we add our signature block will depend on our email provider. The easiest way to learn how to do this is to Google the phrase:

how to add signature block in [your email provider]

Once you've followed your provider's instructions, simply copy and paste your signature block into the designated signature area.

Setting up or updating your email signature is quick, easy, and surprisingly effective.

Most of us send emails every single day - to schools, communities, collaborators, and businesses. So why not use those everyday touchpoints more intentionally? Why not pique people's interest in a fun, natural way, without having to "market" at all?

Most business emails already include signature blocks, because they quietly reinforce who we are and what we do. As authors, we deserve to use that same space to support our visibility and keep our work discoverable.

Remember, your email signature is yet another opportunity to strengthen your author brand. If you have a signature font or a signature color, be sure to use it so your emails become instantly recognizable over time.

Small details like these add up. And when used consistently, they become part of a long-term marketing system that works for us in the background, every single day.

———————— • ◆ • ————————

YOUR TO DOs FOR THIS CHAPTER:

❏ Set up your very own email signature block, then send an email my way so I can admire it - I can't wait to see what you create!

Find all your templates and swipe files using this link below. You may want to bookmark this page, so you can refer to it as quickly and easily as possible.

⬆ *https://www.eevijones.com/marketing-downloads*

LINKS SHARED:

- *https://www.hubspot.com/email-signature-generator*

CHAPTER 24
Expanding Our Visibility Beyond Amazon

Amazon plays a humongous role in getting our children's books into the world. But our book's long-term visibility doesn't have to live on Amazon alone. It can go well beyond it.

Visibility isn't just about where our book is listed. It's about where *we*, as authors, show up. And that's what this chapter is all about.

In this part of the book, we're going to look at small, intentional things you and I can start doing today to build our author visibility beyond Amazon.

These strategies matter because long-term marketing isn't built on a single platform. It's built on multiple touchpoints, different entry doors, and meaningful ways for people to discover our work in places they already spend time. When our book shows up in classrooms, communities, conversations, and collaborations, it becomes more than just a product - it becomes part of everyday life.

———————■ · ✦ · ■———————

REPURPOSING OUR STORY INTO *TEACHABLES*

This approach isn't about promoting our book *as a book*. Instead, it's about transforming it into something that can be taught, shared, and used.

Nearly every children's book carries a message. Maybe it's about kindness. Maybe it's about courage, friendship, grief, or taking care of the planet.

That message can often be turned into classroom materials or homeschool resources - what I like to call *teachables*.

For example, we could create:

- *a short reading comprehension worksheet*

- *a coloring or craft activity related to our book*
- *or a simple discussion guide that helps teachers and parents talk about the story's theme*

We can offer these as free downloads on our own website, or upload them to a platform like *TeachersPayTeachers.com* (↑) to reach educators who might never have discovered our book otherwise.

This can be incredibly powerful when teachers find our resource *first* and then realize there's a whole picture book that goes with it.

It's a completely different visibility path. Instead of trying to convince readers to buy, we're providing value first and letting curiosity do the rest.

This positions us as a trusted voice around our book's topic and makes our story part of something bigger - a learning experience.

So if you've never thought about it this way before, take a look at your book's theme and ask yourself:

What could I turn into a teachable?

Because sometimes the path to visibility doesn't start on a shelf, but in a classroom.

One of my favorite examples of this type of teachable or learning resource comes from the book *Germs vs. Soap* by one of my readers, Didi Dragon.

WWW.DIDIVSDRAGON.COM

On her website, Didi offers

1. fun sheets to help kids retain what they've learned about germs,
2. charts and how-to sheets, and
3. fact sheets to support her book *Germs vs. Soap*.

Another really powerful example comes from the book *My Super Me*, which I co-wrote with Todd Herman - a *Wall Street Journal* bestselling author and the former performance coach of *Kobe Bryant*.

To support parents using his children's book, Todd created a supplementary video with thoughtful questions parents can ask their children at bedtime, turning reading time into something extra special and deeply personal.

WWW.MYSUPER.ME

Another wonderful example comes from my *Children's Book University*® student Heidi Karlsson, an incredibly talented singer and songwriter.

Heidi's books share beautiful life lessons about things like life's ups and downs, being ourselves, and building confidence. These topics naturally lend themselves to classroom conversations.

Heidi created entire downloadable class packs built around her books. These include the book itself, a lyric video, a song, an audiobook version, a recorded lesson, PDF lesson plans, and more.

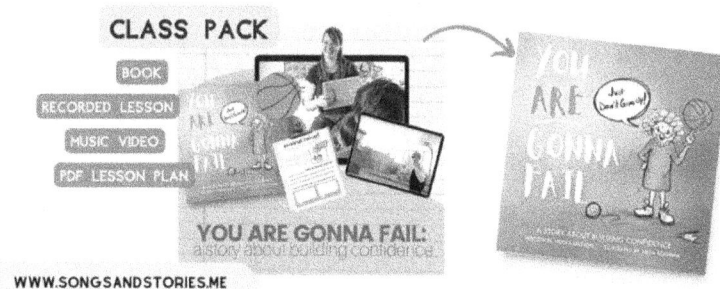

WWW.SONGSANDSTORIES.ME

Some of Heidi's resources are free, like her beautiful songs on YouTube, while others are paid downloadable packages.

I especially love how creative she got with these materials. One of her free class packs even includes a downloadable *Pirate Joke Generator* tied to one of her books. Truly, the sky is the limit here.

NINJA TIP:

If you're creating printables or worksheets, make sure your name and website appear on every page - even if it's just small text at the bottom. That way, every time a teacher shares your resource, your book and brand travel right along with it.

COLLABORATE WITH OTHER AUTHORS & CREATORS

Collaborating with fellow authors and creators can make a big difference when it comes to marketing our children's book.

At its heart, marketing is about connection - and collaboration is one of the most natural ways to create it.

Visibility grows exponentially when we link arms with others who are walking a similar path.

You've probably heard the saying, *"A rising tide lifts all boats."* That's exactly what collaboration is. When we team up with other authors or creators, we get to share audiences, ideas, and energy.

And everyone involved benefits.

Let's look at a few examples that work beautifully, especially for us children's authors.

- **JOINT STORYTIME EVENT:**

  You could team up with another local author to host a joint storytime event - one where each of you reads your book and then, together, host a shared Q&A or craft activity. Parents love this because it feels like a mini author festival. And it takes half the effort because you're doing it together.

- **INSTAGRAM LIVE:**

  You and an illustrator friend could host a short Instagram Live where you talk about why you wrote your beautiful children's book and how you brought stories and art together. It's casual, fun, and gives both of your audiences a peek behind the curtain.

- **MINI GIVEAWAY:**

  You could even collaborate across genres. Maybe your children's book is about mindfulness, and someone else creates guided meditations for kids. You could host a collaboration post or mini giveaway where readers who follow both of you can win a signed copy of your book and access to one of those meditations.

  That way, you're each reaching brand-new audiences who already trust you and the person you're collaborating with.

The beauty of collaboration is that it's never competitive. If we're choosing the right partners, we simply complement each other.

And here's something I've seen time and again: collaborations often open unexpected doors.

Maybe an author you collaborate with later recommends you for a podcast or introduces you to a local bookstore owner.

Those ripples keep expanding.

So if you're feeling a bit invisible, don't isolate yourself. Instead, connect. Reach out to one or two fellow authors whose work you admire and say something as simple as:

> *"Hey, I'd love to do something fun together to support each other's books. Would you be open to brainstorming ideas?"*

That's it. Start small. You'll be amazed how many people are eager to join forces.

NINJA TIP:

When collaborating with others, always tag and celebrate the other person generously - both in your posts and in your stories. That spirit of generosity is what makes people want to work with you again and again.

Collaboration is one of the fastest, most heart-centered ways to grow our visibility, because it's not about chasing followers. It's about creating genuine, lasting connections.

And in the wonderful world of children's books, that's what visibility is really all about.

———————— • ◆ • ————————

GETTING OUR BOOK INTO RETAIL STORES

Getting our beautiful children's book into retail stores is one of the most powerful visibility methods available to us as authors. And I'm not just talking about bookstores here, although those are wonderful too.

I mean *any* retail store.

Gift shops, children's boutiques, toy stores, coffee shops, hospital gift stores, and museum shops.

When it comes to retail stores, here's one important thing to remember:

 People who walk into physical stores are already in a buying mindset.

And when our book is sitting on a shelf right alongside locally made items or adorable gifts, it naturally becomes part of that buying experience.

Now, you might be wondering: if your book is already available on Amazon - the largest online book retailer in the world - what are the benefits of getting your beautiful children's book into physical stores in the first place?

Here are a few reasons why this can be such a meaningful piece of your marketing puzzle.

1. **People that go to stores are already in a buying mindset**
   Shoppers who visit physical stores are often ready to make a purchase. By having your

book on a shelf, you're placing it in front of people who are actively looking for new and interesting items - especially parents, caregivers, and gift-givers who are naturally drawn to children's books.

2. **Less competition**
While online platforms like Amazon are saturated with millions of books, local stores typically offer curated selections. This means far less competition. Your book has a greater chance of standing out in a smaller, more focused environment, without having to compete against thousands of similar titles.

3. **Supporting local businesses**
By getting your book into local stores, you're not just expanding your own reach - you're also supporting the local economy. Many customers intentionally choose independent shops, and this sense of community often leads to long-term loyalty for both you and the store.

4. **Increased visibility and brand recognition**
Being stocked in local stores exposes your book to people who may never have searched for it online. Every time someone picks up and holds your physical book, your visibility grows. That familiarity can lead to word-of-mouth recommendations and future sales, both online and offline.

5. **Opportunities for in-person connections**
Local stores often open the door to in-person events, such as book signings, readings, or community gatherings. These face-to-face interactions help us build genuine connections, grow a local following, and can even lead to future opportunities like school visits or collaborations.

6. **Boosts credibility and legitimacy**
Having your book carried by respected local retailers adds credibility to your work. Being featured in physical stores sends a quiet but powerful message that your book is worthy of shelf space, helping to validate your work in the eyes of readers and other businesses alike.

7. **Diversifies revenue streams**
Selling your book through retail stores creates additional revenue channels, especially when your book is placed in high-traffic locations like gift shops, toy stores, or boutiques. It can even support your online sales, as people who discover your book in stores may later look it up or recommend it to others.

8. **A dream come true**
And lastly, seeing your book on a shelf in a physical store is the realization of a dream many children's authors have carried with them since the moment they first began writing their stories.

Taken together, these reasons beautifully illustrate why retail stores are such a valuable avenue for us children's authors when it comes to marketing and long-term visibility.

THE SECRET TO SUCCESS

The secret to success with getting our book into retail stores lies in preparation. Our goal isn't simply to convince a store to carry our book. It's to make it easy for them to say yes.

That means taking the time to ensure our book aligns beautifully with the store's audience. In many ways, successful retail outreach isn't really about our book at all - it's about the store, its customers, and how our story complements what they already love.

Timing matters, too. When our outreach feels thoughtful, relevant, and well-timed - such as around holidays, local events, or seasonal themes - our chances of hearing that wonderful little "yes" increase dramatically.

When reaching out to potential stores, I always like to keep these guiding principles in mind:

1. It's about relationships, not transactions
When we reach out to retailers, we're not asking for shelf space. We're starting a relationship. The goal isn't to push our book into a store, but to introduce something that genuinely adds value to their customers. Approaching outreach with kindness, curiosity, and respect changes everything.

2. Preparation is your superpower
A retailer's easiest yes comes when we've done our homework. Learning about their shop, their audience, and the products they already carry shows care and professionalism. That thoughtfulness builds trust.

3. Focus on fit over force
Our book isn't meant for every store, and that's okay. The most successful authors don't try to convince everyone. They look for alignment. When a book's theme, tone, or message fits naturally with a store's vibe, lasting partnerships follow.

4. Make it easy to say yes
Store owners are busy. The easier we make the process, the better. That might mean having wholesale information ready, professional images on hand, or a *One-Sheet* (see chapter 16) that answers common questions at a glance. Simplicity builds confidence.

5. Timing is everything
Reaching out ahead of the holidays, before local festivals, or during relevant seasons can make a huge difference. When our outreach feels timely, it feels helpful rather than intrusive.

6. Outreach is ongoing
Getting into stores isn't a one-time effort. It's an evolving process. A "no" today doesn't mean

"never." Staying in touch, celebrating milestones, or reconnecting when you release a new title can turn polite passes into future yeses.

When we view outreach through this lens - relationships, preparation, fit, ease, timing, and consistency - it stops feeling intimidating and starts feeling like a natural extension of sharing our work.

Now, I know this part can feel a bit intimidating.

I hear from so many authors who dream of seeing their book in stores but aren't sure which retailers to contact, how to approach owners, or what to say.

If you'd like to go deeper and map out a personalized outreach strategy, I've created a workbook called *How to Get Your Children's Book Into Any Store* (↑). It walks you step by step through preparing your outreach, crafting your messages, and tracking your progress.

It's a workbook specifically designed to guide you through reaching out to bookstores and relevant retailers, showing you exactly how to approach them and make it easy for them to say yes to carrying your book.

It's a hands-on, step-by-step guide that walks you through:

- *how to select the right stores,*
- *how to write and personalize outreach emails,*
- *how to craft a thoughtful follow-up strategy, and*
- *how to confidently build your own retail network over time.*

It's the exact process I've used myself, filled with templates, examples, and tools to make the process approachable and even fun.

I chose the workbook format because it allows us to create our very own strategy as we learn.

You don't need this workbook to benefit from what we've covered here. Everything you need to understand the *why* and the big picture is already in these pages. But if you enjoy hands-on tools and want extra guidance, it's there for you whenever you're ready.

If you've been dreaming of seeing your beautiful book displayed on an actual store shelf, this workbook can help you make it happen.

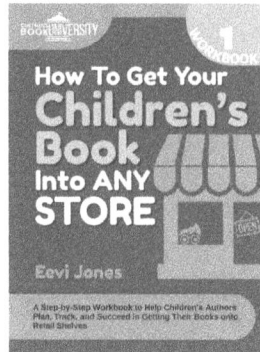

YOUR OWN STOREFRONT - THE INGRAMSPARK STORE

One of the most exciting new developments for children's book authors is IngramSpark's *Ecommerce Storefront* feature - a built-in way for us to sell our hardcover books (and paperbacks) directly through IngramSpark, with no middleman, and earn significantly higher royalties in the process.

Because IngramSpark allows the printing of hardcovers with as few as 18 pages, it's currently the best print-on-demand (POD) option for most children's authors when it comes to hardcovers.

Until recently, IngramSpark only offered three channels for our print-on-demand (POD) hardcovers:

1. **Author Copies:** We could purchase our own books at printing cost (plus shipping) for events or direct sales.
2. **Online Marketplaces:** IngramSpark would list our book on websites like Amazon, Walmart, or Barnes & Noble's *online* stores (not their physical locations).
3. **Wholesale Orders:** Bookstores and libraries could order directly through Ingram's wholesale network, using a wholesale discount we set (usually 40–55%).

Those were the only available options. Until now.

A fourth channel has been added: the IngramSpark direct *Ecommerce* option - and it's a true game changer.

IngramSpark's *Ecommerce* feature allows us, as authors, to create a direct purchase link for our book. This link leads to a professional sales page hosted by IngramSpark, where readers can order directly, without requiring a retailer middleman like Amazon.

Here's what this new feature allows us to do:

- Generate a **unique link** for each book
- Set your **royalty amount**, which automatically determines the purchase price
- Share your book via a direct **URL**, a **QR code**, or an **HTML** embed for your website
- Set **time limits** or **quantity limits** for special promotions
- **Track sales** directly within your IngramSpark dashboard

! In other words, this feature turns your IngramSpark account into your very own online storefront - one that requires no additional setup, shopping cart, or payment processing.

This isn't just a convenience. It's a powerful marketing advantage that helps us keep more of each sale while building stronger connections with our readers.

NINJA TIP:

Think of this as your own online bookstore, powered by IngramSpark, but branded by *you*.

Being able to sell directly through IngramSpark matters because:

- **Increased royalties:** When selling through a third-party marketplace such as Amazon, IngramSpark currently requires a minimum 40% wholesale discount for U.S. sales. For example, if our hardcover costs $8.30 to print and is priced at $16, royalties through Amazon might be only around **$1.14 per copy.**

  When selling directly through your IngramSpark storefront, however, there's no wholesale discount - only an ecommerce fee (currently $3.50). That same $16 book would earn roughly **$4.20 per sale.** That's nearly **four times more income per book**.

  This difference adds up quickly, especially for authors who already have an audience or an email list.

- **Full control and flexibility:** You decide when and where to share your link - whether that's for a limited-time offer, a holiday promotion, or a launch event. You can even set start and end dates for each campaign link.

USING OUR INGRAMSPARK STOREFRONT STRATEGICALLY

To earn the highest possible royalties, we need to be intentional about *when* we share *which* link, and *where* we send readers.

You may be wondering:

"Eevi, if my hardcover royalties are much higher when people purchase directly from my IngramSpark storefront, should I still link to my hardcover on Amazon? Should I still sell my IngramSpark-printed hardcover there at all?"

My answer is yes.

I still recommend offering and linking to your hardcover on Amazon, even though the royalty is lower. And here's why:

Exposure - especially for brand-new authors - is still everything. Amazon is a massive search engine filled with people actively looking to buy books. Having all available formats listed there helps readers who don't yet know you or your book discover it. At the very least, it signals that a hardcover edition exists.

At the same time, we absolutely want to add our direct IngramSpark links to places where *we already have a relationship* with our audience.

Doing so allows us:

1. to share direct links with people who already know us
2. and to create additional pathways for discovery through Google searches

To truly optimize this, we'll want to place our direct hardcover links anywhere we're already sharing Amazon links, such as:

1. on our author website (alongside our Amazon link)
2. in our email signature
3. with our launch team
4. in social media bios or posts
5. as a QR code at book fairs or events

Each of these placements makes it easy for readers to support you directly, while still providing a smooth, professional checkout experience.

This pairing allows you to benefit from Amazon's massive visibility while earning more from readers who choose to buy directly. You get the best of both worlds:

Maximum Exposure + Maximum Royalties

HOW TO SET UP OUR INGRAMSPARK STOREFRONT

Setting up your IngramSpark storefront takes only a few minutes.

NOTE: IngramSpark occasionally updates its dashboard layout. While your screen may look slightly different from the examples shown here, the overall steps and options remain the same.

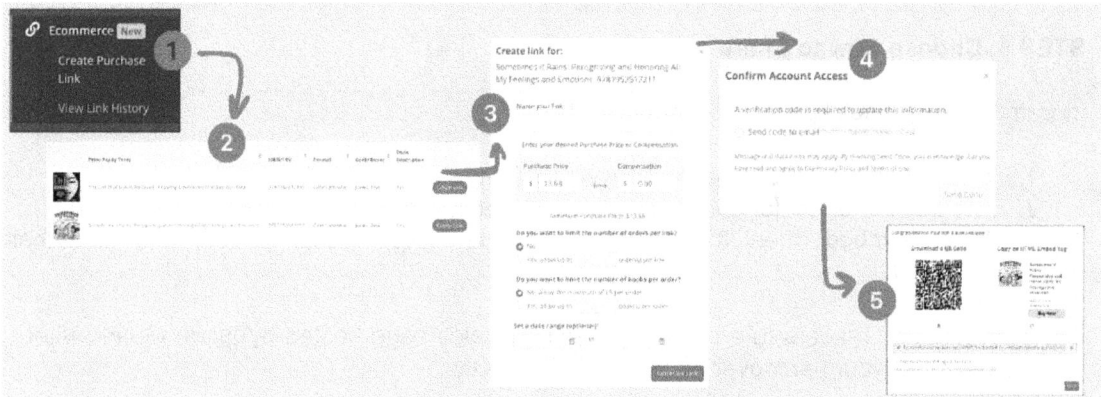

STEP 1: Log in to Your IngramSpark Dashboard

Go to *www.ingramspark.com* and sign in to your account. Once logged in, you'll see an **Ecommerce** tab on the left-hand side of your dashboard. This is where you'll create your direct sales links.

STEP 2: Select Your Book

Click on **Ecommerce**, and a list of your approved print titles will appear. Choose the book you'd like to sell directly.

STEP 3: Create a New Link

Click **Create Link**. A pop-up window will appear where you can:

- **name the link** (for internal tracking, such as "Website Link" or "Holiday Promo")
- **set your compensation** by entering how much you'd like to earn per copy. IngramSpark will automatically calculate the retail price based on your print cost and fees.

You can also:

- limit the **number of orders** per link
- limit the **number of books** per order
- set **start and end dates** if you want the link active only for a specific time (for a launch window or limited offer).

STEP 4: Verify and Generate Your Link

Once your settings are complete, IngramSpark will send a verification code to your email. Enter that code to confirm, and your direct sales link will be created instantly.

STEP 5: Choose How to Share Your Link

IngramSpark provides three built-in sharing options:

1. **Direct URL:** Copy and paste it anywhere (emails, social posts, newsletters).
2. **QR Code:** Perfect for print materials, event tables, or business cards.
3. **HTML Embed:** Ideal for adding a "Buy Hardcover" button directly to your author website.

Each option leads readers to a clean, professional sales page hosted by IngramSpark, where visitors can order your hardcover (or paperback) directly.

NINJA TIP:

Create a unique link for each platform (website, newsletter, Instagram, etc.).

This allows you to track exactly where your sales are coming from and where to focus your marketing energy.

Before this new feature, only you (the author) and official wholesalers could order books directly from IngramSpark. Now, anyone can.

That means you can send readers, schools, or even local gift shops directly to your book - no Amazon, no middleman, and significantly higher royalties for you.

This new storefront option is simple, smart, and strategic. It allows us to treat our IngramSpark account not just as a printer or distributor, but as our very own bookstore on the web.

———————— • ◆ • ————————

GETTING ATTENTION THROUGH BOOK AWARDS

When it comes to marketing, two of the questions I get asked quite often are (1) whether entering book awards is a marketing strategy worth investing in, and (2) which book awards I would recommend.

PLEASE NOTE: My take on book awards may be a bit controversial, but my goal is always to be completely honest with you.

In this part of the book, we're going to look at:

- what a children's book award is
- a very candid look at what a book award can and cannot do for your children's book
- how to choose the best ones for your children's book
- how we can leverage a win
- and finally, what you will want to look out for and stay away from

I have won a number of different awards, from awards for the illustrations in my books, to poetry awards for the poetry in my books, all the way to awards where books were judged in their entirety.

WHAT IS A CHILDREN'S BOOK AWARD?

A book award is usually an annual recognition of exceptional works within the literary world.

Books are entered into different categories, such as genres like poetry, biographies, and children's books, as well as specific elements or components of a book, such as illustrations.

Some awards are absolutely free, while others require an entry fee, usually per category you submit your book into.

Depending on the award, books may be entered or nominated via the publisher directly, or by authors themselves. Some require that the book has been published within the last year, while others are open to older books as well.

Each award has a judging panel whose members read and consider the submitted books, and then announce longlists, finalists, and winners for each category. Prizes depend on the award. They can range from monetary prizes to service prizes such as mentions in a prestigious publication, marketing support, and even potential representation by an agent.

Each book is judged among books in the same category. So if you enter your children's book, you would compete only with other children's books, not with other genres.

For children's books specifically, many awards now also offer sub-categories such as graphic novels, picture books, and young adult.

Some of the bigger awards have in-person ceremonies, while others simply recognize winners online.

There are hundreds of different book awards out there, each with their own submission guidelines, requirements, and deadlines. Most select winners once a year.

And so, I often get asked whether it is worth it to enter our books into awards and contests. I want to share my thoughts and personal findings with you, so you can make an informed decision about whether entering an award or contest makes sense for you and your children's book, and how and if you can benefit from holding an award-winning title.

So let's look at what a book award can and cannot do for your children's book.

WHAT IS THE PURPOSE OF BOOK AWARDS?

When it comes to the purpose of book awards and contests, opinions often differ from person to person. So what follows is based on my own opinion and my own experiences.

Despite what many book award websites claim, here are three things winning an award will likely **NOT** do for you:

1. **Winning an award will most likely not increase your book sales.** While a win *can* create a temporary spike in sales, that's often mostly due to you sharing the win with friends and family on social media.

2. **Winning an award usually does not capture the attention of traditional publishing houses.** There are simply too many awards, and publishers typically do not have the time to track or review them all.

3. **Winning an award usually will not make you well-known throughout the author world.** Most authors who enter awards are focused on their own books. While they may glance at the list of winners, it's relatively rare that they then go out and purchase those books.

There are exceptions, of course. But these are the observations I've made over the years, especially when it comes to children's books.

So if it doesn't increase our book sales, why might we still consider submitting our beautiful work anyway?

ADVANTAGES THAT BOOK AWARDS MAY PROVIDE

Here, the answer depends on what *you*, the author, are hoping to get out of this. What are your main reasons for entering your book into an award?

There are three main things winning a contest, or receiving a title or status, **can** do for you. These are also the reasons why I still enter certain books of mine into awards:

1. **REASON 1:** It can give your book a level of credibility. This depends greatly on the award you choose, and how well-known and accepted it is within the author community and beyond.

2. **REASON 2:** It allows you to showcase your win, which can help set you apart from other children's authors.

3. **REASON 3:** It can bring recognition and validation. It's always meaningful to be recognized for the hard work we pour into our books.

For better or worse, people love social proof. Winning an award validates our work through an outside source, letting others know it isn't just us who believe our book has the potential to impact little ones.

Now, you may have noticed that I said I enter only certain books of mine into awards. While I've written and ghostwritten more than 70 children's books, I enter only a select few into contests. That doesn't mean I don't love and believe in my other books. But like everyone else, I have a budget set aside for things like this, and I try to stick to it.

NINJA TIP:

One of the best pieces of advice I can give you here is to set an awards budget for yourself and stick to it.

Given that there are so many different book awards out there, how should we choose the right children's book award? Let's look at that next.

HOW TO CHOOSE THE RIGHT CHILDREN'S BOOK AWARD

Because there are so many awards out there, there are six questions we'll want to ask ourselves before entering any book award:

QUESTION 1: *What audience does the award site cater to?*

It's important to remember that many contest and award sites are visited mostly by fellow authors. The most beneficial ones, however, are used as a source for other sites and platforms that pull reputable, vetted books.

Just like viewers look to the Oscars or the Grammys to see what movies or songs are worth watching or listening to, so too can an award function as a signal for our books.

The *Mom's Choice Awards*, for example, aren't just for other authors. Their audience can include mom bloggers and sites that are actively looking to feature the best, newest, and already vetted products in different categories.

QUESTION 2: *Does this award offer a children's book category?*

Not all award programs include a dedicated children's book category. When reviewing awards, we want to make sure there is a category that truly aligns with our book's age range, format, and genre.

QUESTION 3: *What other books have previously participated and won this award?*

This is a great criteria to pay attention to. Look for professional-looking work, because we are who we surround ourselves with. Reviewing previous winners is one of the best ways to gauge the quality of an award.

QUESTION 4: *Who is this award associated with or sponsored by?*

A reputable sponsor can be a fantastic credibility booster. The *IRDA Award*, for example, is sponsored by organizations such as Amazon, IngramSpark, and Kirkus Reviews, and had its 2018 winners announced at BookCon in New York City, which I was so lucky to attend as a recipient.

QUESTION 5: *How reputable is this book award?*

Does the award's title speak to me? Besides their own website, who else mentions this award? Are there credible sites that cover it? Does it appear on reputable lists of awards?

QUESTION 6: *Does the award name reference Indie Books or Self-Published Books?*

This question can be controversial, and it depends on your goals.

I personally like to enter contests that include all kinds of books, meaning self-published books, hybrid books, and traditionally published books.

The reason is that if the contest includes traditionally published entries as well, it often carries more weight across the wider publishing world. So I tend to be cautious with awards that include words like "indie" or "self-published," because that can imply they don't include traditionally published titles.

That said, I decide case by case. *The IRDA (IndieReader Discovery Awards)* I mentioned earlier does include the word "Indie," but I chose to enter it anyway because the benefits were strong, including an in-person award ceremony in New York City.

As long as you're clear on your goals and why you're entering any given award, you now have a helpful set of guidelines to base your decisions on.

Now, I mentioned earlier that winning an award can help with credibility, so let's look at how we can leverage a win.

WHERE TO DISPLAY YOUR BEAUTIFUL WIN

As an award-winning children's book author, you'll want to display your win proudly. Here are a few ways to make the most of it:

LEVERAGE 1: *Add your newly won title to your Amazon author profile.*

The below author bio is one of my own. The first sentence reads:

> "German-Vietnamese-born children's book author Eevi Jones is a *USA Today* & *Wall Street Journal* bestselling and award-winning writer, and the founder of *Children's Book University*®."

I made sure to include this badge of honor right away.

Eevi Jones

German-Vietnamese-born children's author Eevi Jones is a USA Today & Wall Street Journal bestselling & award-winning writer, and the founder of Children's Book University®. Writing and ghostwriting under a number of pen names, Eevi has authored more than 40 children's books.

She's been featured in media outlets such as Forbes, Business Insider, Huffington Post, Scary Mommy, EOFire, Kindlepreneur, EP Magazine, SCBWI, and more.

Eevi lives near D.C. with her husband and two children.

Her award-winning books can be found online at www.BravingTheWorldBooks.com.

Follow

LEVERAGE 2: *Weave it into your book description.*

In the example below, I wrote:

> "Help your little ones discover the magic of thinking big and being brave with this *Mom's Choice Awards GOLD Award*-winning book by *USA Today & Wall Street Journal* best-selling author Eevi Jones."

Here too, I mention the award right away.

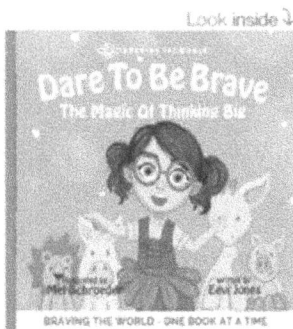

Dare To Be Brave: The Magic Of Thinking Big (Braving The World)

Book 2 of 5: Braving The World

See all formats and editions

Kindle	Hardcover	Paperback
$1.99	$16.00	$9.97
Read with Our Free App	5 Used from $5.18 7 New from $16.00	1 New from $9.97

Help your little ones discover the magic of thinking big and being brave with this Mom's Choice Awards® GOLD Award-winning book by *USA Today & Wall Street Journal* best-selling author Eevi Jones.

Meet Sally O'Nelly,
a brave little girl.
Freckled and kind,
out to take on the world.

LEVERAGE 3: *Add it to your About page on your website.*

Here is another example of mine. It's similar to my Amazon bio, but a bit longer since it's on my own site.

Born in former East Germany to a German mother and a Vietnamese father, Eevi Jones is a *USA Today & Wall Street Journal* bestselling writer & multi-award-winning children's author. Writing under a number of pen names, she has authored and ghostwritten more than 50 children's books that highlight, embrace, and celebrate kids' unique traits and interests.

As the founder of Children's Book University, Eevi has made it her mission to help driven and aspiring children's book authors write.

LEVERAGE 4: *Include your win anywhere else you mention that you are a children's author.*

This could include your LinkedIn profile, Instagram, Facebook, or Goodreads. Here is my Instagram profile, where I mention that I am an award-winning children's author.

Children's Book University®
Public figure
USA Today & WSJ Bestselling Writer
✳ Award-Winning Children's Author
◎ Supporter of Aspiring Kid's Authors
▨east coast living | ▬ born | ▨ roots
www.eevijones.com/vip

You've worked so hard for this, and it's absolutely worth celebrating. Sharing your win on social media allows your friends and family to celebrate right alongside you, so don't be shy about sharing your beautiful news.

Now, with all of that being said, I also want to share what you'll want to look out for and stay away from when researching awards.

WHAT TO LOOK OUT FOR AND STAY AWAY FROM

RED FLAG 1: *Being reached out to*

I've seen many instances where someone creates an award and promotes it heavily on social media, often in Facebook groups.

I urge you to be cautious with award organizers who approach you directly. Legitimate awards with established reputations generally do not recruit entries inside places like Facebook groups.

RED FLAG 2: *Awards that occur more than once a year*

In many cases, you'll also want to be cautious with paid awards that occur multiple times per year. Most legitimate awards run annually.

There are exceptions, of course. But if it's a smaller paid award that isn't widely known, I would think twice before entering.

RED FLAG 3: *No list of previous winners*

Be cautious with paid awards that do not list previous winners. New ones pop up all the time. Do your research using the six questions above, especially when money is involved.

Now, while there are hundreds of book awards to choose from, I wanted to help you get started by putting together a list of awards and contests specifically for children's authors, so the task of finding and choosing the best ones becomes a bit more manageable. You can find them them among the other resources for this book (↟).

————————— • ✦ • —————————

GIFTING AS A MARKETING STRATEGY

If you've ever thought about gifting your beautiful children's book (which I truly hope you have!), the next few pages are for you. They'll help you make the absolute most of every gifting opportunity.

We will look at:

1. **WHY** gifting our book can be such a powerful marketing strategy
2. **WHEN** to gift our book, meaning the different possible occasions
3. **HOW** to gift our book to truly make the most of this opportunity
4. **WHOM** to gift our book

WHY GIFT YOUR BOOK?

Why should we, as children's authors, consider gifting our book to others? How can giving our book away for free be a marketing strategy?

When it comes to gifting our book, my very first and biggest NINJA TIP is all about mindset.

The beauty of this *strategic investment* is that it usually costs us only a copy of our book. The two main reasons for gifting our book are to:

- **increase awareness** that we have written a children's book
- potentially **receive more reviews**

If you're anything like me, you may feel a bit shy about letting others know that you're a children's author. One of the biggest advantages of gifting our book is that it lets people discover this fact without any awkward sales pitching.

And asking for a review after having gifted our book so generously often feels much less uncomfortable, because the pressure of "selling" is no longer there.

WHEN SHOULD WE GIFT OUR BOOK?

The short answer is: **any time**. Any time is a good time.

- When a niece or nephew in our target age group has a birthday.
- When a neighbor's child is celebrating a birthday.
- During holidays when gifting is customary, such as Christmas or Easter.
- And if our book's topic aligns with a holiday where gifting *isn't* usually expected, that's often exactly when we *should* gift it. For example, if our book is about a big, round turkey, gifting it around Thanksgiving is perfect, even though gift exchanges don't typically happen then.
- The same applies to everyday milestones. If our book is about the tooth fairy and a neighbor's child just lost their first tooth, what a perfect moment to gift it.
- Calendar-driven milestones work beautifully, too. The end of the school year, for instance, is always a wonderful gifting opportunity, no matter the topic of our book.

So when it comes to timing, the sky is the limit. Any time is a good time to gift our book.

HOW SHOULD WE GIFT OUR BOOK?

Many authors gift their book without much thought or presentation. But here's where we can do something different. Let's make every gifting moment special and memorable. Because this too is part of our branding.

This doesn't have to cost much, and it may cost nothing at all if we use items we already have on hand. What it *does* take is a bit of planning.

I like to focus on two things:

- *the wrapping*
- *the note we include*

One of my favorite ways to wrap books is with neutral, season-less wrapping paper that I can use year-round. Then I accessorize it with something seasonal or something that ties into the book's theme.

For example:

- If our book contains a recipe, we could add a little cookie cutter. This would also work beautifully for books gifted during the Christmas season.
- If our book is about a dog, we could include a small dog biscuit.
- If our book is about a speedy little car, we could glue a tiny toy car on top of the wrapping paper.
- And if our book is about a playful little cat, we could wrap a bit of yarn around the paper-wrapped book.

The possibilities are truly endless.

No matter how we gift our book, there are two things we always want to include:

- **SIGN YOUR BOOK.** I have dedicated an entire section to why signing our books matters, along with many heartfelt examples of how to do it. Be sure to visit chapter 21 for inspiration.

- **ADD A CARD OR NOTE.** Always include a separate card or note wishing the recipient a happy birthday, happy holidays, or whatever the occasion may be.

Here, our note could even directly mention and ask for a review, like in this example:

"Samantha,

I'm so excited to share my book with you and hope it brings you as much joy as it brought me to write it. If you enjoy the story and feel inspired, it would mean the world to me if you could leave a quick review on Amazon. Your feedback helps others discover the book, and I truly appreciate your support. Happy reading!

Eevi"

To make it even easier, we can include a QR code that leads directly to the book's review page on Amazon.

If asking right away doesn't feel right, we can always follow up later, either after the recipient reaches out to thank us, or with a thoughtful message some time after they've had a chance to read the book.

Here's an example of a follow-up message:

"Hi Samantha,

I hope you and Max have enjoyed reading "Sometimes It Rains" together over the holidays! It was such a joy to create, and I truly hope it brought some smiles to your day.

If the story resonated with you and Max, I'd be so grateful if you could share your thoughts as a quick review over on Amazon. Reviews go such a long way in helping others discover the book.

Thank you so much for your support, and wishing you and your loved ones a wonderful start to the new year!

xo ~ Eevi

P.S. To make it as easy as possible, I've added this link <u>right here</u> that takes you directly to the review page."

WHOM SHOULD WE GIFT OUR BOOK TO?

I like to think about gifting recipients in groups.

GROUP 1: *Teachers & Administrators*

Teachers and school administrators are often the very first people that come to mind. If we have school-aged children, our book makes a wonderful end-of-school-year gift. Teachers may:

1. *add it to their classroom library*
2. *add it to the school library*
3. *take it home to read with their own children*

Either way, it's a win.

NINJA TIP:

Don't forget administrators and support staff. I always include a book in their gift bag as well.

GROUP 2: *Workers*

The second group that comes to mind are all the wonderful workers around us.

If we have yard workers who come by regularly, or a weekly or monthly cleaning crew, and we know they have children, gifting them our book is such a thoughtful way to show our appreciation.

Sharing our book this way may seem like a small gesture, but it can leave a lasting impression. So don't hesitate to gift your beautiful book to the people who come and work in or around your home.

GROUP 3: *Colleagues*

The third group we could be gifting our book to are our colleagues, co-workers, and employees we get to see and work with every day.

Our place of work is such a huge and wonderful pool to dip into. So whether we gift our book directly to someone we're working with, or make our book part of a Secret Santa or White

Elephant gift exchange that our office may be hosting each year, either option provides a wonderful opportunity to share our book.

GROUP 4: *School Bus Drivers*

The fourth group we could be gifting our book to are school bus drivers. This is such a wonderful opportunity, especially if we have school-aged children who take the bus to school.

More often than not, parents already gift a little something to the bus driver, so why not make it our book? And if we usually don't get anything for our son's or daughter's bus driver, even better - because this gesture will stand out even more.

Now, if we don't know whether or not our bus driver has children of their own, we shouldn't let this stop us. Here, we could always say something like this on our card:

"Dear Mr. Todd,

Reading together creates such cherished memories, so I hope you'll enjoy sharing this book with a special little one in your life. Happy Holidays! The Jones Family"

That way, we imply that they can read it with their own children, or share it (and even gift it) to someone else if they don't have children themselves. This is such a versatile message that we could use in any of these situations, no matter whom we are gifting our book to.

And because we will also sign our book along with a special note, the recipient will know that it was us who authored this book.

GROUP 5: *Groups & Coaches*

Whether it's our kids' soccer coach, their swim school, martial arts studio, tumble class, or music class, these are all perfect places to share our beautiful children's book.

Why? Because these are opportunities where just one gifted copy has the potential to reach multiple families. And who knows where that may lead.

If our book's topic ties into any of these environments, even better. For example, if our book is about persistence, we could mention that when gifting it to a swim coach. Or if our book is about martial arts and the lessons this sport teaches, we could share it with a martial arts studio so it can live in the waiting room, where parents and younger siblings often spend time during class.

And if we become close with the other families in our kids' activities, we could even gift each of them their own copy, multiplying our chances of receiving reviews.

These groups don't have to be limited to our kids' activities, either. Knitting groups, yoga groups, pickleball groups, and even Bible study groups are all wonderful opportunities. Most of these groups' members have at least one little one in their lives.

GROUP 6: *Doctors & Dentists*

Group number six we could be gifting our book to are doctors', dentists', and veterinarians' offices.

Remember - gifting our book doesn't have to be limited to holidays. We could bring a copy along to an annual checkup or appointment. This works for all children's books, but if our book's topic relates to the setting, even better.

For example, a tooth fairy book is perfect for a dentist's office. Or if our book is about dogs, why not gift a copy to our vet to be shared in the waiting area?

And this is where one of my favorite gifting-related NINJA TIPS comes in.

NINJA TIP:

It's all about how we frame things.

For example, my reader Didi Dragon's book *Germs vs. Soap* is perfect for a doctor's waiting room. But instead of asking whether it would be okay to place a copy in the waiting area, we could simply gift the book as a way to educate and entertain their young visitors.

That way, it's not a favor we're asking for. It becomes a thoughtful gesture we're extending - and that subtle shift changes everything.

Germs vs. Soap: A Silly Hygiene Book about Washing Hands! (Hilarious Hygiene Battle) Paperback – June 29, 2020
by Didi Dragon (Author), Hannah Robinett (Illustrator)
4.6 ★★★★☆   1,620 ratings

GROUP 7 : *Delivery Drivers*

Group number seven we could be gifting our book to are our neighborhood mail carriers or delivery drivers.

Many of us are fortunate enough to have the same driver year after year. Every year, I like to gift something small, like chocolate or a gift card. And whenever I know someone has children or grandchildren, I love including one of my books as well.

In my neighborhood, for example, we used to have the most wonderful mailman named Robert. He's retired now, but every year he still stops by during our neighborhood Halloween parade to catch up with everyone. Over the years, my family gifted him many books, and he still brings them up during those visits because he loved sharing them with his grandchildren.

GROUP 8 : *Neighbors*

And finally, group number eight we could be gifting our book to is our neighbors. This is another big one, because there is so much potential here.

Every morning at my youngest son's bus stop, there are often 10 to 15 kids, each accompanied by an adult. On the last school day before winter break, I like to gift everyone a small bag with one of my books, while others bring cookies or hot chocolate mixes.

And even if we don't have school-aged kids, neighborhoods are still full of opportunities. Many communities have Little Free Libraries, where people can take a book and leave a book. There are now more than 175,000 of these libraries in over 121 countries. Why not share our book there?

www.LittleFreeLibrary.org

Remember that the two main reasons for gifting our books are to:

1. **Increase awareness** that we have written a children's book
2. Potentially **receive more reviews**

I have received so many reviews through gifting my books in this exact way. So when it comes to gifting, one incredibly important NINJA TIP is this:

We can ask for a review directly in the card or note we include with our book, or we can follow up later, like in the sample email script shared earlier.

Letting others know what a review would mean to us - and to the success of our book - is incredibly important. Most people simply don't realize how helpful reviews are, or how difficult they can be to come by.

There truly are endless opportunities to gift our book intentionally. People around us are often genuinely excited when they learn that we've written and published a children's book. So let's lean into that excitement and allow ourselves to share it.

Being a children's author is about making an impact in the lives of little ones. And so often, we try to reach audiences far away - people we don't know.

But what if we also looked around us? What if we focused on the beautiful people already in our lives? The ones who support us, serve us, and walk alongside us every day?

Especially during the holiday season, gifting our book can be a way to let our story touch the lives that are already touching ours.

I hope that these examples have sparked your creativity and inspired you to start building your own list of people you'd love to gift your beautiful book to - not just as a kind gesture, but as a meaningful way to share your story and make a lasting impact.

———————•✦•———————

When we expand our reach beyond Amazon, we're not just selling a book. We're placing our story into real spaces, real conversations, and real hands. Each classroom resource, collaboration, storefront, award, or gifted copy becomes another touchpoint - another way our book can be discovered, remembered, and shared.

These efforts compound over time. One small action leads to another, and before we know it, our story is traveling in ways we could never orchestrate online alone.

Because meaningful marketing isn't about being everywhere. It's about showing up with purpose - and letting our beautiful children's book find its way into the world, one thoughtful connection at a time.

———————•✦•———————

YOUR TO DOs FOR THIS CHAPTER:

- ❏ Decide which of these marketing strategies you would like to give a try
- ❏ Access and download your curated list of book awards

Find all your templates and swipe files using this link below. You may want to bookmark this page, so you can refer to it as quickly and easily as possible.

⬆ *https://www.eevijones.com/marketing-downloads*

LINKS SHARED:

- *https://www.teacherspayteachers.com*
- *https://www.ingramspark.com*

CHAPTER 25
Meeting Your Audience Face-to-Face

Some of the most meaningful, effective, and lasting marketing we will ever do happens face-to-face - in shared spaces.

Children's books are deeply human. They are meant to be held, read aloud, shared, laughed over, and remembered. And while online marketing plays an important role in our journey, there is something uniquely powerful about meeting our audience in real life. When we show up in the same room as our readers, their families, educators, and community members, our book stops being just a product and becomes an experience.

Face-to-face marketing allows us to create unforgettable moments.

In this chapter, we'll explore several powerful ways to meet our readers where they already are. Each of these opportunities looks different, but they all share the same goal - putting our book into the hands of the people it was written for, in a way that feels natural, meaningful, and sustainable.

If we are willing to step into these spaces, to share our story in person, and to meet our audience face-to-face, we give our book something no algorithm ever can - a memory.

And that is where some of the most powerful marketing begins.

———————— •✦• ————————

BOOK SIGNING

If you've ever wondered whether a book signing event is right for you and your beautiful children's book, then the next few pages are for you.

A book signing is something we, as children's authors, should organize and experience at least once.

I have attended so many wonderful book signings over the years, including events hosted by *New York Times* bestselling authors like Gretchen Rubin and Shawn Achor. What I love about book signings is that the venues are usually completely free, and that anyone can do them. It does not matter whether we are a brand new author or already established, whether we have a large following or are just starting out.

Over the next few pages, we'll look at:

1. **WHAT** book signing events are
2. **WHAT** book signing events are meant to accomplish
3. **WHERE** we should consider hosting a book signing
4. **HOW** to reach out so stores are excited to host a signing for us

WHAT ARE BOOK SIGNING EVENTS?

At a book signing, authors make themselves available to potential buyers by offering and signing their book.

A book signing is as much about networking as it is about the actual signing. This is our opportunity to introduce ourselves, share our story, and invite others to become readers of our beautiful book.

Whether or not we choose to read our book during the event is completely up to us. I've attended signings where the author simply networked with visitors, as well as events that included a reading followed by a short Q&A. Both approaches work beautifully.

WHAT ARE BOOK SIGNINGS MEANT TO ACCOMPLISH?

Oftentimes, authors think of book signings solely as a way to increase book sales. But they can accomplish so much more than that.

Beyond potential sales, there are five additional benefits that make book signing events incredibly powerful.

BENEFIT 1: *Increased Exposure*

Book signings increase our exposure. People who may have never discovered us or our book otherwise might stumble upon us simply because we're signing at a local venue.

Book signings also allow for direct interaction with potential buyers. Unlike vendor events, where multiple sellers compete for attention, book signings typically feature just one author. That means we don't have to compete with other vendors. And that's huge.

BENEFIT 2: *Social Media Growth & Content*

With increased exposure often comes growth on social media.

Live events like book signings give us wonderful opportunities to capture photos and videos that we can later use for promotional materials. Sharing these moments online sparks curiosity and helps bring our book to life for those who couldn't attend.

BENEFIT 3: *Email List Growth*

Book signings can also help grow our email list. These events give us a natural opportunity to invite attendees to stay in touch.

BENEFIT 4: *Practice for Future Events*

Book signings are fantastic practice for vendor events and school visits.

Vendor events usually require a fee, so the pressure can feel higher. Book signings, on the other hand, are typically free and lower pressure. They're also smaller and more manageable than school visits, making them a wonderful starting point if we're just beginning to put ourselves and our book out there.

BENEFIT 5: *Relationship Building with Venue Owners*

Beyond connecting with readers, book signings allow us to build relationships with store owners and venue managers. This can be incredibly valuable. If a store owner sees that our event went well, they may become more interested in carrying our book long-term.

NINJA TIP:

One of our main objectives as the author should be getting to know the venue owner. These relationships can benefit us for years to come.

WHAT PLACES SHOULD WE CONSIDER FOR OUR BOOK SIGNING?

Bookstores are often the first places that come to mind, but we do not want to stop there.

Think beyond bookstores. If our children's book is about a pet, a local pet shop could be a wonderful fit. If our story involves food or a special dish, a gourmet food shop might be perfect. Toy stores are another great option.

Local libraries are also fantastic venues for book signings and readings, especially for us children's authors.

Parents of young children love visiting libraries for regular storytime, which means there is already a built-in audience. Libraries often promote visiting authors through newsletters, websites, social media pages, and local community calendars. Some even share upcoming events with local television stations.

Another powerful benefit is that librarians are incredible networkers. They regularly share recommendations with one another and are members of professional organizations such as the American Library Association and various regional groups.

Most importantly, hosting a book signing in these spaces gives us the opportunity to build relationships with librarians and venue staff. These connections are priceless, especially if we later plan to ask about adding our book to their shelves.

NINJA TIP:

Instead of focusing only on how many books you may sell, see these events as a way to get your foot in the door at places you may want to work with later.

HOW TO REACH OUT SO STORES ARE EXCITED TO HOST OUR BOOK SIGNING EVENT

No matter where we are reaching out, there are five key things we always want to consider.

ONE: *Focus on What Is in It for the Store*

We have to remember that stores and libraries will always be more interested in what is in it for them if they agree to host a book signing, and what is in it for their customers and patrons. Approaching these places from this angle will always make it so much easier to get a yes.

Telling a store owner that we have published a new children's book and that we would love to share it in their venue will never be as powerful and will, in fact, often be the reason why places say no.

So we will want to explain the value or benefit of what we are bringing and offering to them.

For example, we could share that besides bringing in more foot traffic, our book may increase the sale of some of the other items they offer in their store. If, for example, we wrote a children's book about how a little girl prepares for a new pet, we could approach our local pet store and let them know that our book also features all the items a new pet owner would need, like dog food, a dog dish, and a cozy dog bed - all of which could inspire readers to make those purchases in that store.

Or if our children's book is about a little boy who discovers his love of painting, we could approach an art supply store and let them know that our story features a number of art supplies that are, again, available in that store.

TWO: *Lean Into Foot Traffic*

Foot traffic is very important to every store. And because gaining more customers is such a big and important selling point, mentioning this during our outreach can be really powerful.

The mistake many first-time authors often make is expecting the store to be the traffic generator. But if we want to receive an enthusiastic yes from the store owner, and if we want to make our book signing a success, then this should be a combined effort.

So we will want to do our part by bringing our own people in:

- *By inviting friends and family to come by and visit the event*
- *By creating and distributing flyers*
- *By reaching out to local newspapers and local news stations*
- *By sharing the event in local Facebook groups (these could be local mom groups, local playgroups, library groups, or even topic-specific groups like dog clubs, associations, and organizations)*

Again, the more we as the author are willing to do in order to generate traffic, the more successful our event will be, and the easier it will be to get that yes from the store owner. Whatever our marketing plan might be to promote our book signing is something we will want to mention during our outreach.

THREE: *Make Our Outreach as Personal as Possible*

Personalizing our outreach is important because we want to let store owners know that we have done our homework and that we are familiar with their store.

For example, if the store has been owned by the same family for generations, we want to weave that into our outreach message.

Or if the store has won a local award or has been covered in a local newspaper or magazine recently, we again want to make that part of our message.

If we frequently go to this store, visit this particular bookstore often, or are a regular patron of the library, we will want to make sure to let them know. That's truly one of the best ways to get someone's attention and show that we know what they are all about.

All it takes is just ten minutes of our time and a little bit of googling. It makes such a big difference when we tailor each outreach to each individual store we are approaching.

FOUR: *Describe Our Book in One Short Paragraph*

We want to be able to describe our book in as little as one single paragraph - or in 10 to 15 seconds if we are doing so verbally.

This is where our lessons on how to talk about our book from chapter 20 come in really handy. The primary goal of our short pitch is to hook the person and spark curiosity so they want to learn more.

So before reaching out, we have to be clear on how we can sum up our book in a really interesting, intriguing, and concise way.

FIVE: *Mention Relevant Expertise*

This is not a must, but it's always a nice touch.

Sticking with my previous example of a little girl who prepares for a new pet, when reaching out to pet stores, I would want to mention if I am a vet, for example, or if I have volunteered at a dog shelter, or if I've had pets all my life.

If my book is about a little boy who discovers his love of painting, I would want to mention if I've been an avid painter for years or if I've taught a local art class when reaching out to an art store.

Adding our relevant expertise helps us stand out and provides a personal touch that so many pitches are missing these days. To give ourselves and our book an additional dimension, we want to ask ourselves how we, as the author, can tie ourselves to the topic of our book.

THREE MAIN OUTREACH GUIDELINES

When reaching out, we will want to make sure we adhere to 3 main guidelines:

GUIDELINE 1: *Clearly state what we want and what we want the other person to do.*

We want to make sure we clearly convey what we are asking for so the person on the other end doesn't have to guess. We also want to clearly state what we want them to do next - whether that's scheduling a phone or Zoom call, setting up an in-person meeting, or simply replying via email.

GUIDELINE 2: *Provide our contact information.*

If we want the store to contact us via phone, we need to include our phone number. If we are reaching out via email, we want to make sure we are using an email signature (see chapter 23) that includes our name, phone number, and a link to our website (if we have one).

If we are reaching out in person, we may want to have a business card handy (see chapter 22) and consider taking our *One-Sheet* that shares all this information in a clear, easy-to-read format (see chapter 16).

GUIDELINE 3: *Keep our outreach short and sweet.*

We want to limit our email pitch to just a few short paragraphs. Anything longer, and the recipient may not take the time to read it. And if our email doesn't get read, we won't receive a reply.

Let's look at an actual example.

Let's say we want to reach out to a potential book signing venue that is within a 20 or 25 mile radius and that we can easily visit in person. Armed with a copy of our book, our prepared *One-Sheet,* and a couple of business cards, we could simply walk into one of our identified stores and ask to speak with the manager.

Let's say I have written a book about a little girl who prepares for a new puppy. If I'm being strategic about the timing, I would plan to reach out to pet stores a few weeks before the month of May. May is National Pet Month, which is meant to recognize the benefits that pets bring to our lives. It's often during this month that many pet stores host events that promote responsible pet ownership, making it the perfect time for us to approach them.

NINJA TIP:

Pay attention to and take advantage of timing.

For example, if our book's topic aligns with a season, this might be a wonderful time to schedule our book signing around it.

If our children's book is about Santa Claus or a snowman, we may want to suggest a book signing around the Christmas holidays.

If our book is about the first day of preschool, scheduling a book signing around the beginning of the school year could be a great fit.

And if our precious story is about a military family, scheduling a book signing in April would be a wonderful idea, since April is the Month of the Military Child.

We could approach the manager of the pet store by saying something like this:

"Hi Sandra! I'm Eevi, a local vet here in town. And with National Pet Month coming up, I'd love to bring people into your pet store in May by offering a book signing of my award-winning children's book "Cleo and Her New Puppy," which helps kids learn and understand what it means to be a responsible pet owner.

Because you sell almost all the supplies new pet owners would need, I thought [NAME OF PET STORE] would be perfect for this event. To make this fun and easy for you, I've already put together a list of groups and organizations I would contact to help promote the event.

Does this sound like something you would be interested in?"

It's short and concise, yet contains everything we just talked about:

- We know the person's name.
- It outlines the benefits this would bring to the store.
- It clearly states what we are asking for.
- It weaves in relevant credibility markers (being a vet and the book winning an award).
- It ties in timely relevance (National Pet Month).
- It provides a quick summary of the book.
- It shows that we understand the importance of promotion and that we plan to help generate traffic.

By planning our outreach in a thoughtful way that truly considers all involved parties, we make it incredibly easy to say yes.

So instead of asking store owners for a favor, we are offering something that everyone can benefit from.

If you're an introvert like me and prefer to reach out via email, you can absolutely do that as well. To do so, we can find the manager's name and contact information and reach out that way.

Here's what that email might look like:

"Hi Sandra!

I hope this message finds you well. I'm Eevi, a local vet here in town.

With National Pet Month coming up, I'd love to bring people into your pet store in May by offering a book signing of my award-winning children's book "Cleo and Her New Puppy," which helps kids learn and understand what it means to be a responsible pet owner.

Because you sell almost all the supplies new pet owners would need, I thought [NAME OF PET STORE] would be a wonderful fit for this event. To make this easy for you, I've already put together a list of groups and organizations I would contact to help promote it.

Does this sound like something you'd be interested in?

Please feel free to call me at the number below or reply to this email. I'm really looking forward to hearing from you.

Best regards,
~ Eevi"

When it comes to book signing events, it's helpful to keep the following in mind:

NINJA TIP:

Remember to be thankful and to express your gratitude after the book signing event. Ninety-nine percent of authors do not do this. So go the extra mile, because it's never crowded there.

Whether it's a small gift basket, a handwritten thank-you note, or a box of chocolates, make sure to thank the store owner and staff for welcoming you.

And don't forget to thank your friends and family who took time out of their busy day to show up and support you.

NINJA TIP:

Celebrate your book signing event, no matter the outcome.

No matter how many people showed up (or didn't show up).
No matter how many books you sold (or didn't sell).

Each event is a growth opportunity. We learn what worked, what didn't, what went well, and what we can improve. That's it.

If we're just starting out, we may only sell three books. But that's three books more than we sold yesterday.

So see each experience as a stepping stone on your path to helping your beautiful book succeed.

I truly hope you give book signing events a go. They are especially powerful if stores are initially reluctant to carry our book. After getting to know us and seeing how an event goes, they may be far more open to offering our book on consignment or exploring a longer-term relationship.

The same holds true for libraries. If a library has been hesitant to add our book to their shelves, that hesitation often fades once they've had the chance to meet us, hear our story, and experience our book during a signing or reading.

This is marketing in its most human form.

It's not about pushing a product. It's about creating a connection, building trust, and turning a single interaction into an ongoing opportunity. Events like these make putting our foot in the door easier, yes, but they also plant seeds that can grow into bookstore placements, library carry-ons, future invitations, and word-of-mouth we could never manufacture online.

———————— • ◆ • ————————

VENDOR EVENTS & CONFERENCES

These next few pages are filled with information and ideas, so I've organized them into two sections:

1. What to consider and prepare *before* a live event
2. DOs and DON'Ts to help us make any event a success

Most market and fair advice focuses on the during-the-event part and on things like what our booth or table should look like. And that's important, of course. But doing the prep work beforehand is equally important if we truly want to set ourselves up for success.

So let's begin with just that.

When it comes to measuring how successful a market event has been, many authors (and most market vendors, for that matter) only consider how many books they sold during that event.

But attending a fair can be so much more than just book sales.

As children's authors, and as local authors, we have such a wonderful advantage at local fairs. Most fairs or markets do **not** have authors present, let alone children's authors. So there is virtually no competition.

If we prepare properly, a fair can be one of the best networking grounds and can open so many doors and create incredible opportunities for us.

- It might be future buyers who don't purchase at the fair itself, but who learned about us and our book and later look us up and buy it at home.
- It might be a local librarian who comes across our book at the fair and invites us to share our story during the library's weekly storytime.
- It might be a teacher from a local elementary school who encourages us to come in for a school visit.
- It might be a local boutique owner who asks if they can carry our book in their shop.

So when looking at attending a market, I encourage you to look beyond immediate book sales and consider the long-term payoffs as well.

BEFORE THE EVENT: *What Markets Should We Attend?*

With so many different market options out there, how do we decide which ones to attend?

It's always best to start by having a budget for the market fee in mind. Depending on

1. where we live,
2. the type of market or fair, and
3. the season,

the cost of a table or booth may already narrow down which and how many events we can attend.

Once we have a budget in mind, we can look at our options and make a list of potential fairs and markets. To build that list, there are two main approaches I've found to be especially helpful.

1. **SEARCH:** We can search for phrases like "best festivals and fairs near me" and explore the lists that come up.

2. **PERSONAL LIST:** We can also sit down and make a list of the fairs and festivals we personally enjoy attending each year. That's often a great indicator of events loved by members of our local community.

If we can only be a vendor at a few events each year, we'll want to think carefully about which ones would be the most beneficial for us and our book.

We can consider things like:

- *The cost of securing a table*
- *How busy the event usually is*
- *The type of audience most likely to attend*
- *How well our book fits that particular event*

This last point is something many people forget to consider. For example, if my book is about the beautiful colors of spring, a Christmas fair might not be the best fit, even if it's one of the busiest events of the year.

Once we know which vendor events we'd like to attend, we'll want to apply as early as possible and complete the vendor application.

NINJA TIP:

Even if our book isn't published yet, but we have a very specific event in mind that we'd love to be part of, it may be worth applying early.

Each vendor application usually specifies how much space is provided. We'll want to take note of this so we can plan our setup accordingly, including what size table we should bring.

This goes hand in hand with looking at photos from previous years of the event. Those images can help us understand how vendors were set up.

For example:

- *Are there canopies or just tables?*
- *Are the canopies open or enclosed?*
- *How close are vendors placed together?*
- *Are booths set up on one or both sides of the aisle?*

Vendor agreements are often very specific about setup rules. For example:

- *Do our banners or displays have to be located within our allocated space, or would we be able to place them slightly in front of our stand?*
- *Will we be provided with a table, or do we bring our own? If we can bring our own, does it need to be a specific size?*
- *If this is a multi-day event, will we be able to store our belongings and our setup overnight in a secure location, or will we have to take everything home with us each day?*

BEFORE THE EVENT: *Preparing Our Display*

When it comes to our display, we as children's authors want it to be playful and colorful. This helps complement our book and stand out from surrounding booths.

NOTE:

What follows is a list of items that we may want to consider bringing. Please know that we won't need all of these items for our first vendor event. Instead, we can start with the essentials and add to our equipment over time. So please keep this in mind as we look at the different display options.

To make this as easy as possible for you, I went ahead and made a list of all the items I'm about to share that are available on Amazon (↟). You can find the link on the resource page.

TABLE:

A foldable 6 by 3 foot table is ideal. The table itself doesn't matter much, since we'll want to cover it with a tablecloth. A fitted spandex table cover is a great option because it won't blow around in the wind. They're affordable and available in many colors.

The front of our table is a great place to visually attract passersby. A customized table runner is far more cost-effective than a full custom tablecloth. So on top of our plain tablecloth, we can place a runner with a clear, easy-to-read message.

NINJA TIP:

We want our design on our table runner to be evergreen - something we can use over and over again,

- no matter what time of year,

- no matter what type of event,
- no matter how we may grow as authors.

The design below here is a great example for multiple reasons:

- **SIMPLICITY:**
  It is very simple and not too cluttered, with the words really big and the font color clearly standing out from the color of the runner. This makes it easy to read from afar.

- **EFFECTIVE WORDING:**
  The wording immediately piques people's interest.

  - *"Meet the Author"* - lets people know that whatever books are on this table have been written by us.
  - *"Get an autographed copy"* - makes what we are selling instantly more meaningful, especially for those looking to purchase gifts for others.

- **AUTHOR WEBSITE:**
  The runner shares our author website along the bottom, so people know where they can find us and learn more about our books.

- **REUSABLE:**
  This runner is something we will be able to use over and over again, whether we have authored one book or ten. That's why I would suggest not putting a picture of our cover on here, so it stays truly evergreen and can be used for many years to come.

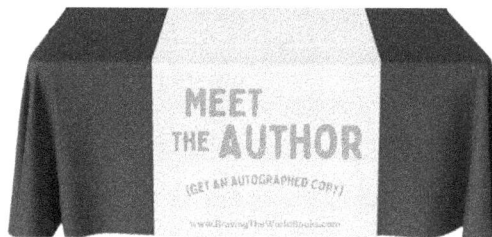

CANOPY

Oftentimes, vendors are not allowed to staple, tape, nail, or otherwise attach posters, displays, or signs to any walls. So we will need to come up with more portable and reusable solutions.

If we have a foldable canopy, I highly recommend using one. This is especially helpful for outdoor events, because standing in the sun for hours can be brutal. Plus, it protects our books if it happens to rain.

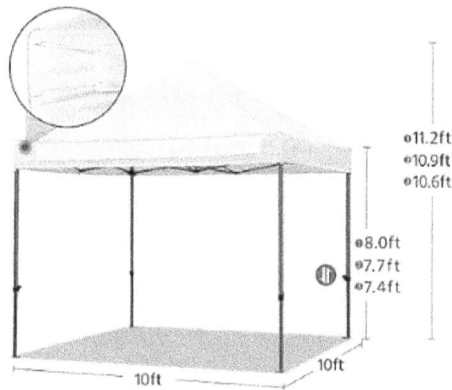

When using a canopy, we can easily hang a sign or banner from the two back poles.

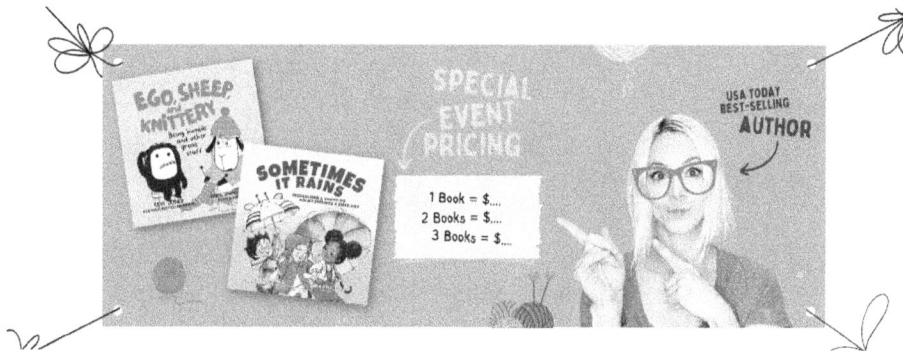

For our banner, we will want to make sure to include a few key elements.

- **ONE**, if we feel comfortable doing so, we could include an author image. Adding a photo also gives us an opportunity to work in some of our accomplishments as authors. For example, I've added my *USA-Today* bestselling title here.

  If our book has won an award or received that coveted bestselling banner, we could have our sign read something like "award-winning author" or "bestselling author." It's social proof, it's hard-earned, and it's deserved, so it's something we should share proudly.

- **TWO**, we may want to add the URL of our author website, large enough so it can be easily read from a distance.

- **THREE**, people love special deals, so we will want to offer some sort of bundle or special pricing and highlight it on our banner to attract potential buyers.

  A great solution for this, without having to commit to permanent pricing, is to have the banner simply read "Special Event Pricing," with an arrow. Before every event, we can then attach a piece of paper right below it that shows our most current bundles and pricing options.

To truly make this banner evergreen, we could leave the cover images of our books off entirely. For this particular banner, however, I decided to include some of my covers.

If this is an indoor event and we don't have a canopy, and there's no option to attach our banner to anything, we may want to consider using a standing sign.

This is a really inexpensive option: a foldable tripod stand and a 24 by 36 inch poster, glued onto a styrofoam board from the Dollar Tree, using all the same design elements we'd include on a banner.

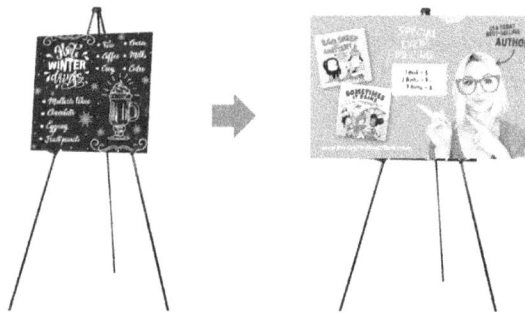

REMEMBER: We don't have to have all of these elements right away. This is something we can build bit by bit over time. Our booth or table setup will evolve and improve each time we set it up and add to it.

BALLOONS

Another fun element we can add to our table or tent setup are balloons. They're simple, but incredibly eye-catching. And the best part is that they're very inexpensive if we use regular balloons and blow them up ourselves.

If we pair them with something like a table arch kit or a column stand kit, we don't even need helium. These kits can be reused again and again.

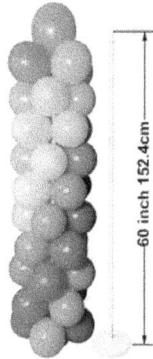

TABLE ARCH   **COLUMN STAND**

INTERACTIVE CUTOUT

Something that can really help with the growth of our social media following is encouraging buyers to take pictures, share them, and tag us.

Large cutouts of our book's characters are a beautiful way to support this. This is a pricier option, so it's something we can work toward over time. It's not something we need right away.

Below is a cutout of one of my book's characters. When planning something like this, we'll want to remember that it's meant for kids. So if little ones are standing right next to it, how big should it be? Anywhere between 3 to 5 feet is a great height. That way, children can look Mr. Sheep right into his big, round eyes.

SOCIAL MEDIA HANDLE

3-5 FEET

NINJA TIP:

Make sure to add your social media handle along the visible parts of your cutout. For example, I have mine placed right at the top, next to the sheep's head. It's large enough to be seen in photos and strategically placed on the opposite side a child would likely be standing on, so the chance of it being covered is quite slim.

To increase engagement even further, we can borrow a page from what influencers do on social media and create small incentives that encourage people to like, follow, tag, and comment on their posts. Oftentimes, these incentives give people a chance to win something.

Here, we can ask ourselves: what would be a fun incentive we could offer to encourage people to post the photo they just took of their kids with our cutout, tag us, and follow our social media account?

These incentives can be small and inexpensive, like giving away a sticker of our character, or something a bit bigger, like taking 5 percent off their book purchase. Giving away a sticker is usually the easiest and most cost-effective option.

We could even prepare small index cards that list the "rules" people need to follow to receive their free sticker. Then we can simply attach the sticker with a piece of tape, making it quick and easy to hand out.

Here, we'll also want to make sure to include the handles of the social media accounts we'd like to grow the most, such as Instagram and Facebook. To make it even easier, we can add QR codes that link directly to our social media profiles or to our website.

A great place to order die-cut stickers is through companies like *Stickermule.com* (↑). They also offer holographic and glitter stickers, which makes this option even more fun.

Now that we have all our larger elements set up, let's take a look at our table itself and a few fun additions that can make it even more inviting, so people feel drawn to check out our books.

BEFORE THE EVENT: *Preparing Our Table*

The best way to display our books is to prop them up using a couple of simple, inexpensive bookstands. This also helps keep our setup sturdier on windy days, so books don't get blown over.

Something I get asked quite often is how to fill our table if we "only" have one book.

In that case, we can display the same book in a few different ways. For example, one copy can be propped up to show the front cover. If the back cover is colorful or interesting, we can display that as well. And we can also have one copy opened to a particularly intriguing spread from the story.

In addition to the propped-up books, it's always a great idea to place several copies directly on the table, perhaps even in a small stack. This makes them easier to grab and helps people feel more comfortable picking one up without worrying about "messing up" the display. We want our table to feel as welcoming and approachable as possible, so people feel that it's okay to pick up a copy and look through it.

If we have a wooden box, we can turn it upside down and place a book on top of it. This creates different levels instead of one flat surface, which makes displays more visually interesting. This works especially well if we have more than one book.

NINJA TIP:

One thing we may want to avoid is using wooden boxes as shadow boxes, where the book is placed inside. This makes it harder to see and grab the book. Instead, simply turn the box upside down and use it to elevate and lift your display.

CRAFTS

Another wonderful addition to our table are small crafts or activity sheets, such as coloring pages or simple mazes.

NINJA TIP:

When adding crafts, make sure they're not random, but directly tied to your book and feature your book's characters.

If our craft requires crayons, scissors, or glue, we'll want to provide those items as well. For example, we could buy a large pack of crayons, take three at a time, tie them together with a small piece of string, and place those individual crayon bundles in a basket next to the activity sheets.

No matter what printouts we prepare, it's important that each one includes our book, our website, and information on where the book can be purchased. Even if someone doesn't buy from us at the event, they may do so later.

And don't forget about the sticker incentive mentioned earlier. Make sure those are clearly visible on the table, too.

EMAILS

Something many children's authors often forget or don't think about is asking for, or collecting, people's email addresses.

If someone is showing interest in our book, we could ask whether they'd like to share their email so they can learn more about it. If that feels a bit awkward in the moment, another great option is to create a small raffle or giveaway.

For example, we could prepare a clipboard with a simple sheet asking for a name and email address in exchange for a chance to win a small, related prize - such as a themed activity pack, a signed bookmark, a printable coloring page bundle, or another fun extra connected to the book.

NINJA TIP:

Try not to make your book itself the prize. While it may feel intuitive, it can unintentionally slow down sales, as some people may hold off on purchasing the book while they wait to see if they've won it instead.

When collecting emails, it's important to clearly state that by providing their email address, they're giving permission for us to email them. A simple note at the top of the sheet will do. This is the equivalent of opting into our email list. Without this clear permission, we wouldn't be compliant with many email providers, and our emails could be flagged as spam.

ATTIRE

A question you may hear over and over again at events like this, even if it's written all over your banners and posters, is whether you are the author. This always makes me smile, because I know it's coming.

So let's lean into it.

Wearing a shirt that says "Author" is such a fun and effective way to do this. It instantly answers the question, sparks conversation, and is something we can wear at every event, making it a great investment.

PRICING & BUNDLES

Let's talk about pricing and payment options, because this is something we want to make as easy and friction-free as possible for everyone.

It's really important to make our pricing very clear. Having prices displayed directly on our banner, as mentioned earlier, and also on the books propped up on stands works extremely well.

It's always easiest to use full dollar amounts, like $10 or $12, instead of $10.99 or $12.99. We also don't want to deal with adding tax on the spot, so ideally all displayed prices already include tax.

For in-person events, bundle pricing is especially effective. The more copies someone buys, the more cost-effective it should feel.

For example, if one copy is $15, a simple bundle might be two books for $28. Whatever bundle pricing we choose, we'll want to make sure it's clearly displayed, either on our banner, a sign on the table, or both.

Bundles don't have to be limited to additional copies of our book. If we really want to go all in, we could turn one of our characters into a stuffed toy, just like author Dr. Danielle Camer did for her beautiful book *Sophie Won't Sleep*. Ordering these items in larger quantities can help keep costs manageable. I've added a few vendor options to the resource page of this book (✝).

NINJA TIP:

There will always be people who ask for the price, even when they already know it, often as a way to try to negotiate or start haggling. Don't do it. Don't give in. These are your prices for a reason, so stick with them!

Instead, we can add value to the conversation. For example, if someone asks about pricing, we could say:

> *"The book is $15. And if you'd like, I'd be happy to sign it for you and add a personalized dedication for whoever you'd like to gift it to."*

That way, people are often less likely to try to haggle with us. This also gives them something they wouldn't get by ordering the book online and often makes pricing conversations feel more comfortable for us, too.

PAYMENT OPTIONS

There are a few payment options we'll want to be prepared for:

- *Cash*
- *Credit cards*
- *Direct money transfers through platforms like PayPal and Venmo*

For cash payments, we'll want to have change ready, either in a lockable cash box or in a fanny pack that allows us to keep it with us at all times.

For credit card payments, a small card reader that connects to our phone works beautifully. I got mine through PayPal, and they're often free for new users or very inexpensive.

For direct money transfers, we can create a simple table display with QR codes that link directly to our *PayPal.me* page or show our Venmo username. These can be printed and slipped into a small sign holder, which looks professional and can be reused again and again.

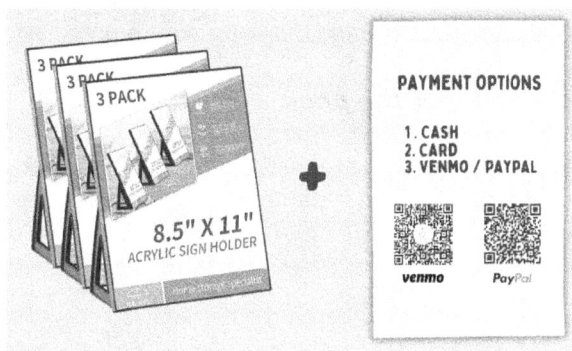

DURING THE EVENT: *Dos & Don'ts:*

Now that we're officially all set up, let's wrap things up by looking at the most important DOs and DON'Ts when attending market events.

NUMBER 1: *DON'T sit down.*

I know how tempting it is to hide behind the table, especially if you're an introvert like me. But every time you feel that urge, remind yourself how much work you've put into your beautiful book and into preparing for this event. This is the moment to let your book shine.

NUMBER 2: *DO talk to everyone.*

I know. It's not getting any easier. But being the one who approaches others (instead of waiting to be approached) will make all the difference. Please believe me!

This is where the *Learning How to Talk about Our Book* chapter (chapter 20) comes in handy, where we already prepared a simple first line we can approach people with. Sooner or later, people will ask what our book is about anyway, and having a short sound bite ready puts us one step ahead.

For one of my books, for example, while holding it in my hands, I might say something like this:

> *"Hi there! Have you heard about "Ego, Sheep, and Knittery," where Ego learns a thing or two about being a bit less braggy and more humble instead?"*

If we're excited and passionate about sharing our book, others will feel that energy too. So have that first line ready and use it as an easy, friendly way to start the conversation.

NUMBER 3: *DON'T assume only moms and grandmas will be interested in buying your book.*

We truly never know who might be looking for a thoughtful gift. So stay open, smile, and approach everyone with that same warmth and one-liner you've prepared.

NUMBER 4: *DON'T forget about the packaging.*

Simple paper bags are a great and inexpensive solution. We can even add branded or customized stickers to seal the bags, which instantly makes the purchase feel more special.

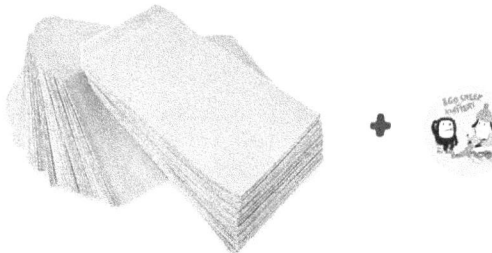

NUMBER 5: *DO make sure to take lots and lots of pictures of the event and your setup.*

These photos are wonderful to share on social media, and they're incredibly helpful when planning future events. They'll also help you remember exactly how you set up your booth or table.

This is something I truly wish I had done more consistently early on, so make sure you do.

NUMBER 6: *DO have your One-Sheet ready.*

We never know what opportunities may come our way during events like this. Having a few copies of your *One-Sheet* (chapter 16) on hand ensures you're prepared when those moments arise.

NUMBER 7: *DO get to know the vendors around you.*

This makes the event so much more fun. Cheering each other on and supporting one another creates a really positive experience. I've had it happen more than once that neighboring vendors bought one of my books for their own little ones, simply because we connected during the event.

NUMBER 8: *DO consider having a buddy with you during the event.*

Having someone with you makes bathroom breaks, quick food runs, and coffee refills so much easier. It also gives you a little extra support during a long day.

NUMBER 9: *DO plan ahead.*

If you plan to participate in vendor events, start researching and applying early. Prepare and order everything well in advance so your signs, cutouts, banners, equipment, and author copies of your books are all ready to go without last-minute stress.

NUMBER 10: *DO have fun!*

These events are all about connection. Be proud of your beautiful book and the time, effort, and love you poured into it.

NUMBER 11: *DO see each event as an experience you can learn from.*

If something didn't go as planned, or if you didn't sell as many books as you hoped, that's okay. There's always a lesson to take with you into the next event.

We either win, or we learn. And either way, it's a win.

SCHOOL VISITS: MARKETING THAT PAYS

While a dedicated book all about school visits is already in the works (because there is simply so much to explore and so many beautiful opportunities for us as children's authors), I want this next section of your marketing book to provide you with a complete, actionable overview of the entire process.

My goal is to empower you right now with practical guidance you can immediately use and build on. School visits deserve a place in every children's author's long-term marketing strategy, not only because they spread awareness of our book, but because they allow us to directly connect with the readers we write for.

What follows is a clear, steady walkthrough of each major stage involved in this marketing strategy.

STEP 1: *Identifying the Focus of Our School Visits*

Before reaching out to any school, it helps to clarify what we are offering and how our book fits into a school setting. Schools book authors for many reasons, but they are most interested in how our visit will support their students' learning, curiosity, and creativity.

So we will want to start by asking ourselves:

- *What grade levels is my book best suited for?*
- *What themes in my book align with school goals (friendship, kindness, SEL, writing craft, courage, identity, etc.)?*
- *Do I want to offer a simple reading and Q&A, or am I excited to give a writing workshop or themed presentation?*

Having clarity here will make our outreach stronger and our sessions more purposeful. Schools appreciate authors who understand their audience and arrive with a clear sense of how they will engage students.

STEP 2: *Finding the Right People to Contact*

Once we have defined our school visit angle, the next step is knowing exactly who to reach out to. Schools are busy environments, and finding the right person helps avoid emails being lost or misdirected.

The main gatekeepers include:

- **School librarians:** Often the primary coordinators for author events, literacy programs, and book fairs
- **Teachers:** Especially those who teach our book's target age group or align with our book's theme
- **Principals & administrators:** Essential when arranging whole-school assemblies
- **PTA/PTO leaders:** Frequently organize and fund enrichment programs
- **Event coordinators:** At larger schools with more formalized programs

We don't need to contact all of them. Instead, we can choose one clear entry point and let that person guide us toward the correct channels inside their school.

STEP 3: *Timing Our Outreach Thoughtfully*

Even the best outreach message can fall flat if sent during testing week or holiday chaos. Schools operate on predictable rhythms, and aligning with those rhythms greatly increases our chances of receiving a "yes."

Ideal windows for outreach:

- August to early October, when schools finalize calendars
- February to April, when teachers and librarians plan spring literacy activities

Times to avoid:

- Standardized testing periods
- The final weeks of a semester
- Major holidays or school breaks

STEP 4: *Craft a Clear, Helpful, Professional Invitation*

Our outreach email is our first impression, and it should feel warm, respectful, and easy to understand at a glance. Schools receive countless emails each day, so our goal is to make their decision process as effortless as possible.

Our message should include:

1. **Who you are** - a short, friendly introduction
2. **Your book's themes & relevance** - not a pitch, but context
3. **What you offer** - for example: reading, Q&A, writing workshop, assembly
4. **Who it's for** - recommended grade levels
5. **Length & format** - 20 minutes? 45 minutes? Virtual or in-person?
6. **Your availability** - general date ranges
7. **Whether you charge a fee** - or offer free sessions while gaining experience

This simple, clear structure honors the school's time while giving them everything they need to make a decision.

STEP 5: *Choose Your Format and Structure*

School visits come in many shapes and sizes, and choosing the right format helps us serve students well while also showcasing our strengths as an author.

Common visit formats include:

1. **Reading + Q&A**
   Perfect for younger grades. These visits are warm, simple, and often interactive.

2. **Large-Group Assembly**
   Ideal for authors who are comfortable presenting on a stage or leading large groups.

3. **Writing Workshops**
   Wonderful for older students. We can teach a writing exercise, character development,

or story structure.

4. **Themed Presentations**
   If our book touches on friendship, bravery, grief, identity, or a STEM topic, our presentation can weave together lessons, storytelling, and student participation.

Regardless of the format we choose, our goal is to keep energy high, transitions smooth, and content appropriate for the students' developmental level.

STEP 6: *Deciding on Fees (or Starting with Free Visits)*

Every author approaches this step differently, and there is no single "right" choice. Deciding whether to offer free or paid author visits depends largely on our goals, experience, and intentions.

FREE VISITS, for example, might open more doors initially, especially if we are a budding author looking to gain exposure, or if this is one of our first author visits. However, they can also imply limitations such as shorter sessions or less in-depth engagement.

PAID VISITS, on the other hand, often come with expectations of a more structured and in-depth experience. They also reinforce our professional role as an author providing meaningful educational value.

Typical fee ranges vary widely based on experience, visit format, time commitment, location, and audience size. These ranges are meant as starting points and should always be adjusted to fit the specifics of each visit.

Type of Visit	Fee Range	Details
New or Emerging Author (Reading Only)	$0 - $400	A simple reading and Q&A session, typically for smaller groups.
Experienced Author (Reading & Q&A)	$400 - $800	Includes a book reading, Q&A, and possibly a short discussion.
Established Author (Reading & Workshop)	$800 - $2,000	Reading, Q&A, and a hands-on activity or workshop.
Full-Day Author Visit (Multiple Classes or Workshops)	$1,500 - $3,500	Full-day event with multiple presentations or in-depth workshops.
Large Assembly or School-Wide Event	$1,000 - $5,000	Large audience, often including a presentation, reading, and Q&A.

Travel Fee (Outside Local Area)	$300 - $1,500	Additional fee for travel expenses, depending on distance and location.
Virtual Author Visit (Reading Only)	$100 - $300	A simple virtual reading and Q&A, ideal for smaller groups or classrooms.
Virtual Author Visit (Reading & Workshop)	$300 - $800	Includes reading, Q&A, and interactive virtual activities or a workshop.
Virtual Full-Day Author Visit	$1,000 - $2,500	Multiple virtual sessions or workshops throughout the day.

If we choose to begin with free visits, that choice is equally valid. Free visits can:

- *build confidence*
- *generate testimonials*
- *help refine our presentation*
- *lead to word-of-mouth recommendations*
- *create relationships that often turn into paid opportunities later*

Our comfort level, experience, and personal goals will guide us here.

NINJA TIP:

If you are feeling unsure about charging for author visits, please know that you are not alone, and your value is absolutely real. As children's authors, we bring creativity, insight, and inspiration to young minds. That is a gift worth sharing, and it deserves to be acknowledged.

When we prepare for school visits, we enter into a mutual exchange of value. Schools want enriching experiences for their students, and we have the opportunity to expand our reach and share our work. Both sides benefit, and that is something to feel proud of.

Remember: your time, expertise, and passion for storytelling are invaluable.

Charging for visits is not about placing a price on creativity. It is about recognizing the worth of the experience you are offering and allowing yourself to continue doing this meaningful work sustainably.

STEP 7: *Handling Book Orders (Before, During, and After the Visit)*

Book orders are often one of the most exciting and practical parts of a school visit, but they also require careful organization and preparation to ensure the process feels smooth for families, teachers, and for us. While every author eventually develops their preferred system, there are a few tried-and-true structures that make this part easy for everyone involved.

Most schools prefer to send book order forms home ahead of time. This allows families to review the options, decide whether they'd like a signed copy, and send payment back to the school through their teacher. We can provide the school with our order form digitally so they can print and distribute it. Keeping the form to one simple, friendly page helps maximize participation.

Our order form might include:

- *our book cover and a short, enticing description*
- *the book's price (tax included, if appropriate)*
- *a line for the child's name and teacher*
- *space for personalization requests*
- *payment instructions (check to the school? check to the author? online payment link?)*

Some authors ask families to pay the school directly, and the school writes one combined check to the author. Others prefer that each family's payment go directly to them. Either method works; the key is clarity ahead of time so teachers know exactly how to collect and organize forms.

If orders come in before the visit, we will have time to sign and prepare each book at home. This is often the easiest method because our signing table is calm and organized, and we can add special touches like bookmarks or stickers. We can then bring the prepared books on the day of our visit and hand them to the coordinating teacher or librarian, who will help distribute them to classrooms.

If the school prefers to collect orders after our visit, that works beautifully too. In that case, teachers will send order forms home the same day we come in, capitalizing on the enthusiasm children feel after meeting "a real author." Orders often increase significantly when sent home post-visit because students go home buzzing with excitement.

Whichever timing we may choose, the most important thing is clear communication. For teachers juggling so much at once, the simpler the system, the more successful the orders will be. We always want to offer to handle as much as possible ourselves (such as bundling books by classroom or supplying labeled envelopes), so the process feels easy and joyful for everyone involved.

STEP 8: *Handling Contracts With Confidence & Professionalism*

Contracts are not meant to be intimidating; they're simply tools that help both us and the school feel clear, supported, and fully aligned about expectations. While many schools might not require a formal contract, offering one shows professionalism and reassures them that you've done this before.

A school visit contract can be very simple. It generally covers:

- *the visit date and time*
- *the number and length of sessions*
- *fees or honorariums (including payment timelines)*
- *whether the school or author provides materials*
- *technology needs (projector, microphone, etc.)*
- *expectations around photographs*
- *cancellation or rescheduling terms*

Many authors begin with a one-page agreement. For clarity's sake, we can also add a second page for optional details (like book order procedures).

NINJA TIP:

Many districts have their own vendor or visitor forms. If a school sends you paperwork of their own, be flexible and gracious. You can fill out their form while still attaching your simple agreement as an addendum. This ensures that no matter which document becomes "official," your needs are clearly stated.

If we're using our own contract, we will want to send it after the school confirms the date. Here, we can send a friendly email like this:

"Hi [NAME,]

I'm thrilled to visit your school! Attached is a short agreement so everything is clear for your team.

Please let me know if you'd like any changes.

Warmly,
[YOUR NAME]"

This sets exactly the right tone - warm, accommodating, and confident.

Keep one signed copy for your records and send a reminder a week before your visit, summarizing the important details. Schools appreciate this more than you may realize.

STEP 9: *Lesson Plan Preparation & Engagement Planning*

A memorable school visit begins long before we walk through the school doors. The secret to a successful visit - one that feels smooth, joyful, and highly engaging - is thoughtful preparation paired with flexibility.

Our lesson plan does not need to look like a teacher's detailed curriculum document. It simply needs to outline a natural flow that keeps students captivated and gives us confidence.

We can start by choosing a structure that fits the time frame the school has given us. A 20-minute session with kindergarten will look very different from a 45-minute workshop with fifth graders. Once we know the session length, we can build a simple arc.

A classic structure includes:

1. A warm, friendly introduction:

Here, we will want to share who we are, how we became an author, and something relatable (e.g., *"I once wrote stories on napkins because I didn't want to forget them!"*). Children love personal details.

2. Our read-aloud or story excerpt:

If students are very young, a full read-aloud is perfect. For older students, a short excerpt paired with behind-the-scenes insights works beautifully.

3. A peek behind our creative process:

Show early sketches, drafts, or funny mistakes. Students are endlessly fascinated by the "messy middle."

4. An engagement activity:

This can be simple: a drawing prompt, a storytelling game, a character-building exercise, or even a moment where students turn and talk to a partner. Interactive sections help bring energy back into the room.

5. Time for Q&A:

Children ask the best questions, so if possible, we will want to leave space for this.

6. A heartfelt closing statement:

We want to end our visit with encouragement (for example, *"You all have stories to tell. I can't wait to read them one day."*).

If we are working with older students, we might turn this structure into a writing lesson, perhaps showing how we revised a scene, explaining how authors develop characters, or guiding them through a short writing exercise inspired by our book's theme.

Ahead of each visit, we could ask the teacher whether students have already read our book. If they have, we can skip the full read-aloud and focus more on process, writing craft, illustrations, or the story behind our story. If they have not, we can keep the presentation simpler and focus on engagement and curiosity instead.

It is always helpful to also have a visual plan. Students respond beautifully to slides or props, even something as simple as a title slide with our book cover, a few artwork snippets, or photos from our writing space. The visuals do not need to be fancy. They simply help anchor student attention.

Lastly, we want to plan for movement. Children need small moments to wiggle, stretch, repeat a line aloud, shout out predictions, or "act out" a character's feelings. Movement is not a distraction; it is part of effective engagement planning.

Our lesson plan is not a script. It is simply our safety net. It gives us enough structure to feel confident, while still leaving room for spontaneity, questions, and the delightful unpredictability of working with children.

NINJA TIP:

Expect occasional surprises, such as bells ringing, schedule shifts, technology glitches, or unexpected interruptions. Flexibility is part of the process, and your calm, patient presence becomes part of the school's memory of you.

STEP 10: *Follow Up Thoughtfully After the Visit*

Many authors forget this step, but it is one of the most powerful parts of our long-term marketing plan. A thoughtful follow-up helps solidify relationships and leads to future opportunities.

Our follow-up may include:

- *a warm thank-you message*
- *a downloadable resource for teachers or students*
- *a reminder of where families can find your book*
- *a request for a testimonial (schools are happy to provide them!)*
- *a photo recap (if allowed)*
- *a gentle invitation to stay connected*

Follow-up is where our visit turns into ongoing recognition, referrals, and invitations, sometimes for years to come.

! BEST PRACTICES for Our Successful School Visits

As we begin stepping into schools and sharing our beautiful children's book, here are a few gentle best practices that will help us shine, support our hosts, and make each visit even more impactful than the last.

PRACTICE #1: *Ask the Teacher to Take Photos*

Photos taken from behind the students (looking toward us as we present) beautifully capture the moment without showing children's faces. These images become powerful credibility markers we can use on our website, in newsletters, and on social media. They also help future schools visualize what our visit might look and feel like.

PRACTICE #2: *Always Ask for Referrals*

After a successful visit, teachers and librarians are often delighted to help spread the word. A simple question such as, *"Do you happen to know any other teachers or schools who might enjoy a visit like this?"* can open the door to district-wide opportunities. Most schools talk to each other, and a single visit can organically grow into many more.

PRACTICE #3: *Request a Short Testimonial*

It's important that we request a short testimonial while the excitement is still fresh. A librarian or teacher can often write a sincere, enthusiastic testimonial within minutes of our visit. These become incredibly valuable additions to our website, media kit, or outreach messages. Testimonials help schools feel confident in choosing us. And they provide a snapshot of the magic we bring into classrooms.

PRACTICE #4: *Bring a Simple Thank-You Gift for Your Host*

A handwritten note, a signed copy of our book for the library, or a small token of appreciation goes a long way. Schools deeply appreciate kindness, and these gestures help create lasting relationships that lead to repeat invitations and enthusiastic word-of-mouth.

PRACTICE #5: *Arrive Early (Even if Only by Ten Minutes)*

A few minutes of buffer time gives us space to check the room setup, test technology, greet teachers, and ground our energy before the students arrive. Schools notice and value our professionalism, and early arrivals prevent stress for both us and our hosts.

PRACTICE #6: *Labeling Everything We Bring With Us*

If we use props, books, puppets, posters, or a laptop, we'll want to label each item discreetly. Classrooms can be busy, materials move quickly, and labeling ensures nothing gets misplaced as we travel between rooms or sessions.

PRACTICE #7: *Prepare a Backup Plan for Technology*

Projectors freeze. Microphones die. Slides won't load. It happens to every author eventually. Having a simple backup (like printed visuals, a few physical props, or the ability to tell our story without slides) ensures our presentation stays smooth and magical no matter what.

PRACTICE #8: *Keep a Running List of Questions Students Ask*

Children ask the most insightful, funny, unexpected questions. Over time, we often notice patterns - questions about where ideas come from, how long illustration takes, or what our childhood was like. These recurring questions can help us refine future presentations, our website FAQ, or even inspire new books.

PRACTICE #9: *Create a Dedicated School Visit Email Folder*

Schools often reach out months before they're ready to finalize details. Having a separate folder (or color-coded system) helps us track inquiries, follow-ups, contracts, and payments. This small organizational step makes a big difference as our school visit requests grow.

PRACTICE #10: *Leave Students With One Clear Takeaway.*

A strong, intentional closing helps anchor the experience. It gives students something concrete to remember and share, and it signals that our time together has a natural, meaningful ending.

You might close with a simple storytelling insight, planting the seed that stories are all around us if we just pay attention. Or we could offer a tiny creative prompt, such as: *"Later today, see if you can spot a story idea hidden somewhere around you."* This sparks curiosity, and it gives teachers an easy extension activity to build on after we leave the classroom.

PRACTICE #11: *Follow Up While the Visit Is Still Fresh*

A warm thank-you email, a shared resource, or a link to where families can find our book helps maintain momentum. Schools deeply appreciate thoughtful follow-up, and this step strengthens our relationship as much as the visit itself.

PRACTICE #12: *Keep a Growing "School Visit Toolkit"*

Over time, we'll want to assemble a folder with our:

- *presentation slides*
- *prop list*
- *book order form*
- *email templates*
- *sample schedules*
- *teacher resources*
- *contract template*

This makes each new visit easier and faster to prepare, and keeps our branding and messaging consistent.

Every school visit helps a child feel seen, inspired, and connected, and every visit helps our author career grow in meaningful, lasting ways. These best practices will support us as we continue shaping remarkable experiences for students and educators alike.

School visits are rich, joyful experiences, and also one of the most powerful long-term marketing strategies we have as children's authors. They spread awareness, deepen relationships, build confidence, and allow us to step directly into the lives of the young readers we cherish most.

While this chapter gives us a full, actionable overview of the entire process (from getting ready to reaching out to delivering a meaningful visit), there is an entire world of wonderful details that deserves its own book. And I'll be writing that book soon, filled to the brim with scripts, lessons, templates, pricing guides, outreach examples, and everything else we might need.

But for now, we have a beautiful place to begin. We have everything we need to start exploring school visits with confidence, clarity, and excitement.

———————•◆•———————

LIBRARIES - USING LIBRARIES TO MARKET OUR BOOK

Libraries are one of the most overlooked marketing channels available to us as children's authors. They may not seem like a traditional "marketing tool," but they are, in fact, one of the most powerful long-term strategies we have - expanding our reach, amplifying our credibility, and introducing our books to readers we may never meet otherwise.

And the very best part?

Library exposure costs nothing but a bit of preparation and thoughtful outreach.

In this part of the book, we will walk through how libraries help market our book, how librarians evaluate titles, how to prepare our book for their shelves, how to approach them confidently, and how to build relationships that may support our author career for years to come.

WHY LIBRARIES ARE A WONDERFUL MARKETING STRATEGY

As authors, we sometimes worry that libraries might deter sales; that if readers can borrow our book for free, they won't feel the need to buy it. But the opposite is actually true. Libraries are one of the most powerful discovery engines for us authors, quietly supporting book sales in ways we don't always see.

Studies show that approximately **35% of library patrons go on to purchase a print or e-book after first borrowing that same title**. This is part of a much larger trend: libraries introduce readers to new authors, and readers then choose to bring those favorite authors into their homes.

In one survey, **57% of patrons said the public library was their primary source of book discovery**, and over half of all library users reported buying books by an author they first discovered on library shelves. Libraries don't replace a reader's desire to own books. They *ignite* it.

And when a book isn't immediately available at the library, patrons don't simply move on. While many place a hold, the next most common actions are to **buy the book online** (23.2%) or **purchase it from a local bookstore** (18.3%). Libraries are not a sales deterrent. They are one of the most consistent and generous pathways to building lifelong readers.

With this reassurance in mind, let's explore what it takes to have our children's book added to a library's collection.

STEP 1: *Getting Our Book Library-Ready*

Before contacting librarians, our book must meet library expectations. Libraries do not judge books the same way bookstores or readers do. They rely on industry identifiers, hardcovers that withstand circulation, and cataloging systems that allow easy shelving.

So here's what our book needs:

A Hardcover Version

Most libraries strongly prefer (or require) hardcovers, because they last longer through repeated handling. If we only published a paperback or eBook, now is the time to create a hardcover edition through a platform like *IngramSpark*.

Our own purchased ISBN (not a free KDP ISBN)

Libraries need real ISBNs that identify *us* as the publisher. Free KDP ISBNs only work on Amazon and cannot be used through IngramSpark's expanded distribution.

A Library of Congress Control Number (LCCN)

This is the number librarians use to order and catalog books, so we will want to make sure to apply for our LCCN through the Preassigned Control Number (PCN) Program before publishing.

Accurate BISAC Codes

Our BISAC categories determine our book's "home" in the library system. The more accurately we categorize our book, the easier it is for librarians to understand our themes and relevance.

NINJA TIP:

We MUST request our LCCN <u>before</u> our book is published. If our book is already live and published, we will no longer be eligible for the **Preassigned Control Number** program, or PCN - the program through which we as independently published authors may acquire our LCCN.

Once our book is selected for inclusion in the Library of Congress's collection, that PCN becomes the official LCCN.

While acquiring an LCCN after publication is still possible, it's not guaranteed, especially for independently-published books.

NINJA TIP:

If you need help with the creation of your hardcover, your ISBN, or your LCCN, you can always watch my separate YouTube videos on each of these topics. They go into great detail on each of the different processes to support you along the way.

STEP 2: *Making Sure Our Book Is Available Where Libraries Buy*

Librarians almost never buy books directly from authors. They also don't purchase books from Amazon, and instead go through trusted distributors, such as:

- ***Ingram*** *(via IngramSpark)*
- ***Baker & Taylor***

- ***Brodart***

It is our job to make sure our book is available through at least one of them, most likely IngramSpark.

When setting up our book in IngramSpark (⬆), we'll want to confirm that:

- *expanded distribution is enabled*
- *our wholesale discount is library-friendly (typically 40–55%)*
- our book is marked as returnable (this significantly increases our chances)

NINJA TIP:

Libraries often prefer ordering through the same distributor they use for all their purchases. When you mention "available via Ingram" in your outreach email, you remove friction immediately.

STEP 3: *Build Your Library Contact List*

Locating the correct decision-maker is half the battle. This step is where many of us authors unintentionally give up; but we won't.

A wonderful tool for this is *librarytechnology.org* (⬆), a directory of public and academic libraries.

Click on Libraries → Select U.S. Libraries → Select State → Visit their Websites → Locate the appropriate Contacts

We'll want to look for:

- *Head Librarian*
- *Library Director*
- *Collection Development Librarian*
- *Acquisitions Librarian*
- *Children's Librarian*

Each library may use different titles, but the goal is always to find the person responsible for selecting and purchasing children's materials.

NINJA TIP:

Start with your local libraries first. They love supporting local authors, and a single local placement can be the start of a beautiful chain of referrals.

NINJA TIP:

Keep a spreadsheet. Track who you contacted, when, whether they responded, and when you plan to follow up. This becomes invaluable as your outreach expands.

STEP 4: *Prepare Your Library Outreach Kit*

Before reaching out, we will want to prepare a simple, polished set of materials that make our book easy to evaluate.

Our library outreach kit includes:

1. **A *One-Sheet*:** our book's "résumé" we already covered and prepared in chapter 16
2. **A clear email template**

Just like pitching schools or podcasts, personalization matters. Librarians receive countless emails; ours should be warm, helpful, and respectful of their time.

To help you get started, here's a sample outreach email that you can adapt for your own book and local libraries:

SUBJECT LINE:
Local Author Submission: *[Book Title]*

Dear [Librarian's Name],

My name is [Your Name], and I'm a children's book author based here in [Your City/State]. I'm reaching out because I would be honored if you would consider my picture book, *[Book Title]*, for inclusion in your library's children's collection.

[Optional local tie-in: "I grew up visiting this library," "My children and I attend storytime regularly," "This community means so much to me," etc.]

My book is a [brief description: "heartfelt story about...," "social-emotional learning tale exploring...," "funny friendship adventure perfect for ages..."]. It's written for children ages [range], and it supports themes commonly explored in early childhood classrooms - such as [theme 1], [theme 2], and [theme 3].

To make ordering as easy as possible, *[Book Title]* is available through **Ingram**. The ISBN is: **[ISBN]**. I've attached a one-page overview that includes the book summary, BISAC categories, reviews, and ordering details.

I deeply appreciate the work you and your team do to support literacy and community connection. If you feel this title would be a good fit for your shelves, it would mean so much to me. I'm grateful for your time and the heart you pour into your library every day.

Thank you again for considering my book, and for all you do for young readers in our community.

Warmly,
[Your Name]
[Your Website]
[Your Email Address]

Here's a breakdown of why this template works well as an outreach message:

- It is **short, warm, and respectful**. Librarians receive many emails, and this is easy to read.
- It includes the **book's age range and themes**, which helps librarians evaluate its relevance.
- It specifies **availability through Ingram**, removing friction.
- It avoids sales pressure and **focuses on service** rather than promotion.
- It includes our *One-Sheet*, which librarians expect and appreciate.
- It politely affirms the librarian's role and values their work.
- It uses a **local connection** when possible, a powerful trust and credibility marker.

NINJA TIP:

Your tone should be one of service, not sales. Librarians respond beautifully when they feel you understand their role.

PRACTICE #1: *Become a Resource, Not Just an Author*

Libraries love building relationships with local authors, especially those who enrich their programming.

Don't just ask for something. Offer something.

Here, we could consider offering:

- *a free virtual storytime*
- *an in-person author meet & greet*
- *a writing workshop*
- *participation in a local author panel*
- *a themed activity tied to your book*

When librarians see our generosity and reliability, they are far more likely to support our work.

This is the difference between transactional outreach and relationship-based outreach; and the latter creates lasting impact.

PRACTICE #2: *Timing Our Outreach Strategically*

Libraries buy books year-round, but their busiest purchasing window aligns with their budget cycle.

Oftentimes, the best months to reach out are **April through July**, when libraries are:

- *closing out their fiscal year*
- *using remaining funds*
- *planning their next year's purchases*

Reaching out during this window greatly increases our chances of a "yes."

PRACTICE #3: *Being Persistent (But Never Pushy)*

Libraries often respond slowly, not because they're uninterested, but because their job includes many competing responsibilities.

For some, it may only take 1 email. Many more need 3-5 nudges. And others may take up to 10-12 emails over a period of 1-2 years.

This is normal, so we'll want to make sure to keep following up warmly and regularly. Persistence is not pestering when done with kindness.

NINJA TIP:

Celebrate every single yes. Your momentum grows library by library.

Libraries are so much more than buildings filled with books. They are places of discovery, belonging, community, and endless possibility. Getting our beautiful children's book onto library shelves is not only a marketing strategy; it is a gift to the families and young readers in our community.

———————————◆·———————————

Whether through a book signing, a vendor event, a school visit, or a library program, each face-to-face interaction gives our book the opportunity to be experienced, not just seen. These moments turn stories into memories, readers into advocates, and single events into long-term opportunities.

This is marketing at its most human.

By showing up where our audience already gathers, we allow our marketing to feel natural, meaningful, and sustainable. We are not just promoting a book. We are building relationships, creating moments that matter, and giving our story the chance to live on in the hearts and hands of our readers.

And that is the kind of marketing that truly lasts.

———————————◆·———————————

YOUR TO DOs FOR THIS CHAPTER:

❏ Decide which of these marketing strategies you would like to give a try

Find all your templates and swipe files using this link below. You may want to bookmark this page, so you can refer to it as quickly and easily as possible.

⬆ *https://www.eevijones.com/marketing-downloads*

LINKS SHARED:

- *https://www.eevijones.com/amazon_author_event_items*
- *https://www.stickermule.com*
- *https://www.ingramspark.com*
- *https://www.eevijones.com/youtube*
- *https://librarytechnology.org*

CHAPTER 26
Sustaining Momentum Over Time

Sustainable success as a children's author is not built in a single moment. It is built through continued presence.

Sustaining momentum means learning how to keep our book relevant, visible, and meaningful long after launch day has passed. It means understanding how readers actually discover books over time, how trust is built through repetition, and how small, thoughtful actions compound into long-term visibility.

Long-term marketing is all about positioning our book so it continues to show up in conversations, classrooms, libraries, gift moments, and reader lives throughout the year. It is about creating systems that support our book even when we are not actively promoting it every single day.

In this final chapter of our continuous and long-term marketing phase, we'll explore how to extend the life of our book through strategies that work together: seasonal relevance, series-building, evergreen visibility, and intentional scaling when the time is right.

When we learn how to sustain momentum, we give our stories what they deserve: the chance to be discovered again and again, by the readers who need them most.

———— • ◆ • ————

KEEPING OUR BOOK RELEVANT ALL YEAR LONG

Launches are exciting. Holiday spikes are wonderful. Those moments matter.

But if our marketing efforts only live inside those short windows, our books fade from view far too quickly.

Long-term marketing is not about doing more. It's about continuing the strategies from this book that have proven to work for our children's book and staying visible in ways that feel natural, intentional, and aligned with how families, educators, and librarians actually discover books throughout the year.

One of the biggest differences between a book that continues to sell and one that quietly disappears is not luck, budget, or algorithms. It is how actively we, as authors, continue to share our work with the world, and how willing we are to position it in fresh, relevant ways.

Most authors stop too soon, and only a small handful keeps going. And it is that handful that sees long-term success.

So let's look at seven practical, creative, and highly actionable ways to sustain momentum and keep our beautiful children's book relevant all year long.

STRATEGY 1: *Tapping Into Seasonal Reading Themes*

This is one of the most powerful free marketing tools available to us for our long-term success.

Schools, libraries, and families think in seasons. They actively seek books that align with what children are experiencing at that moment in the year. When we learn to position our book alongside those seasonal rhythms, it naturally stays relevant twelve months out of the year.

- In **January and February**, families often focus on new routines, kindness, and love. A book that celebrates courage, resolutions, or friendship feels perfectly timed. Here, we could position our book as *"a story to kick off the new year with bravery and heart."*
- In **March and April**, themes of growth, renewal, and Earth Day take center stage. Stories featuring nature, curiosity, or new beginnings shine here. A social media caption like, *"Just as flowers are blooming, this story celebrates how little ones bloom in courage and kindness,"* makes it instantly seasonal.
- During **summer**, libraries launch reading programs and parents look for engaging read-alouds and road trip books. Fun, adventurous, or educational stories fit seamlessly into this season. Here, we could share pictures of our book in a beach bag or tucked next to a picnic blanket.
- In the **fall**, back-to-school emotions dominate. Books about belonging, friendship, and facing fears become especially meaningful. So if our book touches on any of these themes, this is the time to emphasize it.

By aligning our book with what is already happening seasonally, we are not creating demand from scratch. We are stepping into conversations that are already taking place.

To help you get inspired year-round on how all of this can tie into our calendar, remember to use my *Social Media Wizard* (↑) that I first introduced in chapter 17. It creates daily content prompts and ideas for us children's authors.

STRATEGY 2: *Integrating Our Book Into Classrooms and Libraries*

We have already talked about the power of schools and libraries in the context of connecting with and meeting our readers. We can supercharge these previously discussed marketing strategies by keeping our book tied to what is currently happening in educational spaces throughout the year.

And that matters because schools and libraries do not simply buy books. They build programs around them.

They host storytimes, themed weeks, reading challenges, and curriculum tie-ins all year long. When we position our book as a resource that supports those activities, it gains long-term staying power.

- In **February**, schools might be running a kindness campaign. So if our book is about empathy or friendship, we could pitch it as a perfect read-aloud.
- In **April**, libraries might host Earth Day storytimes. So if our book has animals or nature themes, we can suggest it for their storytime.

By offering storytimes, author visits, or read-aloud opportunities tied to the current season, we are expanding our book's lifespan far beyond a single purchase moment.

STRATEGY 3: *Creating "Evergreen Awareness Hooks"*

"Evergreen awareness hooks" is a term I like to use to refer to recurring opportunities to talk about our book without relying solely on major holidays.

For example:

- *World Kindness Day* in November is perfect for books that highlight empathy.
- *National Puppy Day* in March is perfect if our book has a dog character.
- *International Day of Friendship* in July is ideal for books about connection and belonging.

They can also include recurring content themes we create ourselves. For example:

- **Motivational Monday** can be celebrated by sharing an inspiring line from our book.
- Or **Feel-Good Friday** could be celebrated by sharing a fun behind-the-scenes moment or a character highlight.

Because these hooks repeat every year (or week), they become part of a sustainable social media content strategy rather than one-off ideas. They keep our content fresh without requiring constant reinvention.

For example, if we have a book about kindness, we could share something like, *"Today is World Kindness Day, and this story is all about helping little ones see just how powerful kindness can be."* That feels relevant, timely, and yet remains evergreen, because it works every year.

STRATEGY 4: *Refreshing and Repurposing Our Content*

One of the most overlooked marketing tools we have is our book's sales page.

Our Amazon description, A+ Content, and even keywords can be updated at any time. When we treat our sales page like a storefront rather than a finished product, we unlock powerful seasonal relevance.

Small changes make a big difference:

- In **August**, it could be as simple as adding a line to our description like, *"A heartwarming story to ease first-day-of-school jitters."*
- In **December**, we could add, *"The perfect stocking stuffer for little readers."*
- And in the spring, we could say, *"A delightful Easter basket surprise."*

We can do the same with our **A+ Content** by swapping in seasonal graphics. For example, snowy backdrops in December or sunny picnic scenes in July. These small updates keep our book page fresh and signal to buyers that our book is alive and relevant. And we can reuse these visuals every year.

We could also do the same with our **keywords**. People's search habits and search vocabulary change throughout the year. So we can reflect that in our keyword lists as well, since that is something we can update at any time.

And don't forget about **social media**. Here, we can repurpose our content seasonally too. We can absolutely repost already shared illustrations or posts by simply adding a seasonal spin to them.

Refreshing doesn't mean starting over or creating new material every time. It means reimagining what we already have through a seasonal lens to make it instantly more timely.

STRATEGY 5: *Bundling Our Book With Experiences*

Books do not have to stand alone. With this strategy, we want to think about how we can package our book with other items or experiences that make it a perfect gift or teaching tool.

Since we are most likely publishing through a print-on-demand platform, it might be more challenging to combine our book with something physical, like a stuffed animal or stickers. Instead, we can focus on something digital or experiential.

For example:

- If our book is about starting preschool or heading off to kindergarten, we could create a little *Confidence Kit* for parents and their little reader. This could include
    - printable first-day checklists with fun icons that remind kids what to pack or bring along
    - affirmation cards that little ones can read aloud to boost their confidence
    - a short guided video where we walk children through a breathing exercise or repeat positive affirmations together
    - a printable thank-you card that kids can fill in for their new teacher on the very first day of school

- Or if our story is about getting a new pet, we could put together a *Pet Welcome Kit.* This might include
    - a printable pet chore chart that helps children keep track of feeding or walking their new friend
    - custom coloring pages featuring the characters from our book
    - a simple PDF with kid-friendly tips on how to care for their pet
    - a fun activity like a 'Make Your Own Pet Story' worksheet, where kids can draw or write their own mini-adventure starring their real-life pet alongside the character from our book

- If our book focuses on nature or the environment, we could create a *Nature Adventure Kit.* This could include
    - a printable nature scavenger hunt with prompts like 'find a red leaf' or 'spot a bird'
    - along with a simple nature journal kids can use to draw or write about what they discover outside
    - a short video lesson where we talk about the importance of caring for the earth
    - a recorded short audio meditation for children, inviting them to imagine lying in a sunny meadow, listening to the sounds of nature around them

- And if we want to create something more universal, we could create what I like to call a *360-Experience Bundle.* This could include
    - a printable activity pack with coloring sheets, puzzles, or word searches inspired by our book
    - a video read-aloud where we share our story in our own voice

- a behind-the-scenes video where we show early sketches or talk about how the book came to be
- a short set of reflection questions or journal prompts that parents or teachers can use with children to extend the conversation

When we create a digital or experiential bundle, we are not just selling a book. We are building an ecosystem around our story. This makes our book feel more interactive and valuable, and because these resources are digital, they can be delivered instantly with no added cost.

STRATEGY 6: *Tying Our Book to Current Conversations or Current Events*

While we don't want to jump into every news cycle, it is always helpful to listen to what parents, teachers, and communities are already talking about. From there, we can show how our book naturally fits into those conversations.

If parents are talking about back-to-school anxiety, we can share how our book helps kids feel brave. If kindness campaigns are trending online, we can highlight the empathy message in our story. If a movie featuring dinosaurs is released and our book has dinosaurs too, we can ride that wave of interest.

This works especially well on social media by using hashtags that align with what's trending.

The key here is to join the conversation in a way that feels authentic. If our book naturally connects to what people are already talking about, that's the perfect moment to step in and share.

STRATEGY 7: *Positioning Our Book as a Go-To Gift*

Books are one of the most versatile and meaningful gifts, and there are so many moments throughout the year when parents, grandparents, and teachers are looking for exactly that.

Here, we want to think beyond the holidays.

- *Birthdays happen every single month.*
- *Baby showers happen year-round.*
- *Teacher Appreciation Week is every May.*
- *And graduation is not just for high school. It is for preschool and kindergarten too.*

So instead of only talking about our book as a holiday gift, we can position it as the perfect birthday surprise, a beautiful baby shower keepsake, or a meaningful graduation gift.

By framing our book as a go-to gift for multiple life moments, we are no longer dependent on December sales. We have given our book gift-giving power all year long.

———————— • ✦ • ————————

THE *EVERGREEN AWARENESS CALENDAR*

Relevance comes from contextualizing our book within readers' lives. Instead of pushing the book itself, we frame it as the solution or perfect companion to something already happening, whether that is holidays, seasons, awareness days, school events, or everyday parenting challenges.

Our book does not just have one season to shine. It has twelve. And by aligning with what is already happening in the lives of parents, teachers, and librarians, we give our story the staying power it truly deserves.

What begins as launch momentum becomes long-term visibility when we give our book new reasons to be shared, discussed, and discovered throughout the year.

The strategies above help us keep our book relevant year-round and long after launch by tying it to awareness days, celebrations, and recurring moments throughout the year.

To make this approach simple and sustainable, I created a companion resource called *The Evergreen Awareness Calendar* (⬆).

This calendar is filled with celebration days, awareness months, and thoughtful, real-world examples for every single month of the year. You will see exactly how a children's book can be naturally and meaningfully connected to a new moment or conversation each month, without forcing it or starting from scratch.

It is practical, easy to use, and removes the guesswork from long-term planning. You can access the *Evergreen Awareness Calendar* alongside the other resources created for this book.

THE MARKETING POWER OF WRITING A SERIES

Creating a series instead of a single standalone book can be one of the most effective long-term marketing strategies available to us as children's authors. A series naturally builds familiarity, trust, anticipation, and momentum. So many popular children's books are part of a series in pretty much every single age group, from simple board books and picture books all the way to middle grade chapter books and graphic novels.

AGE: 1-3   AGE: 5-8   AGE: 3-6   AGE: 6-9

When little readers fall in love with a character, a world, or a theme, they don't want that connection to end. And from a marketing perspective, this creates something incredibly valuable: readers who return, not just once, but again and again. A series gives families, teachers, and librarians an easy reason to follow our work more closely, to buy the next book, and to continue sharing our stories with the children in their lives.

Even if we are currently planning to write only one book, understanding the strategic advantages of series-writing can help us make more informed, intentional choices, and perhaps even plant seeds for future stories that grow naturally out of the one we are writing today.

In this part of the book, we'll explore why a series can strengthen our visibility, boost our discoverability, and help us maintain momentum long after our first book has launched. Whether we eventually write one book or ten, this insight will serve us well as we continue building our beautiful author career.

ADVANTAGES TO WRITING A SERIES

Creating a series has a number of really fantastic advantages:

ADVANTAGE #1: *A Separate Sales Page*

By creating a book series, we are able to create a separate sales page specifically for this series over on Amazon. This series sales page is separate from (and in addition to) our individual books' sales pages. This is really helpful because, as a separate sales page, it also gets its own URL. So if we wish to share our entire series with someone (instead of just one book), we can share our series URL instead.

Below is an example of one of my own series, called *Life's Biggest Moments*. This particular series isn't for children, but the principle for children's books is exactly the same.

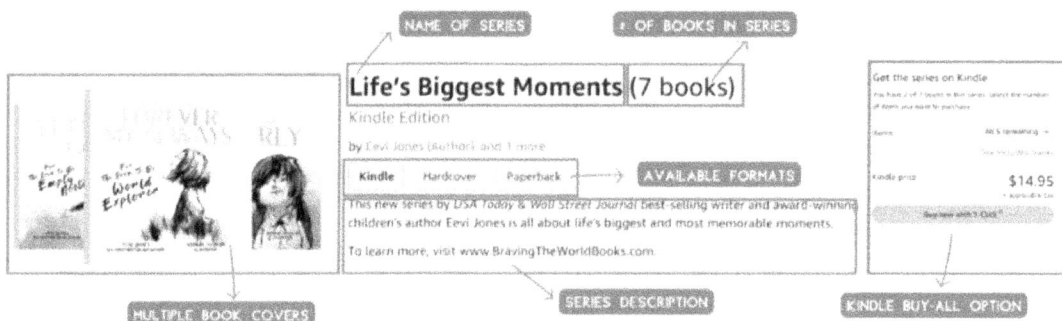

The first series-specific element on this series page is that the image shows multiple covers instead of just one.

It also displays the name of our series and how many books are in this particular series. In this case, the name of the series is *Life's Biggest Moments*, and it shows that there are currently 7 books in this series.

We can also see the different available formats, so we can easily select a different format, whether that's an ebook, hardcover, or paperback.

As we set up a series, we can also add a description specifically for our series.

If the Kindle format is selected, the buyer can also see a ***Buy All*** option to the right - a very series-specific feature that gives everyone the opportunity to add all our books in this series to their shopping cart quickly and easily with one single click.

Below this series introduction, all the books that are part of this series are listed individually as well, along with each book's cover, a short description, the number of reviews, and a purchase button.

ADVANTAGE #2: *Sharing of the Other Books in Our Series*

Amazon automatically shares the other books that are part of our series on each of our books' regular, individual sales pages. This is absolutely free cross-promotion. If someone is looking at one of our books, they can immediately see the other books that are part of that same series as well.

Below is a regular sales page of my book *Forever My Always.* The name of the series this book is a part of is *Life's Biggest Moments,* which is displayed in parentheses right behind the book title. Right below the title, buyers are provided with a hyperlinked series title and the number of books that are part of the series, leading to the series' separate sales page I shared earlier.

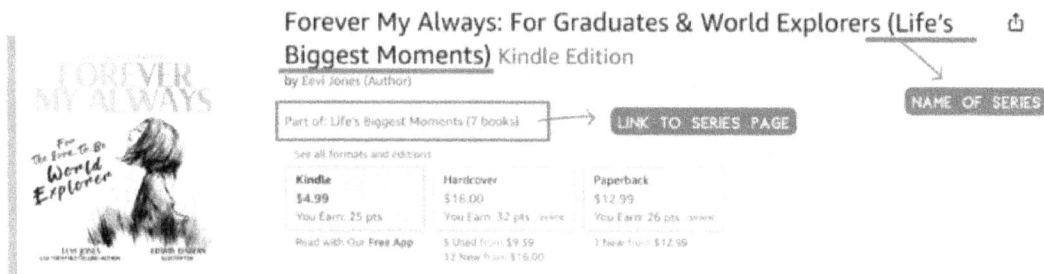

Right below this section, Amazon also displays an entire row of some of our other books that are part of this series, all clickable. This is quite remarkable, because Amazon usually preserves this prime real estate for other sponsored, competing content. But because our book is part of a series, we have our books displayed there instead - for free.

Books In This Series (7 Books)

NAME OF SERIES

INDIVIDUAL BOOKS IN THIS SERIES

ADVANTAGE #3: *An Additional Keyword Opportunity*

By creating a series, we are provided with yet another opportunity to weave in additional relevant keywords into our book's metadata, which in turn really helps with our book's discoverability.

The more we optimize our book, the better. That's how we're setting it up for success.

ADVANTAGE #4: *Boost in Sales*

A series can help with our sales, because every time we're launching a new book in our series, we are potentially bumping up the sales of the other books in that same series.

Whenever we're launching a new book, whoever we're sharing our new book with inevitably gets to see the other books in this series as well, which often sparks interest in those previously published books, provided the books in that series relate to each other somehow.

For example, when I launched my book *Sometimes It Rains - Recognizing and Honoring All My Feelings and Emotions*, the sales of my book *Ego, Sheep, and Knittery - Being Humble and Other Great Stuff* went up as well, without me having shared about this book at all.

So by promoting and driving traffic to one, we are indirectly also driving traffic to all other books in that series.

WHEN TO SET UP OUR SERIES

There are two different times we can set up a series for our book.

BEFORE PUBLISHING:

If we already know that we want our book to be part of a series, we will be able to set this up during the regular, initial book setup over on KDP by clicking on the "Add to series" button in the Series box.

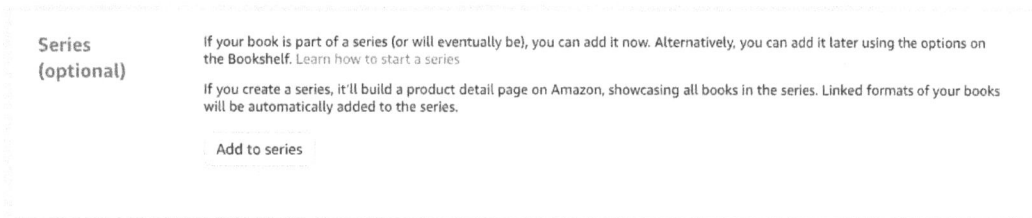

If this is the very first time we're setting up our series, we will create a new series by selecting "Create series."

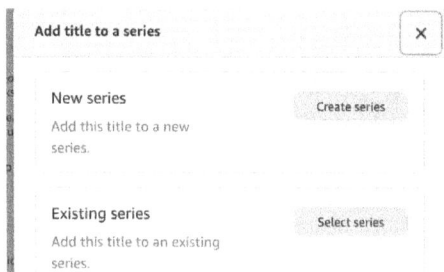

Next, we have to enter how our book relates to the series. If it's a regular book in our series, we will want to set it up as "main content."

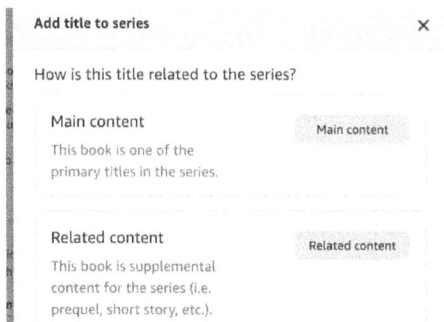

Finally, we get to enter our series details, such as the title of our series, whether or not we want our books to be displayed in a certain order, and a description for our series.

AFTER PUBLISHING:

If we have already published our book and we decide we want to make it part of a series, we can do so at any time.

All we have to do is log into our KDP account, find the book we want to create a series for on our bookshelf, click on the three dots next to any of the formats, and select "Edit details."

NINJA TIP:

We usually only have to add one of our formats to a series; the other formats should then be automatically added as well. So if I go through the process for my ebook, then my paperback and hardcover should be automatically added too.

But just to make sure, go ahead and check the other formats anyway - just in case.

The remaining process will then be exactly the same as described above.

Adding the series title to our cover is completely optional and not required. If we do decide to display the series title on the cover of our book, it is usually displayed right above the actual title, often in a much smaller font size.

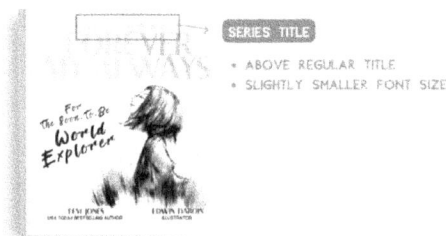

PRACTICE #1: *Mention the Series*

Whenever and wherever we're sharing our book description, we will want to make sure this description mentions that this book is part of a series. Whether that's in our description on Amazon, our description on our website, or a pitch to a media outlet. That way, people will know right away that there are more titles, no matter where they come across our book.

PRACTICE #2: *Mention the Series Inside the Book*

This is something I also shared in my book *How to Self-Publish a Children's Book*, where I suggested adding a page that shows the covers of any other books we may have already published.

If a book is part of a series, we showcase the covers of the other books in that series toward the end of the book. If a book is not part of a series, we simply add a few of our books that we think the reader of this particular book might be interested in.

This right here is my *Life's Biggest Moments* series, showcasing the covers of the different books in this series.

OTHER WORKS BY THIS AUTHOR

AND MANY MORE

To take full advantage of cross-promoting your books, make sure to update this page in your already published books every time you publish a new book in that series.

PRACTICE #3: *Adding the Series in Our A+ Content*

We will want to make our series part of our A+ Content (see chapter 7) on our Amazon sales page, whether that's in the form of an enticing image with the different covers on it or in the form of a table.

The fact that we, as independent authors, can now add this type of content to our book's sales page on Amazon is such a game changer.

Using the *Children's Author Blueprint* series as an example, this is the A+ Content in the "From the Publisher" section of the sales page.

And adding a table module makes each of the books in this series clickable, all while informing potential buyers about the different features of the books.

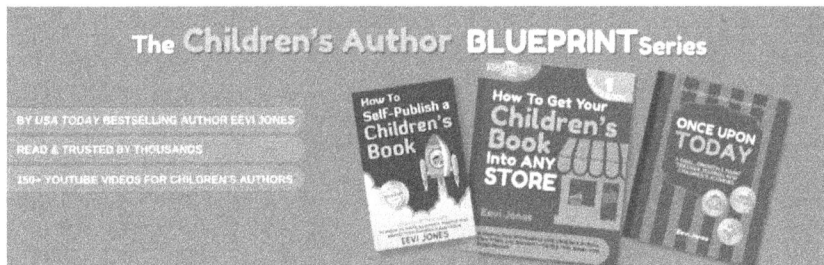

	Once Upon Today: A Goal, Growth & Habit Tracker Journal for Children's Author...	How To Self-Publish A Children's Book	How To Get Your Children's Book Into Any Store
	Add to Cart	Add to Cart	Add to Cart
SYTLE	Accompanying Journal	Step-by-Step Guide	Step-by-Step Workbook

Writing a series isn't something we have to decide right now. We can simply keep an open mind, knowing that we can always add our book to a series later, even after it has been published. It's something we can do with our first book or with our third, as long as we have the intention of writing more than one book eventually.

AMAZON ADS: A GENTLE INTRODUCTION (For When You're Ready)

When it comes to marketing our children's books, most of the strategies in this book have one thing in common: they can be done on a lean budget. They build momentum slowly and steadily, without requiring a large financial commitment.

Paid Amazon ads, however, sit in a different category. They can be a powerful tool (truly powerful), but only after our book has gained enough traction to make ads worth the investment. Amazon ads typically require consistent funding, ongoing testing, and a willingness to let our ads run long enough to collect meaningful data. For many authors, this can take months. And for authors on a tight budget, that level of trial-and-error can feel stressful rather than supportive.

So rather than walking you through a step-by-step ad setup (which could unintentionally lead to overspending), my goal in this part of the book is to give you a high-level understanding of why Amazon ads work, when they make sense, and what the most important insights are, so that when you are ready, you can approach ads with clarity instead of overwhelm.

And don't worry! You won't have to figure this out alone. At the end of this section, I've added a supportive decision tool to help you decide whether Amazon ads make sense for you at this stage.

IF ADS, WHY AMAZON ADS?

What makes Amazon ads so unique is that they show our book to people who are already looking for a book to buy. After all, that's why they're on Amazon.

Unlike Facebook or Instagram ads (which interrupt a reader's scrolling), Amazon ads place our book right where book-buying decisions are already happening:

- *in the search results*
- *on other book product pages*
- *inside "customers also bought" carousels*

In other words, ads catch readers in "shopping mode," often moments before they decide what to buy.

THE TWO FACTORS THAT MATTER MOST

The entire Amazon ad system can feel technical, but really, it boils down to just two core factors:

1. **Your bid:** How much you're willing to pay when someone clicks your ad.
2. **Your relevance:** How closely your book matches what the shopper is looking for.

Relevance is especially important for us children's authors, because Amazon rewards ads that point readers toward the *exact* type of book they want, whether that's a bedtime story, an emotions book, a spooky adventure, or a puppy book.

THE BOOK SELLS THE BOOK: OUR PRODUCT PAGE MATTERS

When it comes to ads, we will want to remember this:

Our ads can drive traffic, but it is our book page that must then convert that traffic into buyers.

This means that before we ever spend a dollar on ads, our book must be "ad-ready." That's why we must first review our book's five conversion assets:

1. *Cover*
2. *Description*
3. *Price*
4. *Reviews*
5. *Title & Subtitle*

If any of these are unclear, confusing, or misaligned with our target reader, ads will simply reveal those weaknesses faster.

NINJA TIP:

Ads magnify what already works and what already struggles. If your book page doesn't convert well organically, ads won't fix that. They will amplify it.

THE THREE CAMPAIGN TYPES

While we won't be setting up campaigns in this book, it's helpful to know that ad experts repeatedly see success with three core campaign types:

1. **Automatic targeting campaigns**, where Amazon tests hundreds of keywords and related books on our behalf to determine when and where our ad is most relevant.

2. **Category targeting campaigns**, which place our book in front of readers who are actively browsing specific Amazon categories related to our book's topic or age range.
3. **Brand keyword campaigns**, where we target keywords related to our own books, author name, or series name, allowing us to promote multiple books together and capture readers who are already familiar with our work.

A strong ads strategy doesn't require dozens of campaigns. In fact, starting with only three (each with a clear purpose) often outperforms huge, complicated accounts.

BUDGET CONTROL: PROTECTING OUR WALLET

One of the most reassuring tools inside Amazon ads is the ability to set monthly budget caps through something called *portfolios*. This means we can tell Amazon not to spend more than this amount per month.

For authors working with careful budgets, this feature is essential.

What many new authors don't realize, however, is that Amazon doesn't always spend our full budget. Some days, even high-budget campaigns are barely spent at all, because Amazon didn't find enough relevant, high-quality matches for our ads.

This is why it's so important to start when your book is ready, not simply because ads exist.

THE BIG-PICTURE MINDSET: ADS DON'T WORK IN ISOLATION

Fellow authors often share their ACOS (Advertising Cost of Sale) with me, wondering whether their number is "good" or "bad." But I personally believe that Amazon ads should never be judged by ACOS alone.

Why?

Because ACOS only measures the books we sold *directly* from our ads, not the readers who:

- *buy Book 2, 3, or 4 after finishing Book 1*
- *discover our work through Also-Boughts created by ads*
- *purchase our paperback after borrowing the ebook*
- *discover our books organically because our bestseller rank improved*

For authors who write series, ads can look "unprofitable" if we judge them by Book 1 sales alone. But once we include all the additional books readers go on to buy after finishing Book 1, those same ads often become much more profitable.

SO... SHOULD WE RUN AMAZON ADS?

Here is my honest, gentle guidance:

Start ads only when your book page is strong, your foundation is laid, and your organic marketing strategies are already working.

Ads are an **amplifier**, not a replacement for foundational marketing. They can absolutely help us scale our visibility (especially for a series), but they require:

- *consistency*
- *patience*
- *budget*
- *data-driven decision making*
- *an emotionally calm approach (not panic-clicking every 24 hours!)*

In this book, we have mainly focused on lean and sustainable marketing strategies that build momentum without financial strain. Once that momentum is in place (once we have sales history, reviews, and visibility), that is the perfect time to consider Amazon ads.

ARE YOU READY FOR AMAZON ADS?

To help you determine whether you truly are ready to run Amazon ads, here is a clear decision tree. Each question simply guides you toward what would serve you right now, based on where you are in your author journey.

1. Has your book been fully optimized?

Do you feel confident that your:

- cover
- book description
- price
- reviews
- title and subtitle

are all strong, clear, and aligned with your specific target reader?

➡ **If YES:** Great! Move to Step 2.
➡ **If NO:** Pause here. Remember: Ads will magnify whatever is already working... and whatever isn't. Strengthening your book page is the best next step.

2. Do you already have some organic traction?

Examples:

- Slow but steady sales
- A handful of reviews
- Readers finding you on their own
- Positive response from schools, libraries, influencers, or your launch team

➡ **If YES:** Wonderful! Move to Step 3.
➡ **If NO:** Ads will struggle without a foundation. Build momentum using the strategies in this book first.

3. Do you have a stable monthly budget you're comfortable spending, even if you don't see immediate returns?

This doesn't have to be large, but it should be *steady*.

➡ **If YES:** Move to Step 4.
➡ **If NO:** Ads can wait. Your time is better spent using the dozens of low-cost, high-impact methods in the rest of this book.

4. Are you emotionally prepared to let ads run without checking them constantly?

Amazon ads need time to stabilize. Turning them on and off too quickly prevents the system from learning.

➡ **If YES:** Move to Step 5.
➡ **If NO:** That's completely okay. Your organic marketing will serve you well for now.

5. Do you have time to check your ads once or twice a week?

You don't need hours; just enough time to review your data, make small adjustments, and let the campaigns continue learning.

➡ **If YES:** Move to Step 6.
➡ **If NO:** Save ads for a season in your life where weekly check-ins feel manageable.

---

6. Are you writing (or planning to write) a series?

Ads are especially powerful when you have multiple books, because even if Book 1 barely breaks even, Books 2 and 3 often turn the whole series profitable. This is called *readthrough*.

➡ **If YES:** You're a strong candidate for ads.
➡ **If NO:** Ads can still help, but only once your organic momentum is strong.

---

7. Does the idea of experimenting slowly (rather than rushing results) feel doable for you?

➡ **If YES:** You are likely ready to begin exploring Amazon ads thoughtfully.
➡ **If NO:** Keep nurturing your organic strategies. Ads will always be there later.

If most of your answers were a **YES**, then Amazon ads might be a supportive next step for you - not as a *first marketing strategy*, but as a *scaling strategy* once your foundation is in place.

If many of your answers were **NO**, the good news is:

- You don't need ads just yet.
- Your time and energy are far better spent on the sustainable, free, momentum-building strategies throughout this book.

Either path is the right path, as long as it aligns with where you are today, not where you think you "should" be.

And whenever you're ready to come back to the world of ads, this chapter and this decision tree will be right here waiting for you.

———————•◆•———————

YOUR TO DOs FOR THIS CHAPTER:

- ❏ Access & download your *Evergreen Awareness Calendar*
- ❏ Decide which of these marketing strategies you would like to give a try
- ❏ Go through the Amazon Ads *Decision Tree*

Find all your templates and swipe files using this link below. You may want to bookmark this page, so you can refer to it as quickly and easily as possible.

⬆ *https://www.eevijones.com/marketing-downloads*

LINKS SHARED:

- • *https://www.eevijones.com/social-media-prompt-generator*

FINAL THOUGHTS
What Happens When You Keep Showing Up

I wrote this book because I saw a gap. And more importantly, I saw us children's authors standing inside that gap.

This book was written with deep respect for the unique nature of children's books and the people who bring them into the world. It honors the fact that our stories are created with care, intention, and heart, and that sharing them requires a different kind of approach. One rooted in trust, patience, and genuine connection.

Children's book marketing is about meeting readers and buyers where they already are. It is about understanding families, educators, and librarians who discover books thoughtfully and often through repeated exposure. It is about showing up in meaningful ways over time, allowing familiarity to grow naturally, and giving our books space to find their audience.

This book was written to support that kind of journey.

Throughout these pages, we explored marketing as something far bigger than promotion. We looked at visibility as something that can begin long before launch and continue long after it. We talked about baking marketing into the creative process itself, rather than tacking it on at the end. We reframed marketing as connection, conversation, and care.

This book exists to offer clarity, structure, and reassurance. Not by telling you what to do, but by helping you understand when and why different strategies make sense.

As you move forward, remember this: you are never meant to do everything at once. The most sustainable way to use this book is in rounds. Choose a small number of strategies that feel aligned right now, give them the time and space to work, and then pause to reflect. Decide what to carry forward, what to gently release, and what to try next. This is how momentum builds - intentionally, steadily, and without burnout.

Marketing matters.

Not because numbers define our worth. Not because success is measured only in sales. But because stories cannot change lives if they are never discovered.

Marketing is simply the bridge between your story and the child who needs it. And when done with care, intention, and heart, it becomes an extension of the very message your book carries.

If this book helped you reframe what marketing truly is, feel less overwhelmed, more confident, and more supported, then it has done what I hoped it would do.

Your story has a place in this world. And now, you have the tools to help it find its way.

Thank you so much for trusting me with this part of your beautiful journey, my sweet friend!

xo
~ Eevi

If you found this book helpful, it would mean the world to me if you'd consider leaving a heartfelt review. I've been so incredibly fortunate to support tens of thousands of fellow children's authors through my book *How to Self-Publish a Children's Book*, and my deepest hope is to now walk alongside you through the marketing phase as well.

Your review is what allows this book to reach the authors who are still searching for guidance, reassurance, and a path that feels aligned. It is also what gives me the encouragement, clarity, and confidence to continue creating thoughtful resources that truly serve you and this beautiful community.

Thank you for being here, for showing up for your book, and for helping your story find its way into the hands of the children who need it most.

I'm cheering you on, always!

https://www.eevijones.com/marketing-book-review